IMAGES
of Aviation

AKRON AVIATION

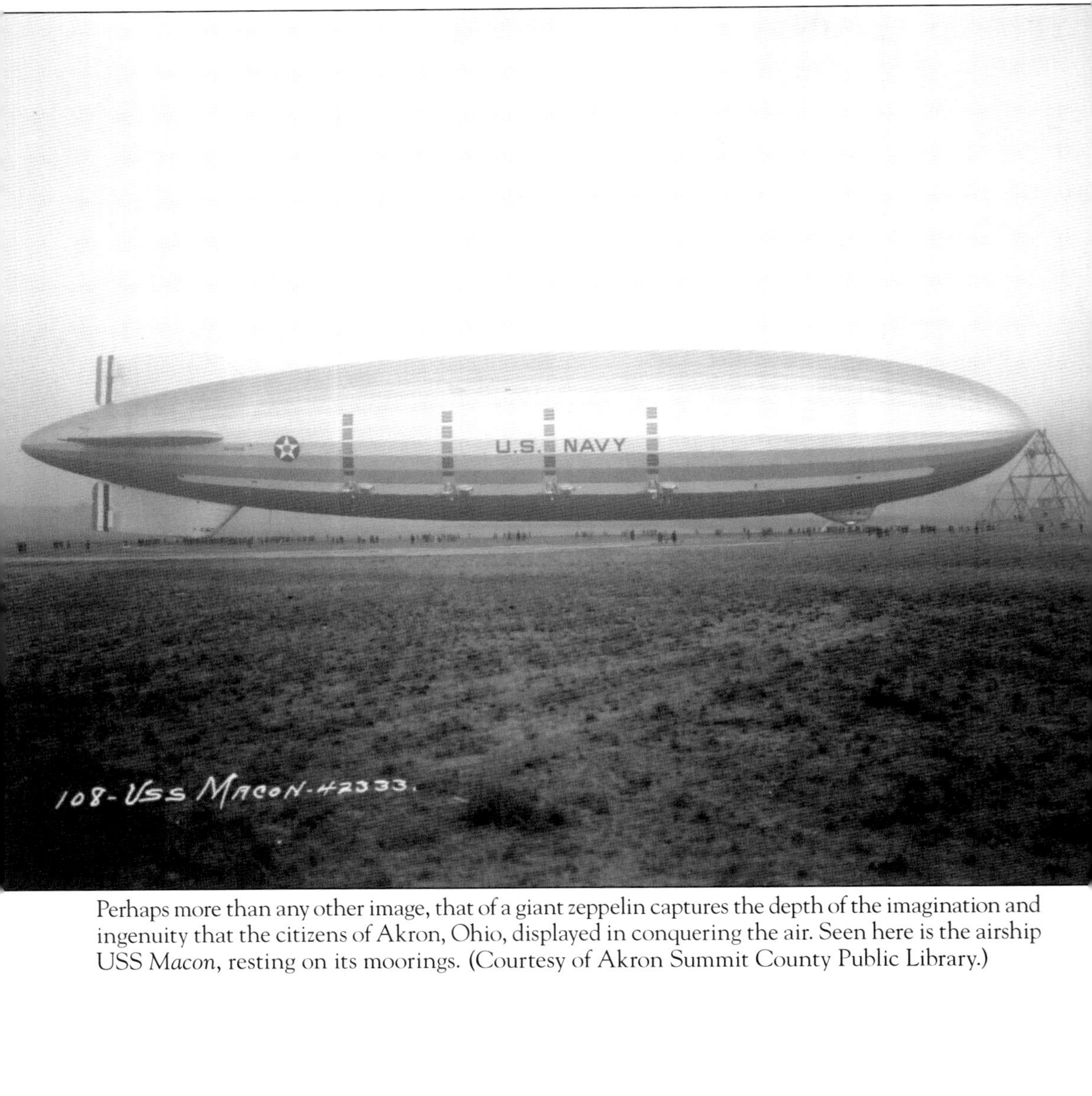

Perhaps more than any other image, that of a giant zeppelin captures the depth of the imagination and ingenuity that the citizens of Akron, Ohio, displayed in conquering the air. Seen here is the airship USS *Macon*, resting on its moorings. (Courtesy of Akron Summit County Public Library.)

On the Cover: This 1935 photograph shows people touring a DC-2 or DC-3 United Airlines Mainliner. The tour was part of the ceremonies inaugurating flight service at the Akron Municipal Airport. The DC-3 was the first airliner to make a profit by carrying passengers only. It could be fitted as a sleeper for 14 passengers, or as a day plane seating 28. (Courtesy of Akron Summit County Public Library.)

IMAGES
of Aviation

AKRON AVIATION

James I. Pryor II

ARCADIA
PUBLISHING

ISBN 978-1-4671-1132-4

Published by Arcadia Publishing
Charleston, South Carolina

Printed in the United States of America

Library of Congress Control Number: 2013943645

For all general information, please contact Arcadia Publishing:
Telephone 843-853-2070
Fax 843-853-0044
E-mail sales@arcadiapublishing.com
For customer service and orders:
Toll-Free 1-888-313-2665

Visit us on the Internet at www.arcadiapublishing.com

This book is dedicated to Joel, Benjamen, Lukas, and Aiden; may you dream dreams and have the courage and determination to conquer new worlds.

Contents

Acknowledgments 6

Introduction 7

1. Wings and Wheels 9
2. The Kitty Hawk of Lighter Than Air 17
3. Incredible Triumph, Unspeakable Tragedy 31
4. A Giant Aircraft Factory 49
5. Mr. Fulton and His Flying Field 63
6. The College of Lighter Than Air 93
7. Naval Air Station Akron 97
8. The Aviators Visit Akron 113

The Not-So-Final Story 127

ACKNOWLEDGMENTS

The accomplishments of the citizens of Akron in their endeavors to conquer the air are well known, especially in regards to lighter-than-air activities. That is why it is especially gratifying to have worked with Mary Plazo of the Akron-Summit County Library, who provided the vast majority of the images used to tell the story in this book. Unless otherwise noted, all images are from the archives of the Akron-Summit County Public Library. Further acknowledgement goes to my editor at Arcadia Publishing, Mary Margaret Schley, whose guidance and encouragement was of infinite value. A very special thanks must be given to the University of Akron's Archival Services, Frank Arre of the US Naval History and Heritage Command, Alvaro Bellon of the Lighter Than Air Society, and the State of Hawaii Department of Transportation, without whose cooperation this book would not have been possible.

INTRODUCTION

In the autumn of 1875, Akron held two Summit County fairs. Such fairs were the main events for the community every year. In 1875, the festivities were promoted by rival groups, and as a result, Akronites had the thrill of witnessing a balloon ascension that, by all aeronautical logic, should have resulted in death for the daring aeronaut who attempted to pilot the craft.

On September 27, to provide a stellar attraction that would draw crowds, the seeding faction engaged a Professor Wise, intrepid aeronaut of Philadelphia, to come to Akron and make a flight. His balloon arrived on Monday, September 7, but the good professor did not. He wired that he was ill and would be unable to make the flight.

The promoters were quite disturbed at the news of Professor Wise's sudden illness. At the last minute, they caught a break in the form of a young farmer from Northhampton Township. Jack C. Johnston volunteered to make the flight, taking the place of the presumably prostrate Professor Wise. So, at exactly 3:22 p.m. on Tuesday, as a great crowd watched in nervous anticipation, Johnston climbed into the basket, the ropes were released, and into the sky and the annals of Akron aviation history he soared. Caught by a north wind, the balloon, named the *Summit*, drifted southward, at an elevation of approximately 4,000 feet, to Summit Lake. As it passed over the lake, the balloon rose to 6,500 feet, entered a different air current, and started back north.

Over the Little Cuyahoga Valley it serenely drifted, then over North Hill, and over the main Cuyahoga River. Then, just as it approached the village of Cuyahoga Falls, the balloon abruptly exploded. Downward the balloon plunged. People watching below saw Johnston frantically throwing out ballast and pulling ropes. The daring young man fell 4,000 feet. The folks below feared a fatal crash. Then, either a miracle happened, or the varnished cotton held. Part of the balloon blossomed out and formed a parachute! The downward dive was slowed, and Johnston landed in a plowed field, badly scratched and bruised but otherwise uninjured. And so it was that from this event the citizens of Akron had their appetites whetted for conquering the mysteries of the air. Those dreams of conquest would eventually become reality and in much the same manner as Jack Johnston's inaugural flight.

A few decades after Johnston's aerial adventure, the Goodyear Tire & Rubber Company began building tires and wheels for "aeroplanes," thus marking the birth of the aviation industry in Akron. The Wright brothers were building their airplanes with wooden skids or sled runners for landings. The company responded to the landing-gear problem by introducing a rubber tire that was lightweight, held to the wheel, was puncture-resistant, and was easy to replace if it failed. The result of this design work was the Goodyear Wing Aeroplane Tire. This was the first tire built to specifications for aviation use and was the first complete tire, rim, and wheel assembly in aviation history. This success led to a discovery that influenced early aviation for decades: a wing and fuselage fabric dubbed "Stay Tight." This product was a combination of specially woven linen impregnated with a light film of rubber to maintain tightness and rigidity. It was the discovery, and widespread use, of this fabric that took Goodyear, the B.F. Goodrich Company, and other rubber manufacturers into an entirely new direction in aviation.

The aviation accomplishments and innovations by companies and individuals in the Akron area runs parallel to the growth of the United States in the early and mid-20th century. Among the city's aviation triumphs are the following: Akron's first fixed-wing flight (1906), the first complete aircraft tire assembly (1910), the development of rubberized aircraft fabric, the construction of racing balloons for competition, the manufacture of airships and balloons for use in World War I, airships made for the US Navy and the US Army during the depths of the Great Depression, establishment of a municipal airport at a time when Depression-era economic effects were ravaging the city, and the establishment of the Guggenheim Airship Institute.

The years between the world wars are often described by historians as aviation's "Golden Age." Akron and its citizens had a front-row seat to the period's achievements. In nearly every major aviation development during that time, Akron played a role. The city was visited frequently by such noted aviators as Charles and Anne Morrow Lindbergh, Jimmy Doolittle, Clearance Chamberlin, Douglas "Wrong Way" Corrigan, and Wiley Post. Akron played host to a wide variety of women aviators, including the following: Helen Ball, a stunt pilot from Pittsburgh; Gretchen Reighard, a champion glider pilot who made parachute jumps to finance her glider flying; Louise Thaden, winner of the 1936 Bendix Trophy; and the mysterious German aviatrix Antonie Strassman, who would later be revealed as a Nazi spy.

Akron continued to look to the skies for growth and opportunity, regardless of the effects of the Great Depression. In 1929, the Goodyear Zeppelin Corporation, a division of the Goodyear Tire & Rubber Company, was awarded a contract from the US Navy to build two airships for duty with the fleet. The USS *Akron* and USS *Macon*, at 785 feet long and 113 feet in diameter, would become the largest aircraft ever built. This required the largest hangar facility ever built. The Goodyear airdock, or Goodyear Zeppelin Airship Factory, as it was originally named, was completed in November 1929. The airdock measured 1,175 feet long, 325 feet wide, and 211 feet high. It was the largest freestanding structure in the world.

Due to the construction of the airdock and airships, the City of Akron began to see the need for expanding its airport. One man's persistence and vision made that need a reality. Bain E. "Shorty" Fulton, described as a man with "zip," came to Akron in 1916 looking for opportunity in this city built on rubber. In 1920, he conceived plans for a flying field that would ultimately serve Akron, and in 1924, those ideas became the plans of the present Akron Municipal Airport. "Shorty" Fulton's drive and unwavering vision, coupled with a keen sense of business and politics, served to eventually make the "port" a part of everyday life in Akron.

In September 1939, war was declared in Europe, and the United States began making war plans. Orders for military aircraft parts began rolling into Akron and, in particular, the Goodyear Aircraft Corporation. In 1939, Goodyear Aircraft had only 30 men on its payroll; by the end of World War II, the company employed 33,500 workers producing 4,008 Navy Corsair fighter aircraft and 156 type "K" airships for the war.

On January 14, 1948, Naval Air Station Akron was established at the airport. The station would gain Korean War fame with the overseas deployment of fighter squadrons VF 653 and VMF 231. These squadrons served with conspicuous gallantry during that conflict.

One

Wings and Wheels

In 1909, Akron, Ohio, was at the beginning stages of an economic boom, thanks to Henry Ford and his model T. This new era of "motor madness" brought with it the need for tires to satisfy the country's insatiable appetite for Ford's "Flivver."

Akron rubber companies expanded to meet the demand and also began developing new rubber products. One of the smaller rubber companies in 1909 was the Goodyear Tire & Rubber Company. Nestled securely along the Little Cuyahoga River on Akron's industrial east side, the company was growing fast, due mainly to the success of its detachable automobile tire. Goodyear management saw an opportunity to expand its rubber markets by developing the first pneumatic rubber airplane tire, advertised as the Goodyear Wing Aeroplane Tire. Use of the "wing" tire necessitated a special rim to bolt the tire, making the package the first complete tire, rim, and wheel assembly in aeronautical history.

Goodyear would go on to develop an improved airplane tire, the Goodyear No-Rim-No Cut Aeroplane Tire. Soon to follow was the first airplane tire testing machine and the first set of airplane shocks and springs. The success of these products within the aviation community eventually led to the invention of a product that would impact the manufacture of airplanes worldwide for decades.

In 1910, the wings of airplanes were canvas-coated, with varnish or paraffin to make the fabric airtight and moisture-proof. The coated fabric had several drawbacks. The slightest break or scratch in the coating permitted moisture to enter the wing, causing the fabric to shrink or warp. The exposed area would rot and give way, with often catastrophic results.

Goodyear arrived at a solution to the problem by developing a rubber protected airplane wing fabric, popularly known as Stay Tight fabric. The success of the new material was instantaneous. Several world-record airplane flights, including the first US transcontinental flight and the first airmail flights were made with Goodyear-equipped airplanes.

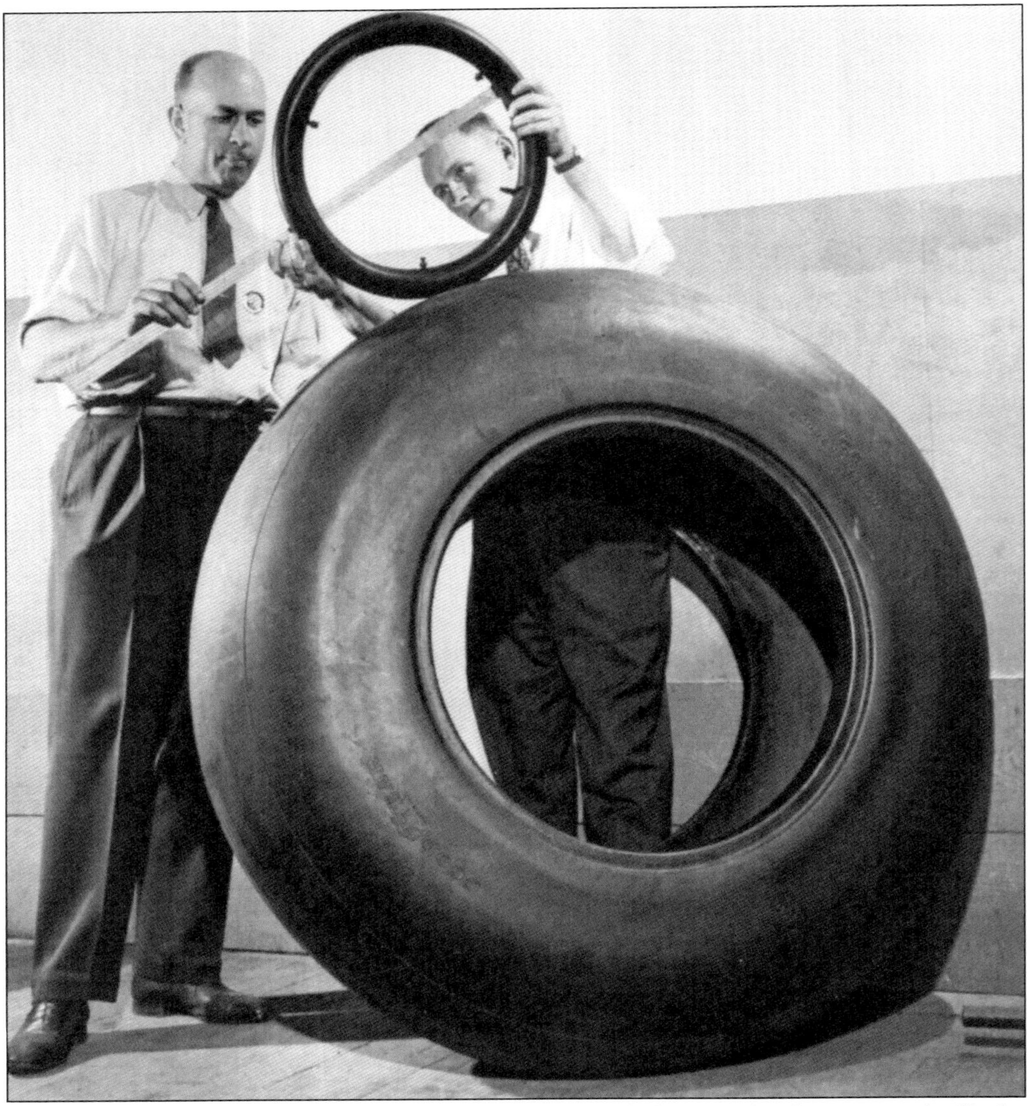

In the Goodyear Tire & Rubber Company's 1943 book *Trail Blazing in the Skies*, written by Shafto Dene, the Goodyear Wing Aeroplane Tire is seen here. Measuring 20 inches in diameter, it is being compared by two unidentified men to a "modern" 1940 aircraft tire measuring 56 inches in diameter. It was the largest aircraft tire ever built at that time. (Author's collection.)

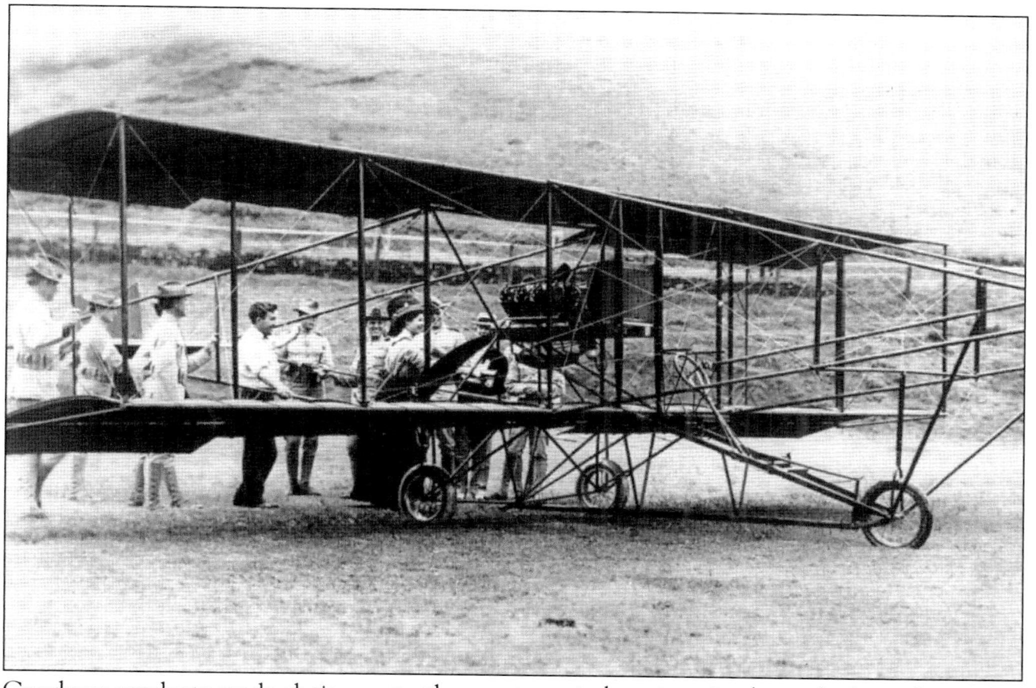

Goodyear products made their way to the most exotic locations in the early days of aviation. The Goodyear Wing Aeroplane Tire is seen here riding the skies of Hawaii with Bud Mars, the first man to fly an airplane in Hawaii, on December 31, 1910. Piloting a Curtiss B-18 biplane, he flew to 500 feet over Moanalua Polo Field, Oahu. (Courtesy of the State of Hawaii Department of Transportation.)

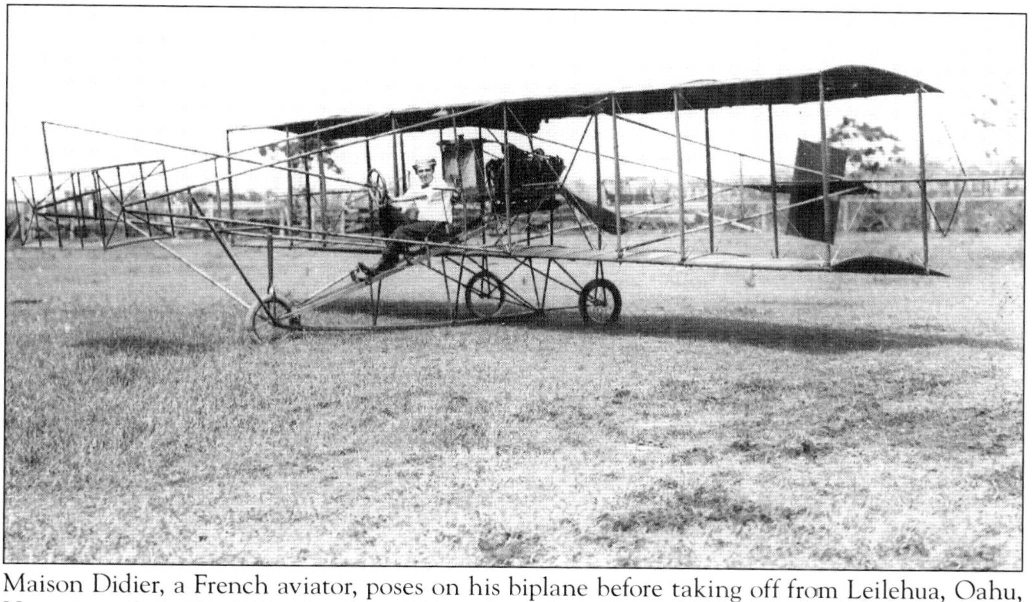

Maison Didier, a French aviator, poses on his biplane before taking off from Leilehua, Oahu, Hawaii, on June 22, 1911. Goodyear Wing Aeroplane Tires and Stay Tight wing fabric were on board. Didier crashed after this photograph was taken. (Courtesy of the State of Hawaii Department of Transportation.)

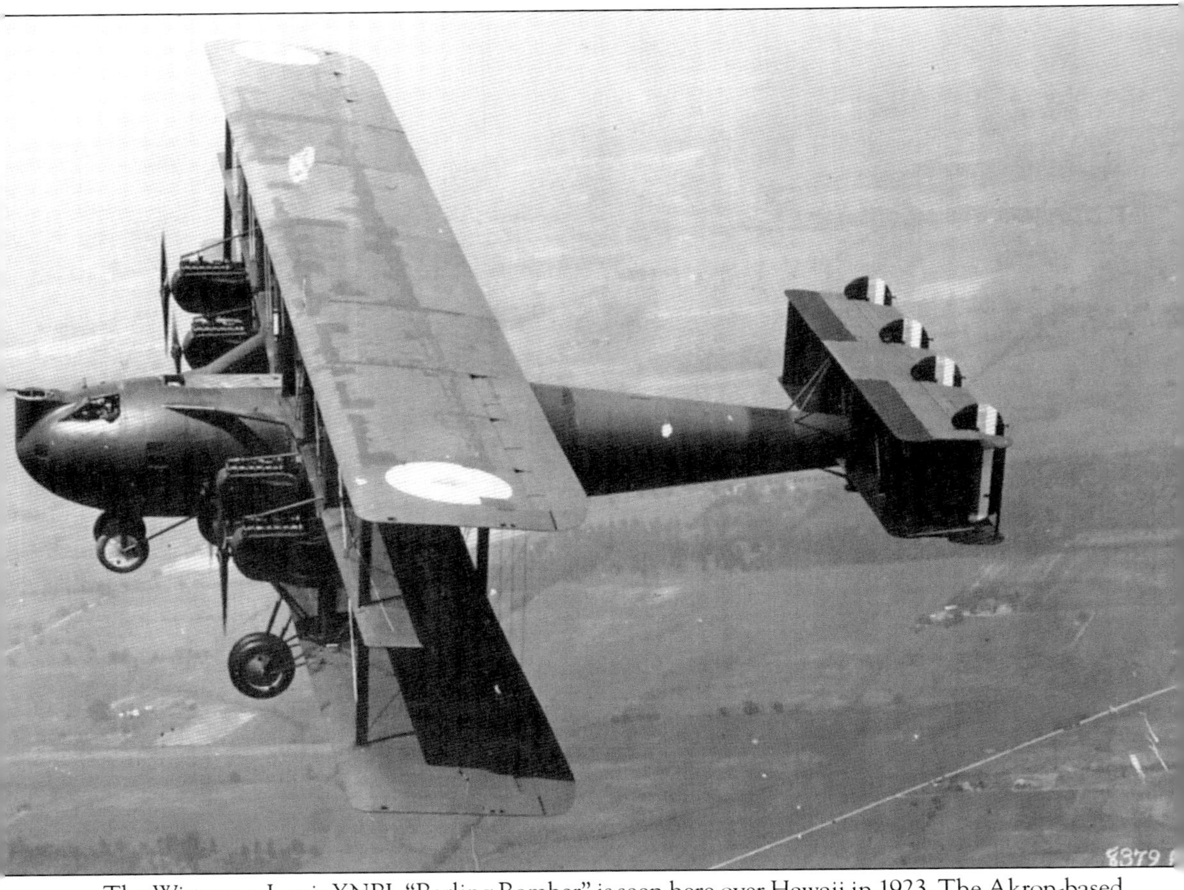

The Witteman-Lewis XNBL "Barling Bomber" is seen here over Hawaii in 1923. The Akron-based B.F. Goodrich Company found their products taking to the skies. This aircraft landed on no less than 10 aircraft tires built by the company. Remarkably, this aircraft actually flew. (Courtesy of the State of Hawaii Department of Transportation.)

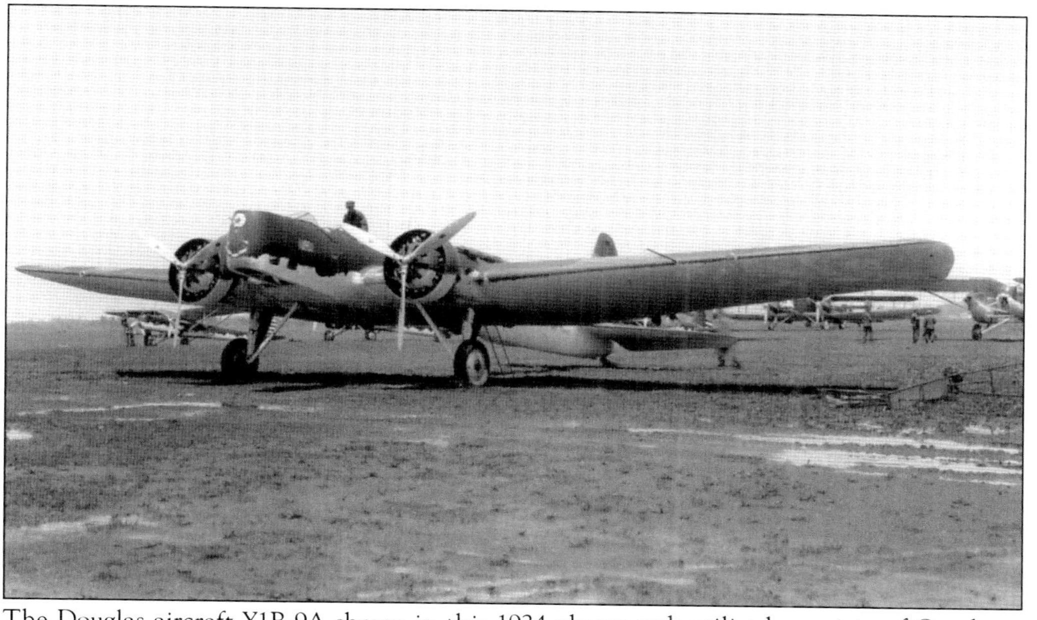

The Douglas aircraft Y1B-9A shown in this 1924 photograph utilized a variety of Goodyear aviation products, primarily in the complete wheel assembly. (Courtesy of the State of Hawaii Department of Transportation.)

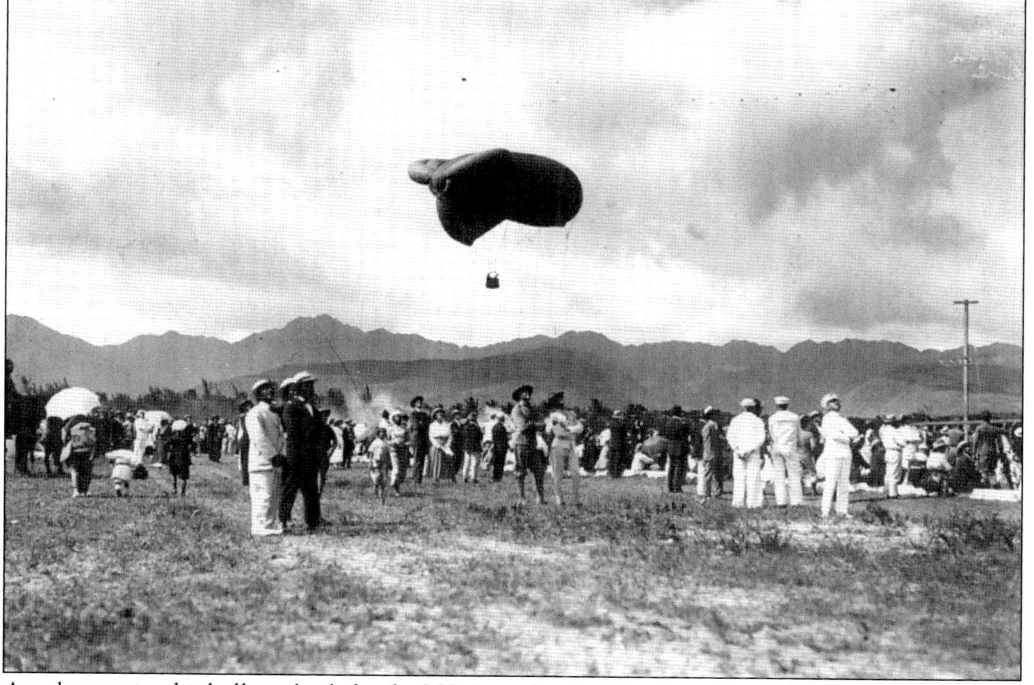

An observation kit balloon built for the US Army by the Goodyear Tire & Rubber Company can be seen floating above the crowd at Kapiolani Park in Honolulu, Hawaii, during a Fourth of July or Army Day celebration around 1920. Note the intrepid aeronauts in a basket suspended beneath the kite by cables. (Courtesy of the State of Hawaii Department of Transportation.)

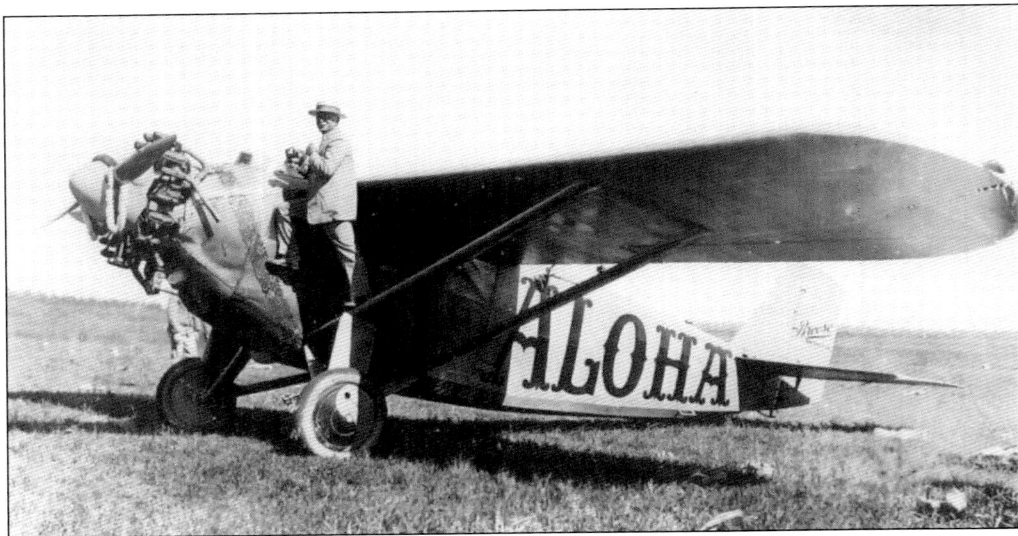

Martin Jensen poses in his aircraft, *Aloha*, after finishing second in the famous Dole Pineapple Race of 1927. Jensen, flying his Breese monoplane equipped with Goodyear No-Rim-Cut Aeroplane tires, flew from San Francisco to Honolulu in approximately 28 hours. (Courtesy of the State of Hawaii Department of Transportation.)

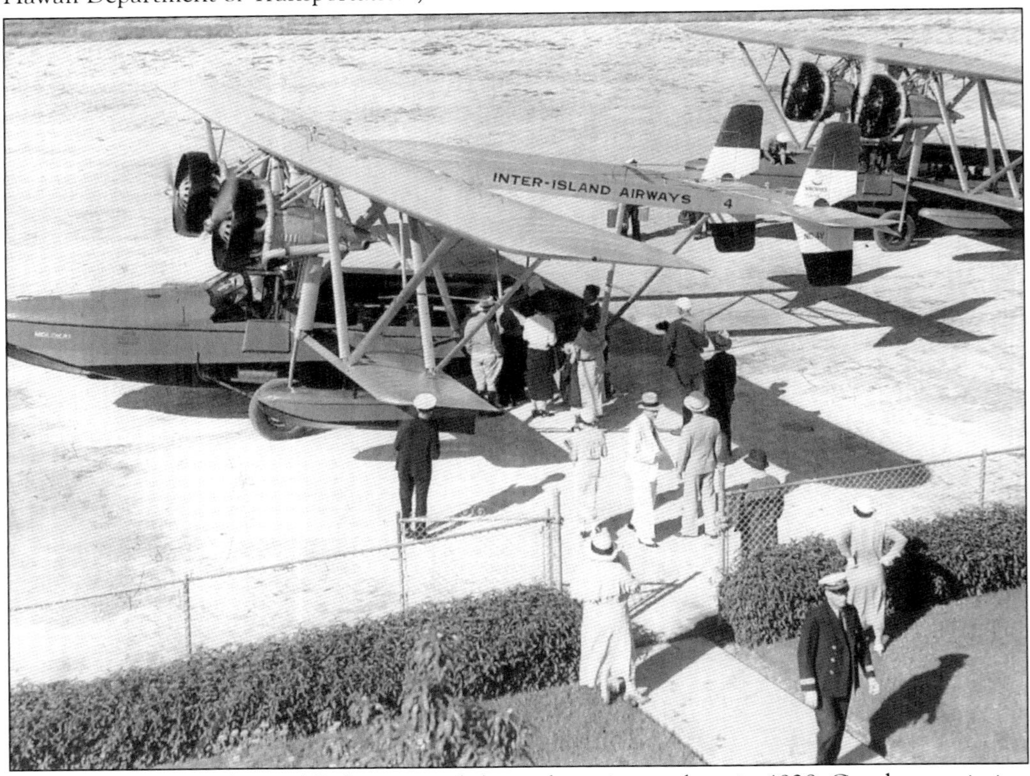

The Sikorsky S-38, the world's fastest amphibian plane, is seen here in 1928. Goodyear aviation products, including Stay Tight wing fabric, flew the romantic skies of Hawaii with Inter-Island Airways. (Courtesy of the State of Hawaii Department of Transportation.)

This Inter-Island Airways amphibian, a Sikorsky S-43, flies low over Honolulu Harbor. The improvement in Goodyear aircraft tires in both design and size can be seen here. The tire's profile is neatly tucked away in the aircraft hull. (Courtesy of the State of Hawaii Department of Transportation.)

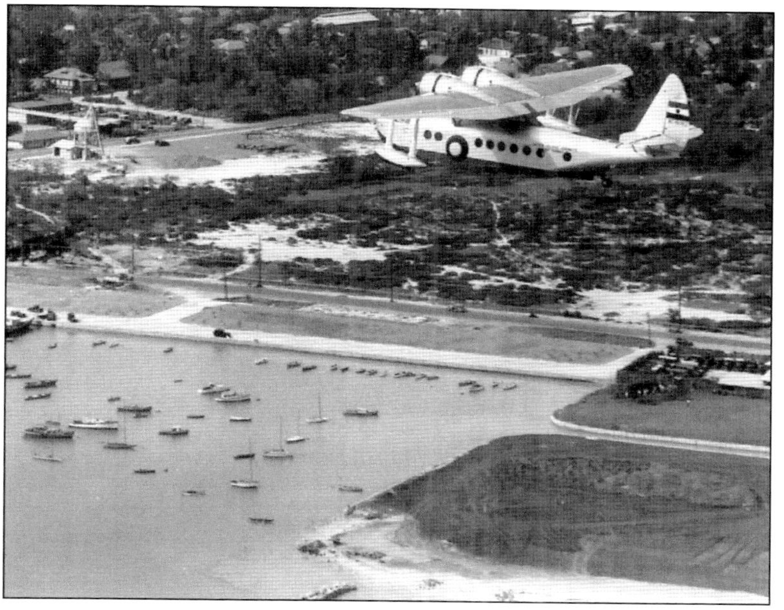

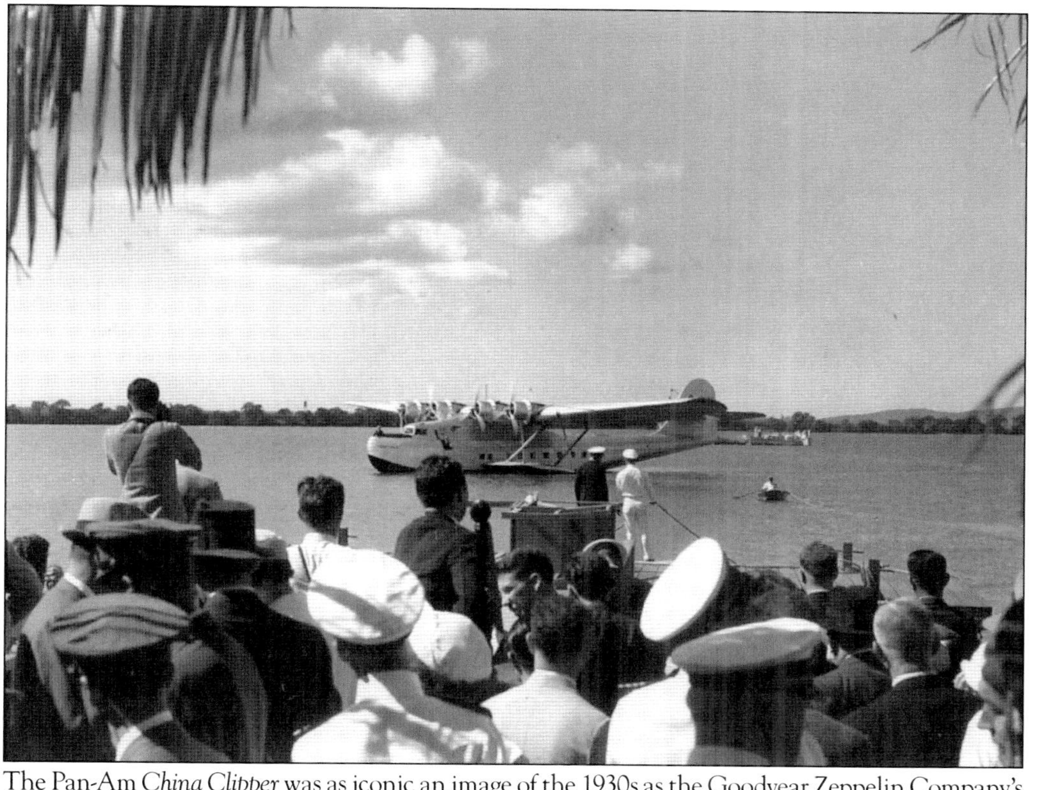

The Pan-Am *China Clipper* was as iconic an image of the 1930s as the Goodyear Zeppelin Company's airships. This craft, equipped with Goodyear tires and components, rests quietly in the bay at Pearl City, Hawaii. (Courtesy of the State of Hawaii Department of Transportation.)

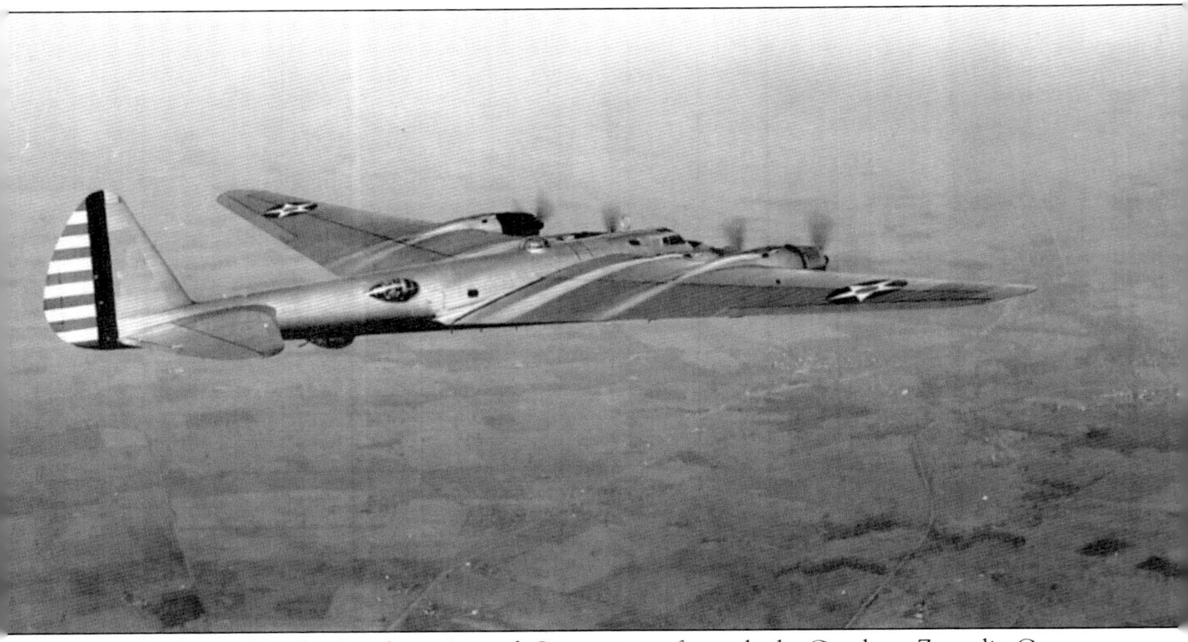

By the late 1930s, the Goodyear Aircraft Corporation, formerly the Goodyear Zeppelin Company, was involved in producing a variety of aviation-related components for various manufacturers, including Boeing Aircraft. Pictured here is Boeing's XB-15 in flight around 1938. Goodyear Aircraft Corporation would go on to produce an untold number of aircraft components for Boeing and for nearly every major aircraft manufacturer in the country. (Courtesy of the State of Hawaii Department of Transportation.)

Two

The Kitty Hawk of Lighter Than Air

The Goodyear Tire & Rubber Company's Wingfoot Lake Airship Base, sometimes called "The Kitty Hawk of Lighter than Air," is the oldest airship base in the United States. In 1916, Goodyear bought 720 acres of land southeast of Akron to serve as a flying field and manufacturing site. Construction of the big hangar began in March 1917. The initial structure was 100 feet wide, 90 feet high, and 200 feet long. Its length was soon doubled to 400 feet.

Airship production also started in March 1917, when the Navy ordered 16 B-type airships—nine from Goodyear, five from Goodrich, and two from Connecticut Aircraft. Since the hangar at Wingfoot Lake (WFL) was not ready, the B-1 was erected in a large amusement-park building in Chicago. It first flew on May 24, 1917. Then, five days later, it was flown nonstop to within a few miles of WFL. The B-2, also built in Chicago, soon joined the B-1 as a training ship at Wingfoot Lake.

The Navy ordered 15 (later reduced to 10) C-type airships in 1918. Goodyear erected the C-1 at WFL. It was flown to the Navy facility at Rockaway, Long Island, via Washington, DC, on October 22. The C-2 was used as a trainer at WFL. Most of the B-type and C-type ships built by Goodyear were shipped to the Navy for final assembly and flight-testing.

WFL was the training site of the first class of Navy airship pilots. With Goodyear personnel as instructors, some 600 Army and Navy officers and enlisted men were trained to fly and maintain B-type and C-type airships, kite (observation) balloons, and free balloons. The Navy took over the facility and operated it as a US Naval Airship Training Station from 1917 to 1921. It served as a construction, test, and development base and consisted of 26 buildings by the end of World War I. The first commanding officer was Lt. Lewis H. Maxfield. The last commanding officer was Lt. Comdr. Zachary Lansdowne.

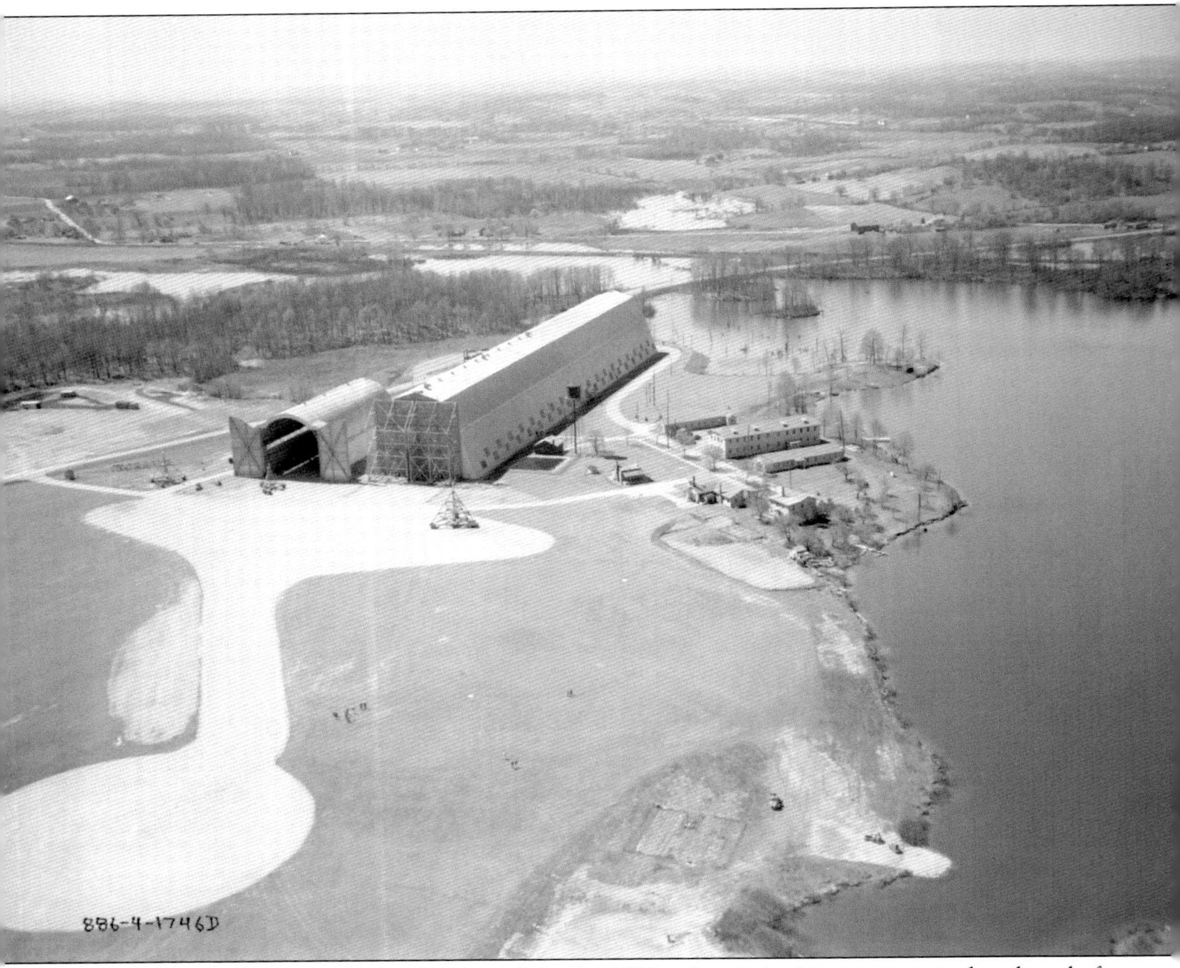

Known as the "Kitty Hawk of Lighter than Air," Wingfoot Lake Hangar is poised and ready for action in this 1946 photograph. The building to the left, known as the small hangar, was used for building L-type and G-type airships. The housing and training complex can be clearly seen on the right. The first cabin in Portage County can be seen just north of the water tower. Wingfoot Lake would play a major role in the development of lighter-than-air flight. Built in 1917, the hangar immediately began producing airships for use in World War I. The facility would go on to serve the nation in World War II, producing the major portion of airships needed by the US Navy for coastal defense. (Courtesy of the University of Akron Archives.)

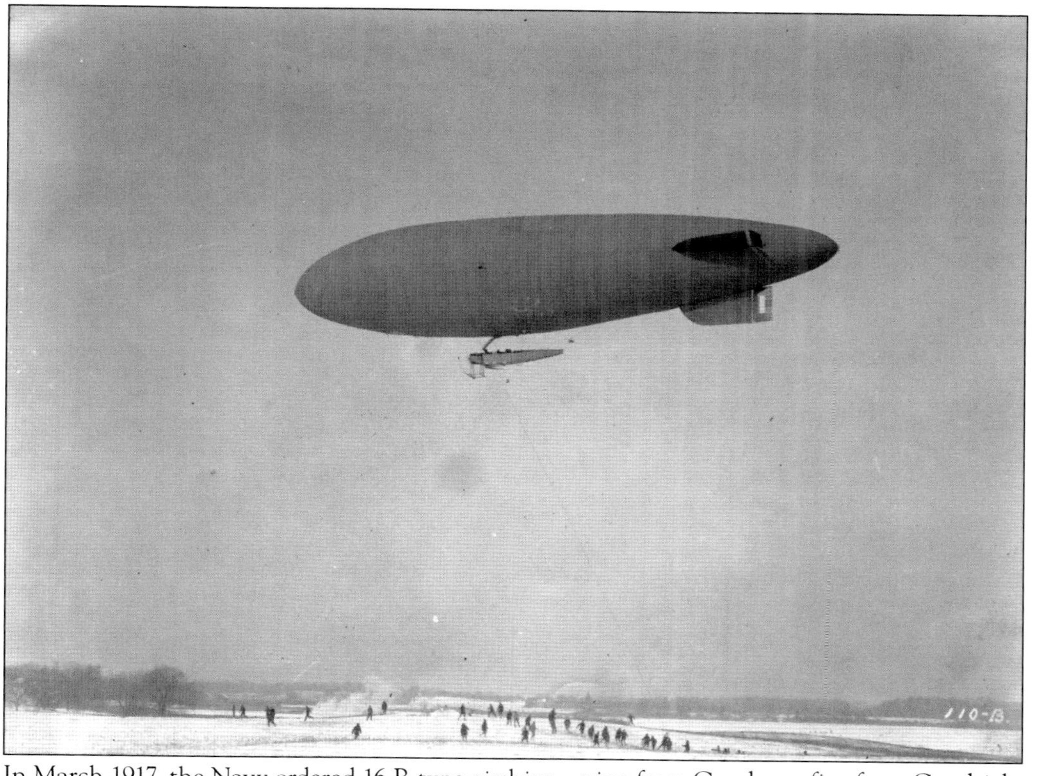

In March 1917, the Navy ordered 16 B-type airships—nine from Goodyear, five from Goodrich, and two from Connecticut Aircraft. Since the hangar at Wingfoot Lake was not ready, the B-1 was erected in a large amusement-park building in Chicago. It first flew on May 24, 1917. Note the snow-covered fields and the open cockpit gondola suspended beneath the airship envelope.

From 1917 to 1922, Wingfoot Lake Airship Facility would become Naval Air Station Akron, producing airships, observation balloons and kites, and providing training for the US Navy during World War I. In this 1918 photograph, a Goodyear/Navy C-type airship is under construction.

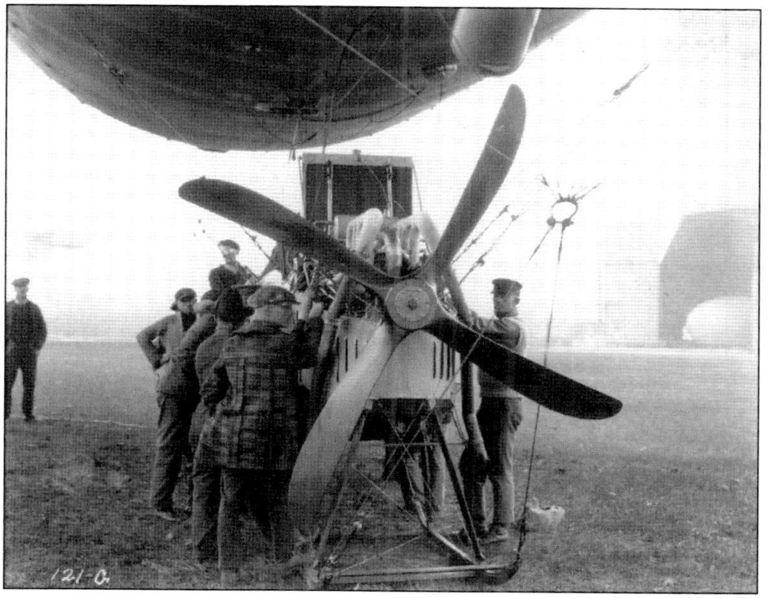

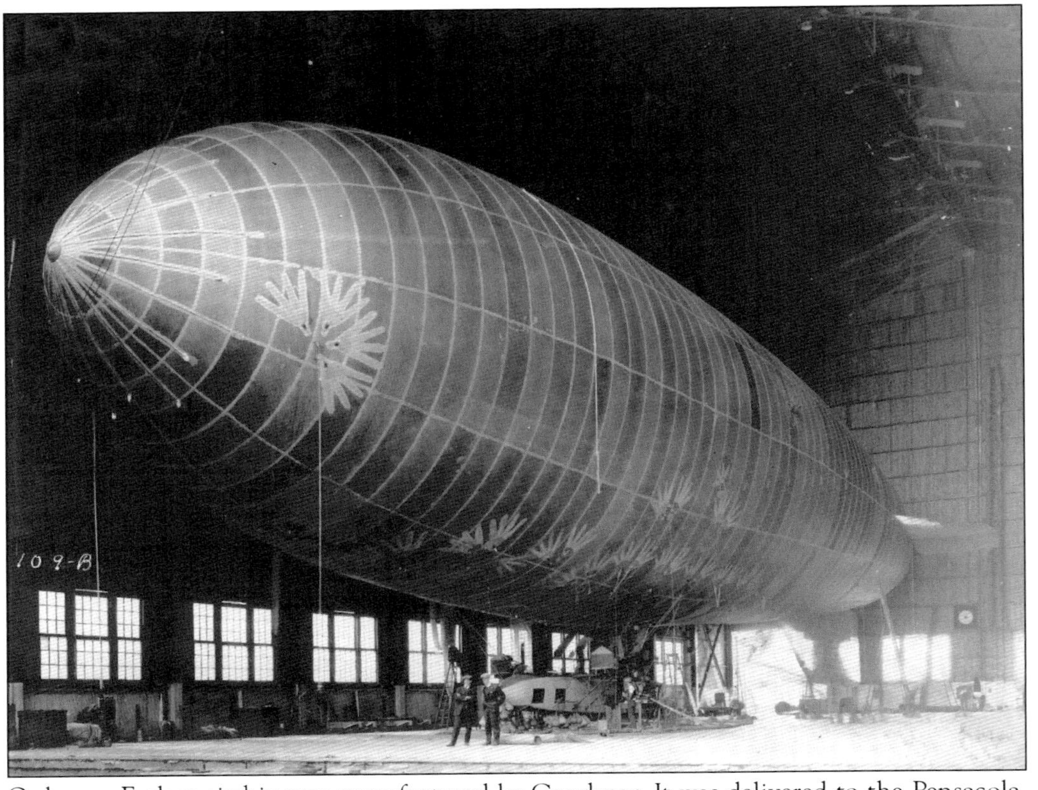

Only one E-class airship was manufactured by Goodyear. It was delivered to the Pensacola, Florida, airship school. In Pensacola, the E-type blimp was flown only as a training device. It used a Thomas motor. The E-1 blimp was made at the same time as the F-1 and the Army airship A-1. Note the size and weight of the early aircraft engines.

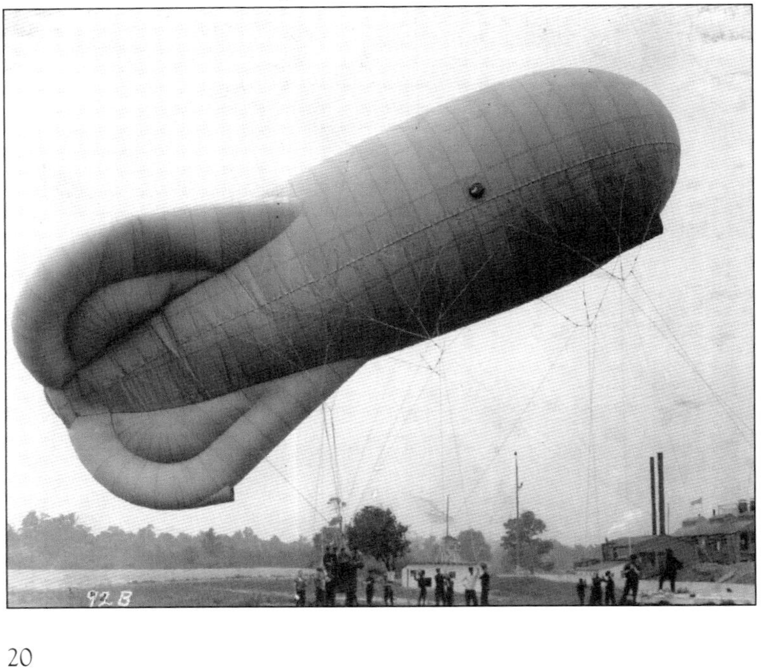

The C-class blimp was made by both Goodyear and Goodrich. These airships, larger than B-class blimps, had two motors and longer endurance. C-class blimps were used for patrol purposes. On September 30, 1918, the C-type airship made its maiden flight at Wingfoot Lake in Akron, Ohio.

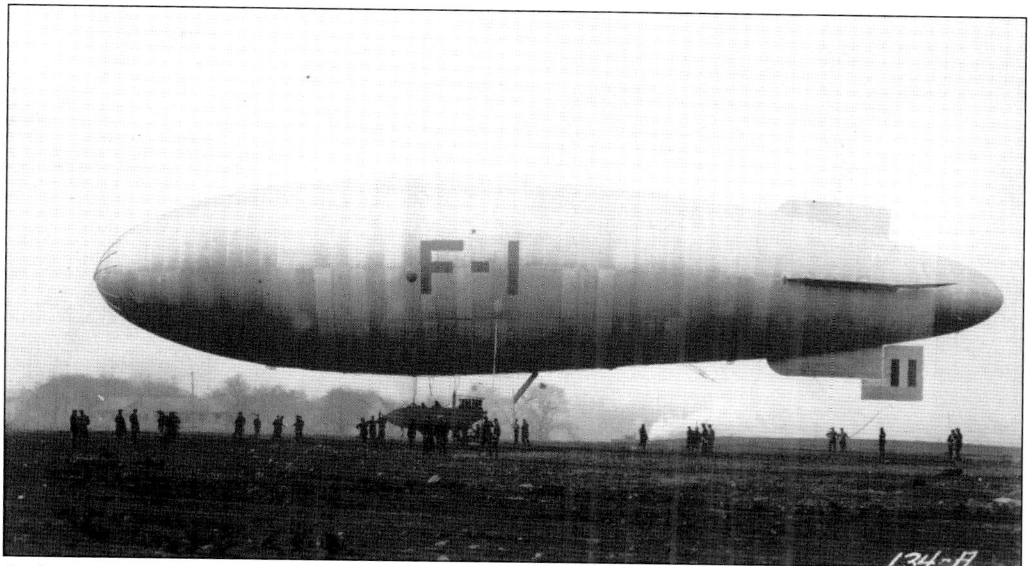

Only one F-class airship was manufactured by Goodyear. The F-1 spent its entire career at Hampton Roads in Norfolk, Virginia. The F-1 was made at the same time as the E-1 and A-1. The F-class of US Navy blimps, comprised of a single airship, was built at the Wingfoot Lake Airship Facility during World War I.

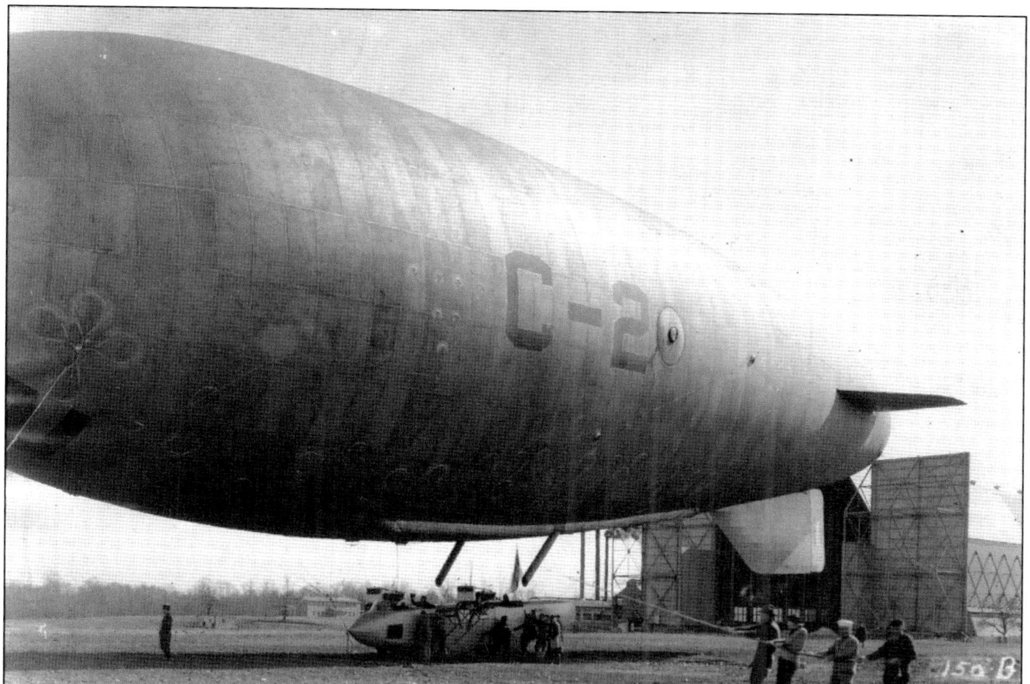

The C 2-class blimp was made by both Goodyear and Goodrich. They had two motors for longer endurance and were designed for coastal patrol purposes. On September 30, 1918, this C-type airship made its maiden flight at Wingfoot Lake in Akron, Ohio. The C-2 never saw active service. Note the ground crew holding the ship down.

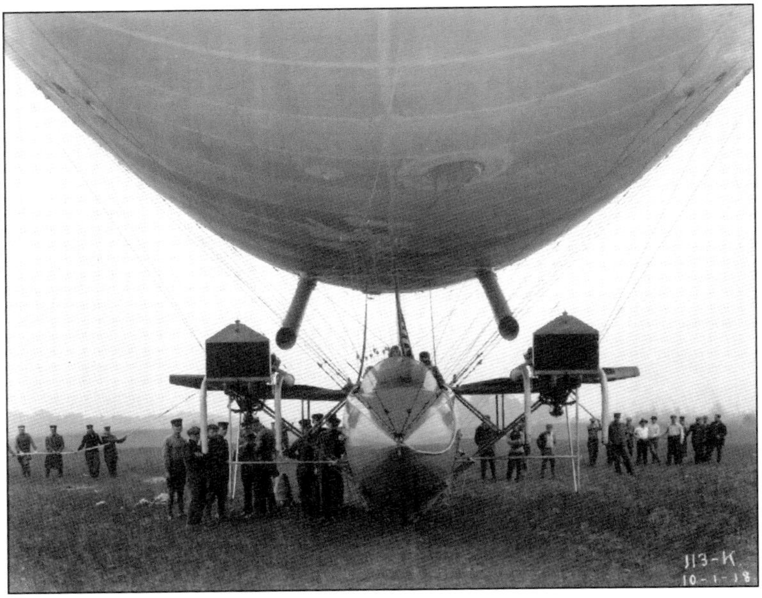

This is the front of a C-1 gondola. The C-class blimp was made by both Goodyear and B.F. Goodrich. It was larger than the B-class ships, and it had two motors and longer endurance. C-class blimps were used for patrol purposes. On September 30, 1918, the C-type airship made its maiden flight at Wingfoot Lake. Note the crew positioned directly behind the engines.

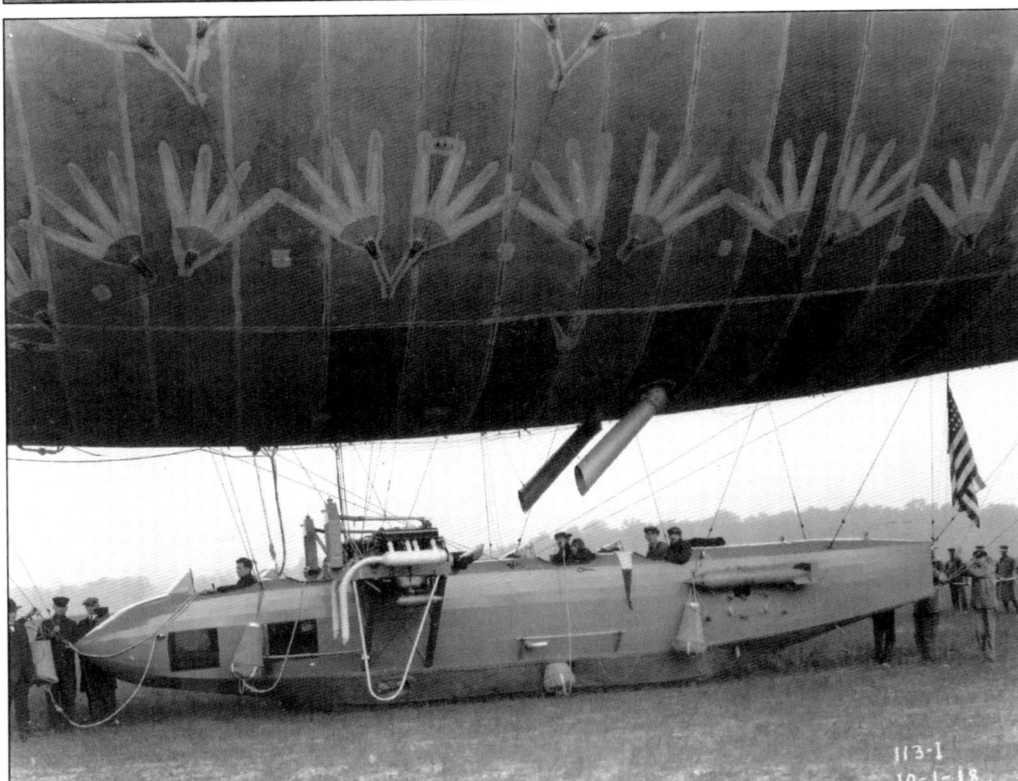

In this side view of a C-1 gondola, note the pilot with no flight gear. The observer in the center foreground appears to be the only crewman wearing goggles and a leather helmet. The gondola is complete with full crew positioned behind the engines, exhaust, and propellers. The C-1 is armed and, in true naval tradition, displays the Stars and Stripes abaft.

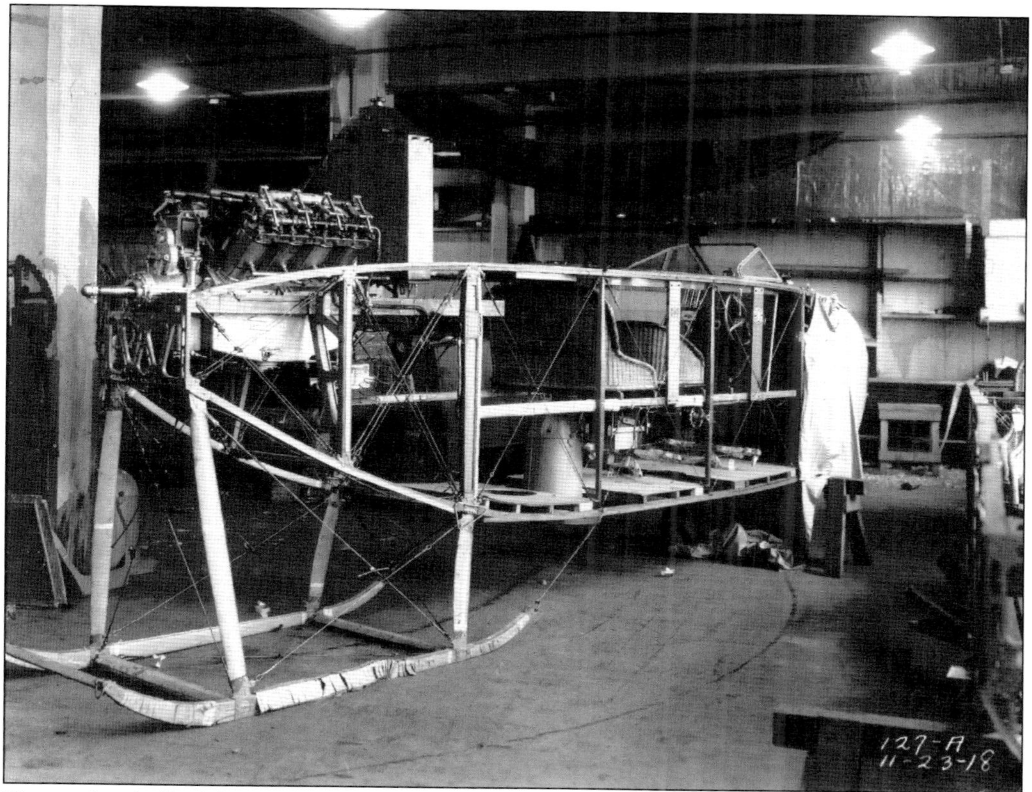

This is the shell of the gondola for the Army A-1 airship. Only one A-1 airship was manufactured by Goodyear. The A-1 was the first blimp operated by the Army. The ship's Curtiss OXX engine was a water-cooled V8 aero engine derived from the Curtis OX. The A-1 was made at the same time as the E-1 and F-1.

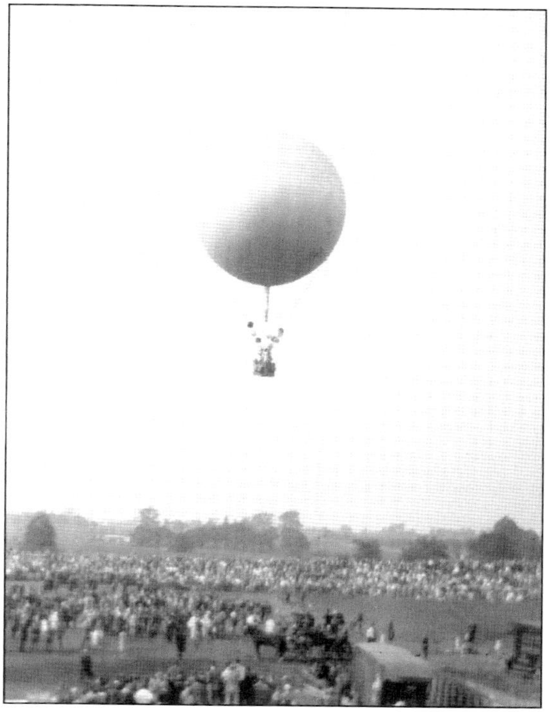

The Goodyear Tire & Rubber Company and the B.F. Goodrich Company manufactured balloons during World War I, from 1914 to 1918. The balloons were fabric envelopes filled with dangerous, flammable hydrogen gas. After World War I, these balloons were filled with nonflammable helium. Used for observation purposes, they were tethered to a steel cable and elevated around 3,000 feet.

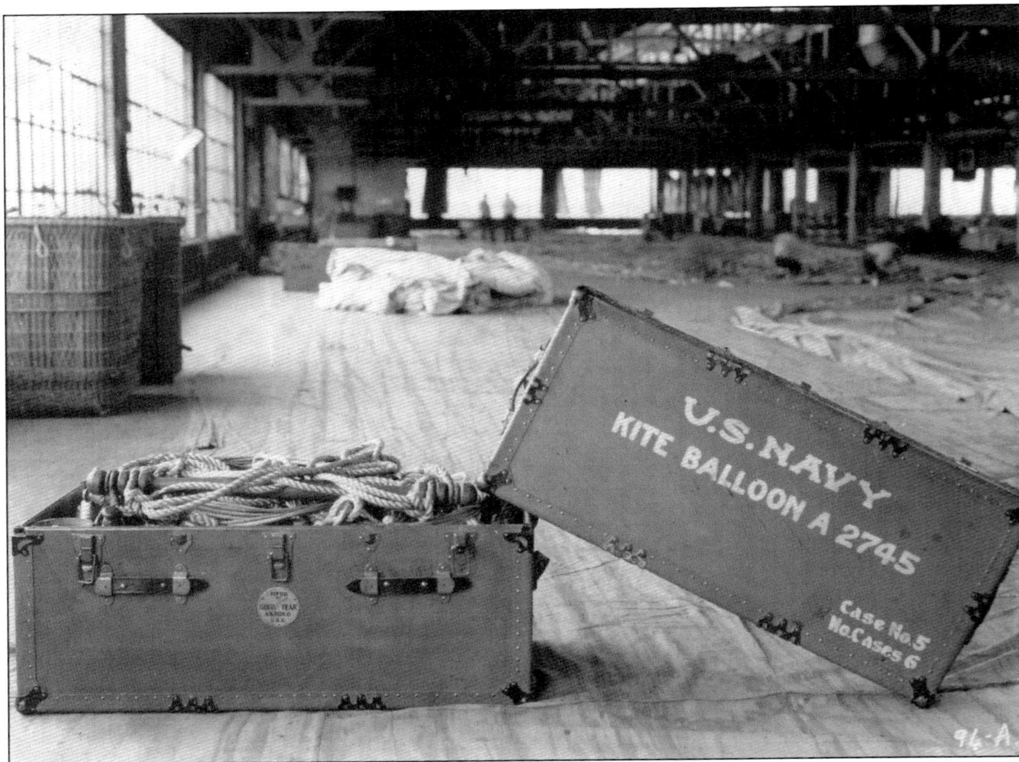

This 1918 photograph shows a Goodyear Kite Balloon ready for shipment. Note the rope ladder rungs on top. This method of shipping balloon equipment was commonplace. There was very little protection from damage.

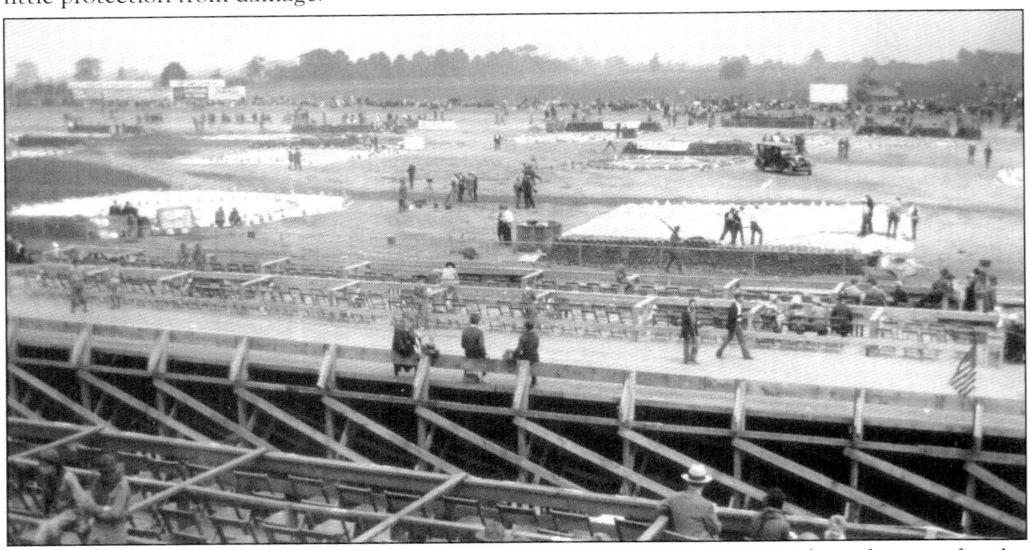

Flight crews at the 1927 National Balloon Race prepare their respective launch areas for the prerace inflation process. The protective ground cloths are weighted down around their perimeters with sandbags. In the foreground is the banked wooden track of the Akron-Cleveland Speedway, where the race took place.

In this photograph, two sailors stand guard at the hydrogen tanks as the US Navy balloon entry in the 1927 National Balloon Race is undergoing inflation behind them. The race took place at the Akron-Cleveland Speedway in Northampton Township. Note the storage of the hydrogen cylinders, with the end caps pointed directly at the sailors.

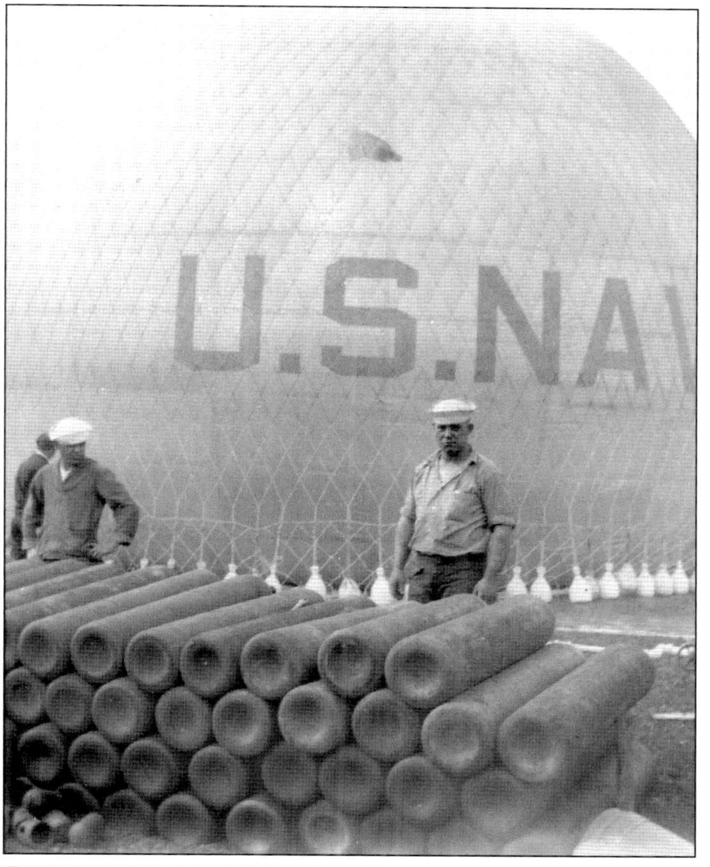

Two planes can be seen flying above the field as inflation proceeds prior to the start of the 1927 National Balloon Race at Akron-Cleveland Speedway. In the center of the photograph is the US Navy entry.

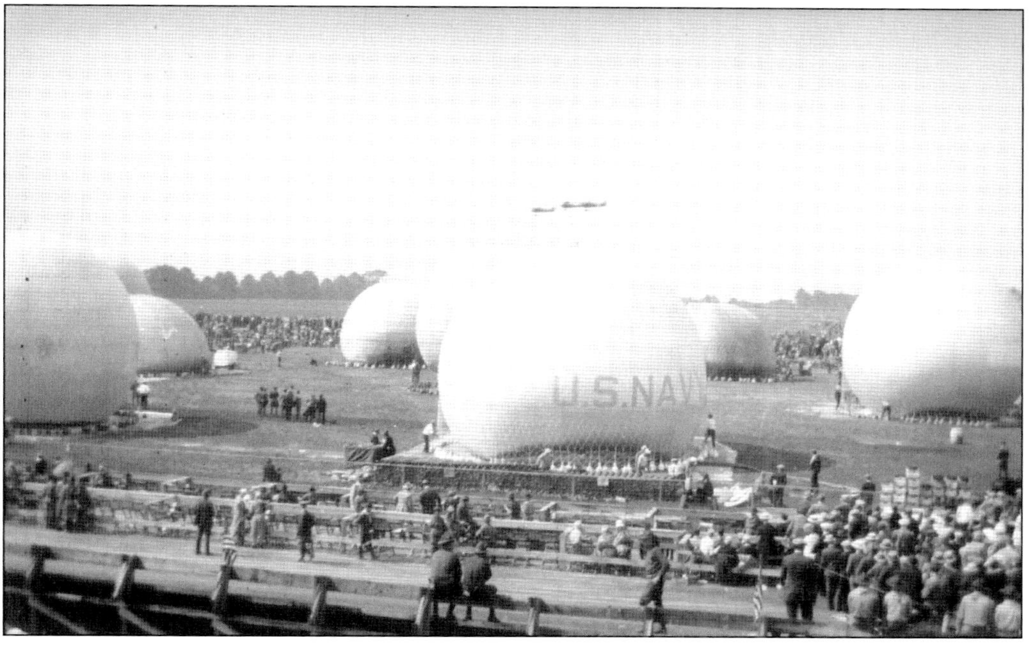

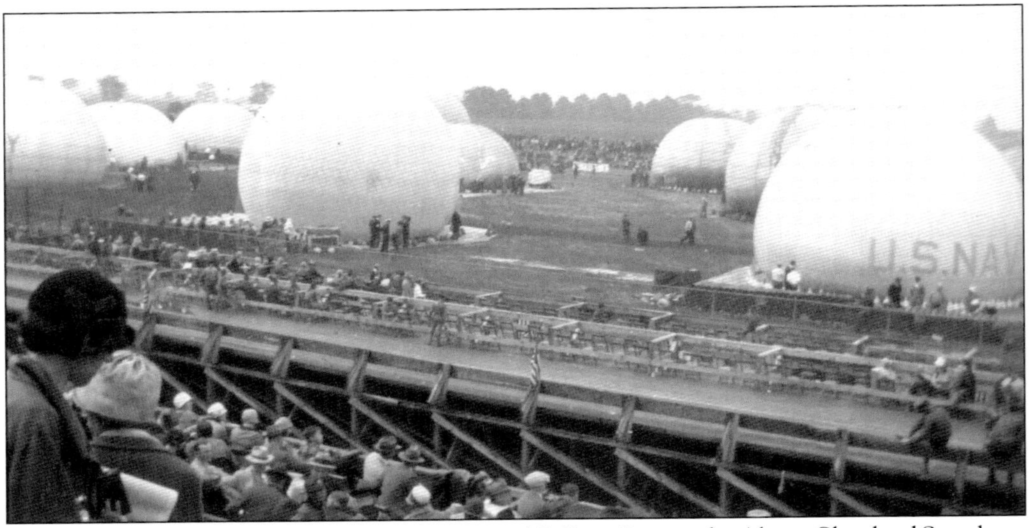

In this view of the preparations for the 1927 National Balloon Race at the Akron-Cleveland Speedway, the US Navy entry is at the far right. The US Army entry can be seen at the far left.

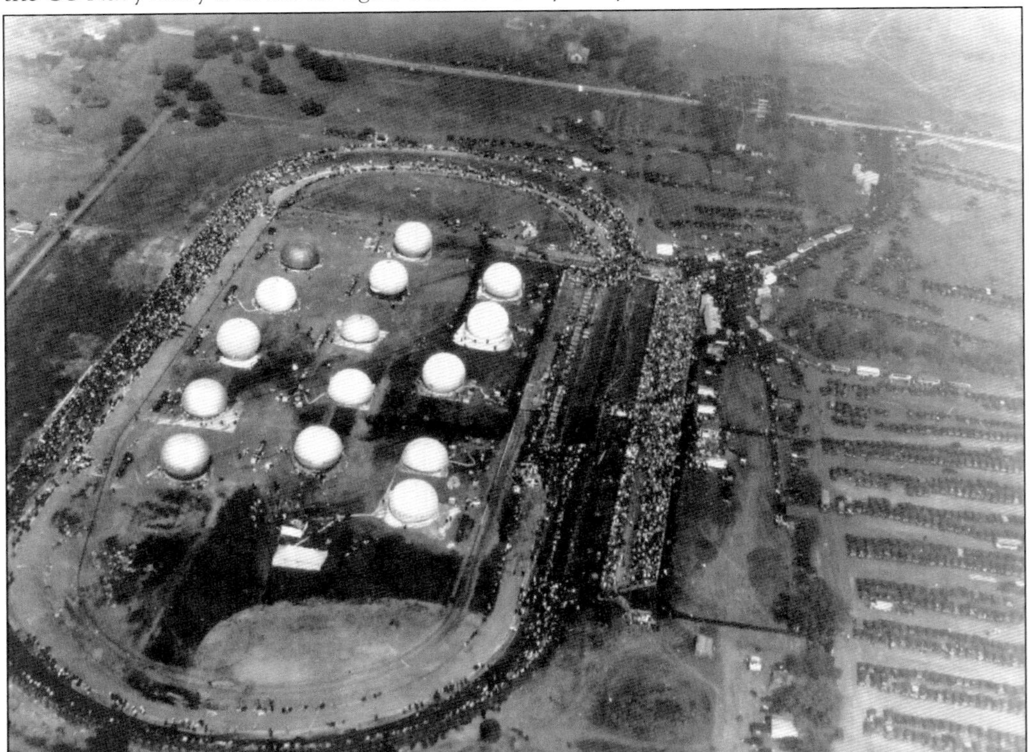

The Akron-Cleveland Speedway in Northampton Township was the starting point of the 1927 National Balloon Race, which took place on May 30. This aerial photograph shows the contestants in varying stages of inflation before the start of the race. The entrants were vying for the coveted Litchfield Trophy, awarded to the balloon that landed the greatest distance from the starting point.

As the crowd looks on, the first balloons begin their ascent at the 1927 National Balloon Race out of the Akron-Cleveland Speedway. The balloons took off at intervals, as the race was for distance, not speed.

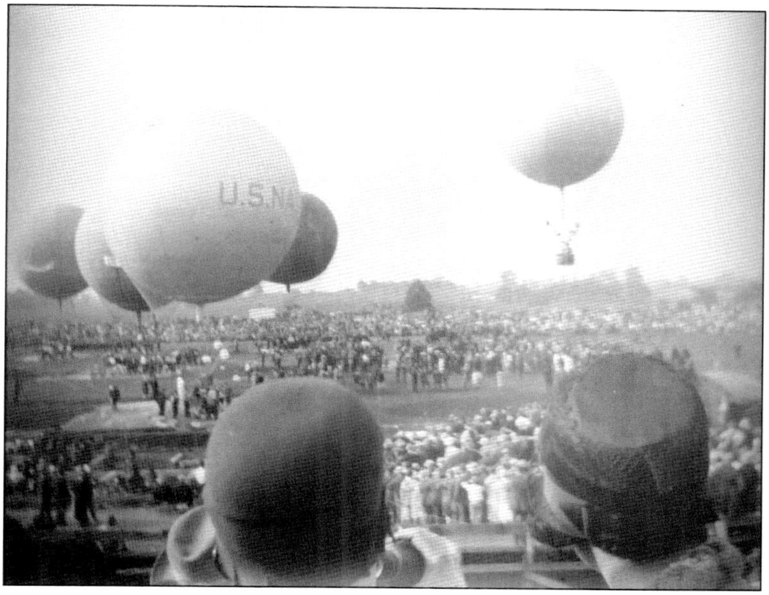

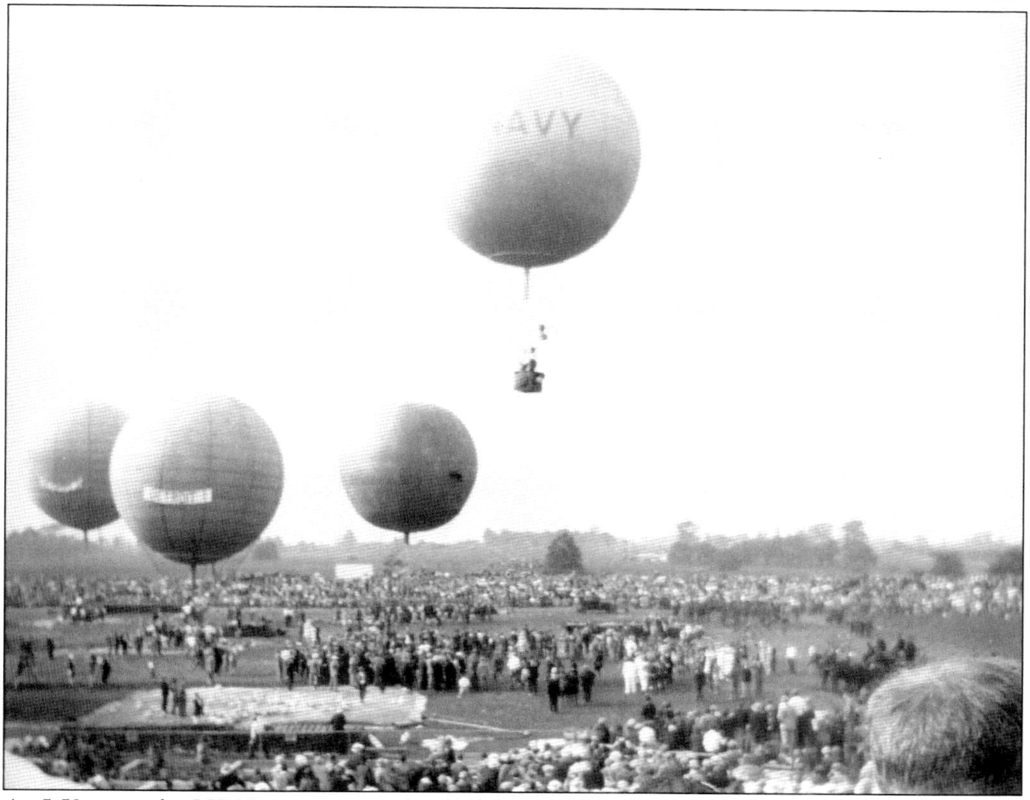

At 5:52 p.m., the US Navy entry in the 1927 National Balloon Race leaves the ground. It was piloted by Lt. "Tex" Settle and Chief Boatswain's Mate George Steelman. Although their 393-mile flight to Pope Mills, New York, was not far enough to place in this race, Settle would go on to place first in the 1931 National Balloon Race, which had its starting point in Akron.

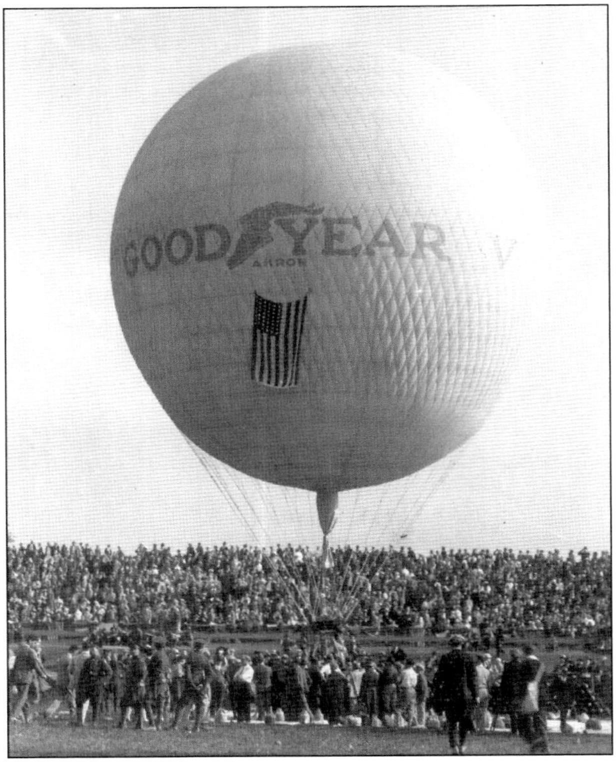

The winner of the 1927 National Balloon Race out of the Akron-Cleveland Speedway was the *Goodyear V*, piloted by Ward T. Van Orman and his aide, Walter Morton. This photograph was taken just before they left the ground at 5:20 p.m. Their 718-mile flight to Bar Harbor, Maine, took approximately 26 hours.

Ward T. Van Orman (far left) and Jack Yolton (far left) stand between two unidentified men in front of an early Akron balloon. Van Orman, a Goodyear balloonist, also won the US Gordon Bennett Races in 1929 and 1930 with his copilot, A.L. McCracken. Jack Yolton was the pilot of the *Pilgrim*, the first blimp designed to be inflated with helium.

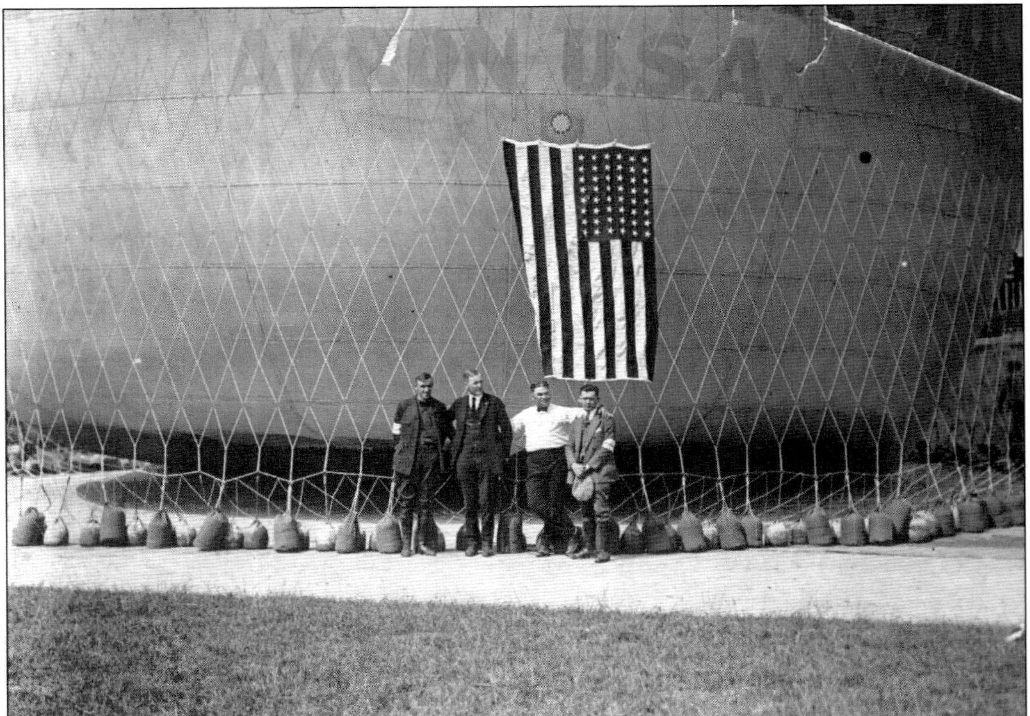

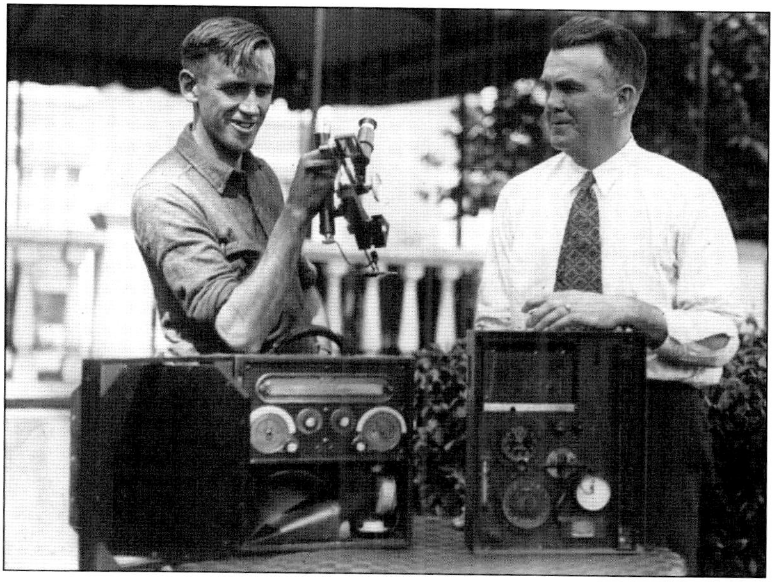

Ward T. Van Orman (left) is seen here with Walter M. Morton. Van Orman (1894–1978) was a Goodyear balloonist. In 1926, he won the US Gordon Bennett Races with his copilot, Walter M. Morton. Tragically, a lightning bolt killed Morton in a balloon race in Pittsburgh, Pennsylvania, in 1928.

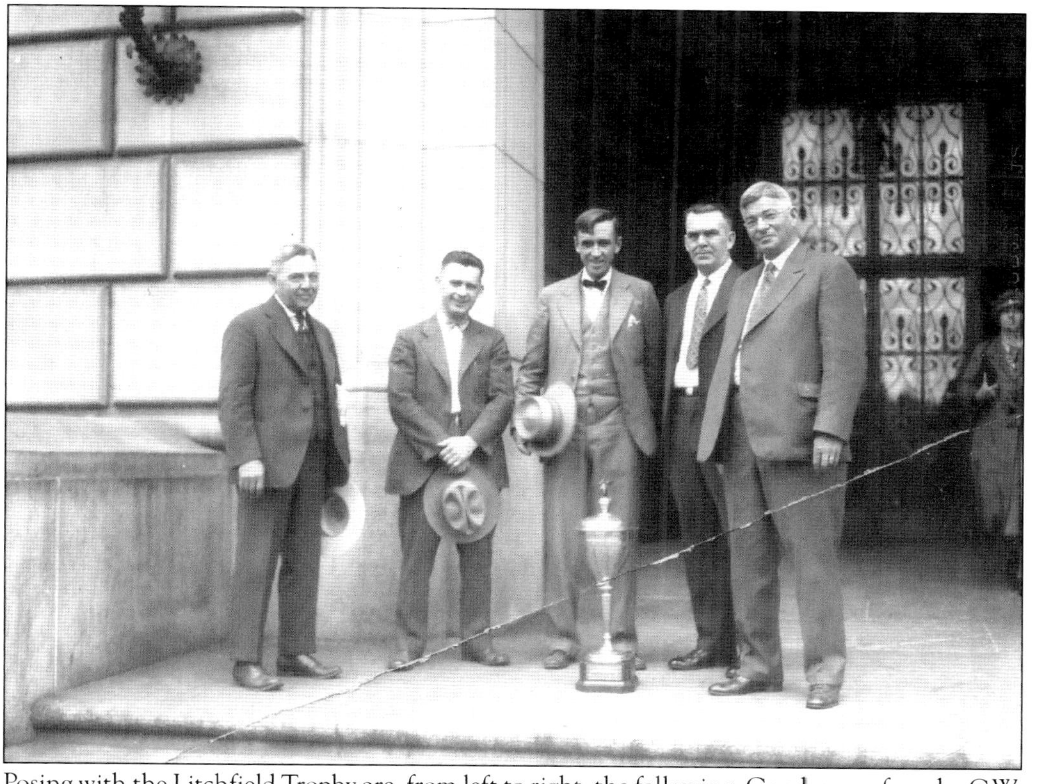

Posing with the Litchfield Trophy are, from left to right, the following: Goodyear cofounder C.W. Seiberling; Goodyear pilot Carl Wollam; winning pilot Ward T. Van Orman; Van Orman's aide, Walter Morton; and Goodyear vice president Fred Harpham. This was the third consecutive time that Van Orman had won the national race, which enabled him to take permanent possession of the Litchfield Trophy.

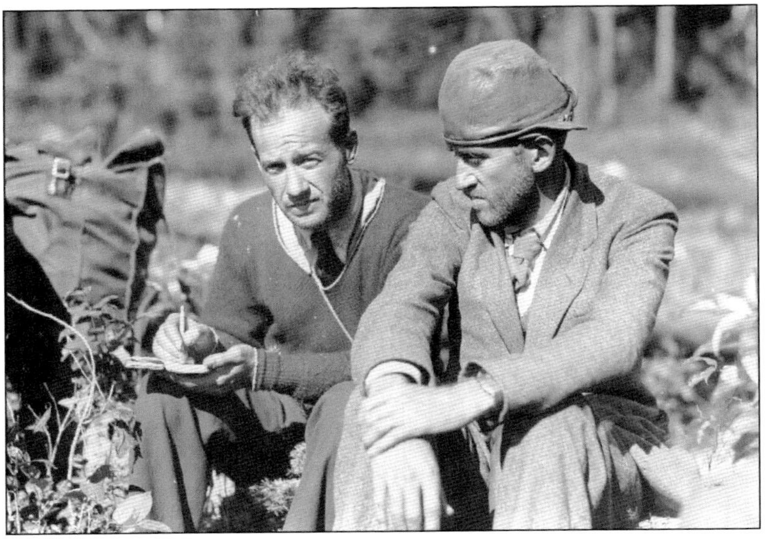

During the 1933 Gordon Bennett International Balloon Race, Frank Trotter (left) and Ward T. Van Orman (right), pilots of the *Goodyear XI*, crashed in Ontario, Canada. Here, Trotter and Van Orman await rescue. Sadly, Frank Trotter was killed in an airship accident in July 1942.

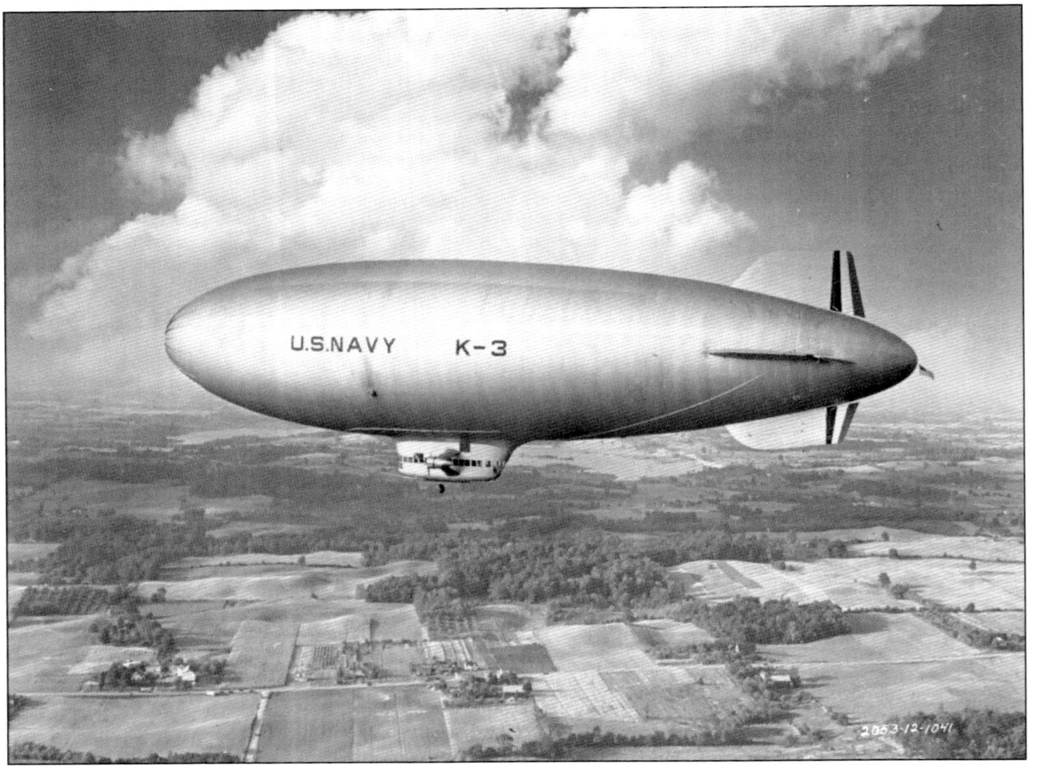

The Goodyear-built K-type airship is seen here in 1943. The ship was as iconic an image to Wingfoot Lake Airship Facility as the USS *Akron* was to the Goodyear Zeppelin Airship Factory. During World War II, 156 airships of all types were built for the US Navy for patrol duty. None were quite as successful as the K ship, assembled at Wingfoot Lake. (Courtesy of the University of Akron Archives.)

Three

Incredible Triumph, Unspeakable Tragedy

With the end of World War I, governmental support of all branches of the service was greatly curtailed, partly for reasons of economy and partly in keeping with the trend of global disarmament. It was a time of hopeful thinking that the "war to end all wars" had been fought.

Akron, though, would benefit from these events in ways never conceived. Under the terms of the Treaty of Versailles, Germany was to build a rigid zeppelin airship and turn it over to the US Navy. At the same time, the Navy proceeded with plans to build a two-million-cubic-foot airship. In 1928, the German-built *Graf Zeppelin* amazed the world by completing a 6,630-mile flight from Freidrichshafen, Germany, to Lakehurst, New Jersey. This flight proved the reliability of the dirigible. That same year, the US Navy awarded an $8 million contract to the Akron-based Goodyear Zeppelin Company to build two giant airships. The plans called for these leviathans to have lifting gas capacity of 6.5 million cubic feet. At a length of 785 feet, they were longer than a city block.

When the Goodyear Zeppelin Company was formed, expert zeppelin designers were brought to Akron. They immediately started work on designing huge airships, with the hopes of commercial applications. With contract in hand, Goodyear had to build a mammoth hangar to construct the airships. The company wanted the hangar as close to its factories as possible. That need would lead to the creation of the Akron Municipal Airport. In point of fact, the airport, Goodyear, and the City of Akron would grow up together in times of incredible triumph and moments of unspeakable tragedy.

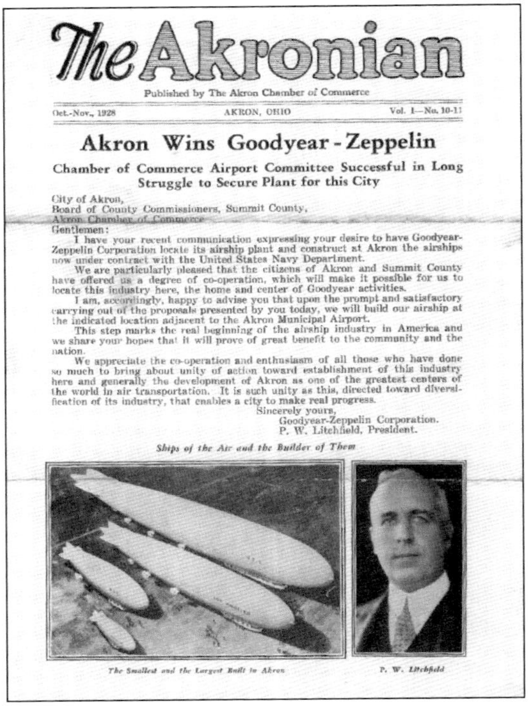

The Akronian

Published by The Akron Chamber of Commerce

Oct.-Nov., 1928 — AKRON, OHIO — Vol. 1—No. 10-11

Akron Wins Goodyear - Zeppelin

Chamber of Commerce Airport Committee Successful in Long Struggle to Secure Plant for this City

City of Akron,
Board of County Commissioners, Summit County,
Akron Chamber of Commerce
Gentlemen:

I have your recent communication expressing your desire to have Goodyear-Zeppelin Corporation locate its airship plant and construct at Akron the airships now under contract with the United States Navy Department.

We are particularly pleased that the citizens of Akron and Summit County have offered us a degree of co-operation, which will make it possible for us to locate this industry here, the home and center of Goodyear activities.

I am, accordingly, happy to advise you that upon the prompt and satisfactory carrying out of the proposals presented by you today, we will build our airship at the indicated location adjacent to the Akron Municipal Airport.

This step marks the real beginning of the airship industry in America and we share your hopes that it will prove of great benefit to the community and the nation.

We appreciate the co-operation and enthusiasm of all those who have done so much to bring about unity of action toward establishment of this industry here and generally the development of Akron as one of the greatest centers of the world in air transportation. It is such unity as this, directed toward diversification of its industry, that enables a city to make real progress.

Sincerely yours,
Goodyear-Zeppelin Corporation.
P. W. Litchfield, President.

Ships of the Air and the Builder of Them

The Smallest and the Largest Built in Akron — *P. W. Litchfield*

The October-November 1928 issue of the *Akronian*, the official publication of the Akron Chamber of Commerce, heralds the signing of the contract with the US Navy to manufacture two giant zeppelins. This contract sealed a place in aviation history for Goodyear and Akron. It would also give rise to one of the most unique manufacturing enterprises ever devised.

No sooner had the ink dried on Goodyear Zeppelin Company's announcement, than work began on constructing the airship factory. In this 1929 photograph, excavation is being conducted to remove one million cubic yards of earth. Nearly 1,300 concrete piles were driven to rock as a base for the structure, each pile being able to withstand a weight of 30 tons.

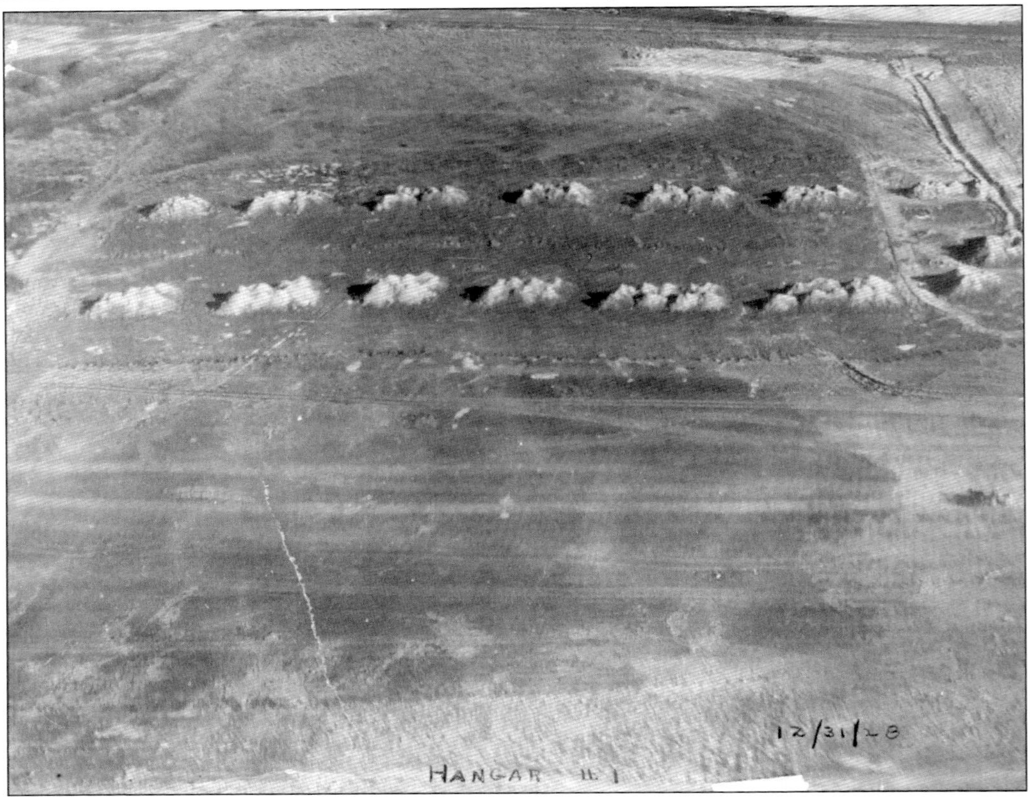

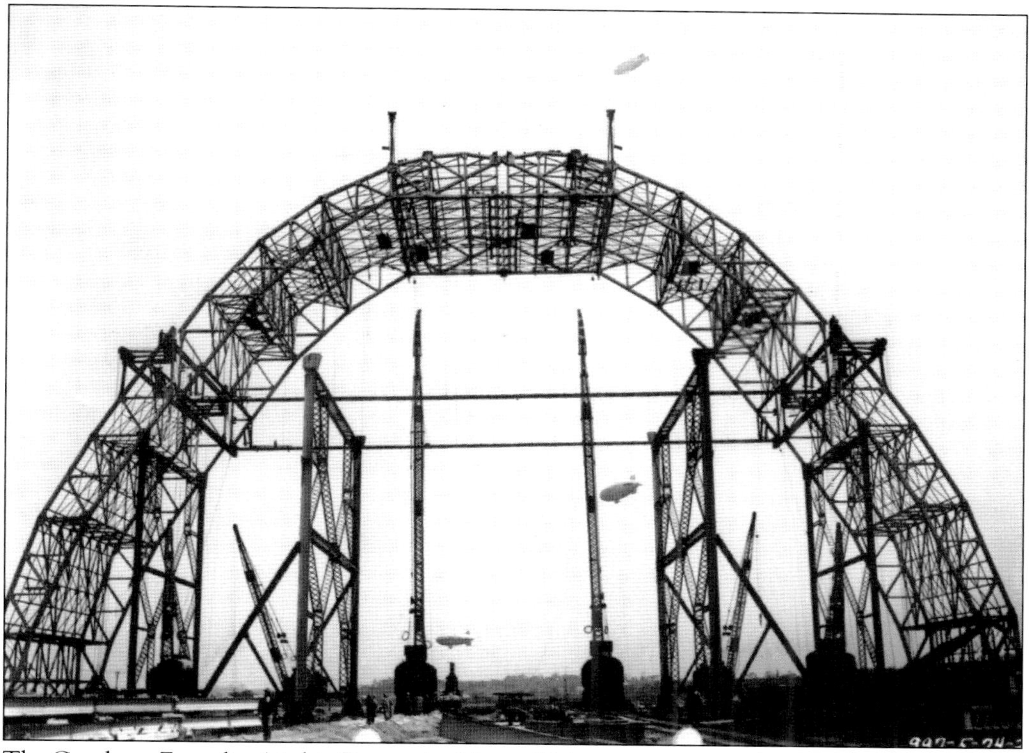

The Goodyear Zeppelin Airship Factory in Akron, Ohio, was constructed in 1929 by the Goodyear Zeppelin Corporation from plans created by the Wilbur Watson Engineering Company of Cleveland, Ohio. In this 1929 photograph, the center support sections are under construction, while a fleet of smaller Goodyear Tire & Rubber Company airships pass in review.

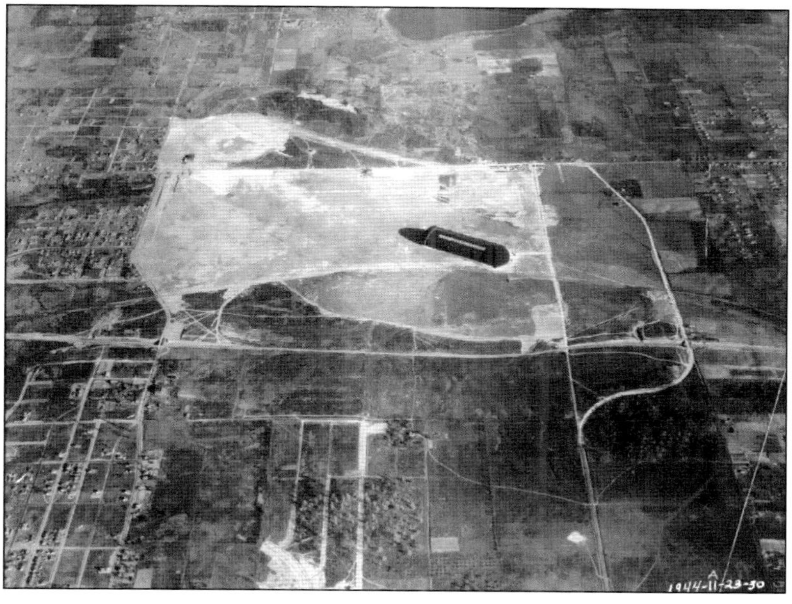

In this photograph, taken on November 23, 1930, the newly completed Goodyear Zeppelin Airship Factory is seen standing nearly alone. Bain E. Fulton's "Flying Field" can be seen in the upper left.

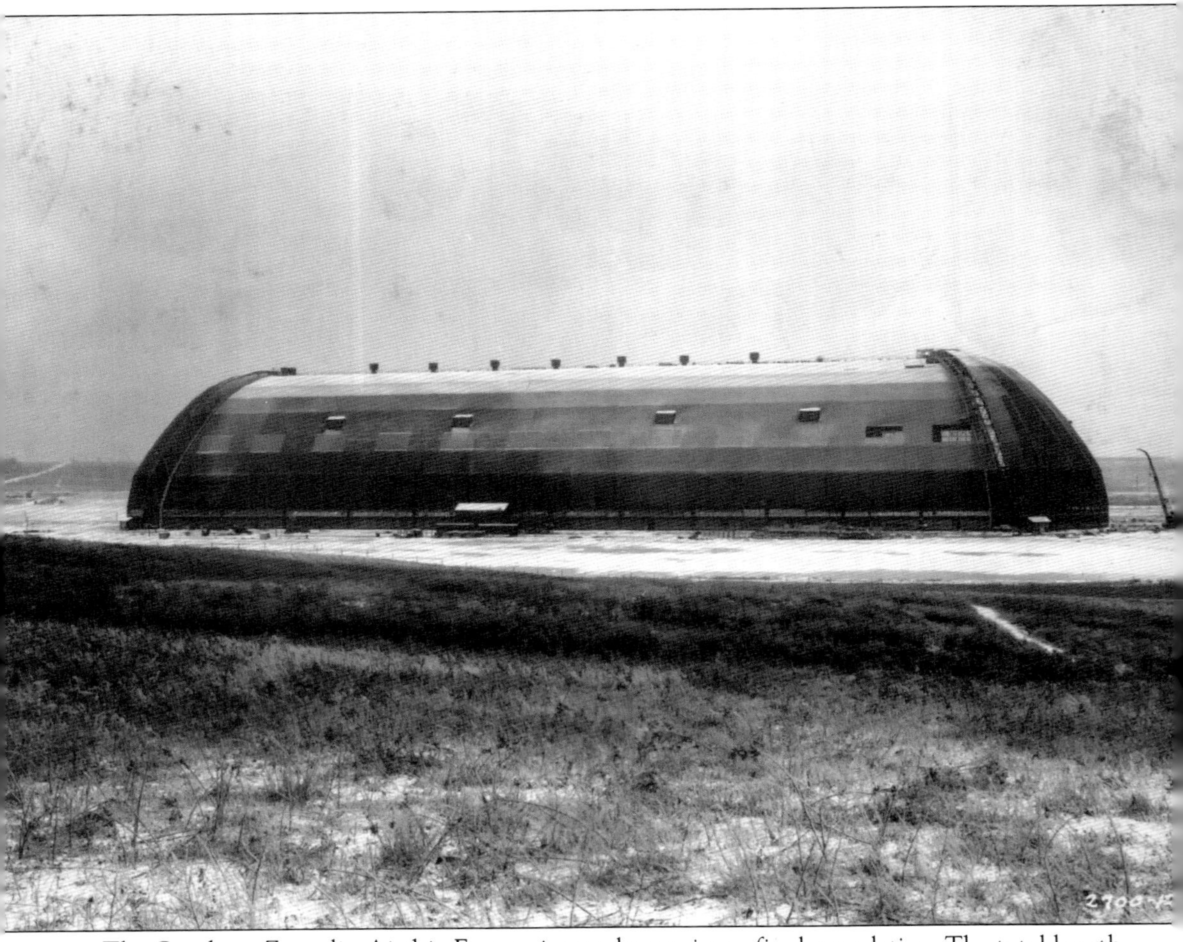

The Goodyear Zeppelin Airship Factory is seen here prior to final completion. The total length of the hangar is 1,175 feet, its total width is 325 feet, and its height is 211 feet. The orange-peel parabolic hangar doors weigh 600 tons each. It is the largest freestanding structure in the world, capable of housing two World War II–era aircraft carriers along with the Washington Monument and the Statue of Liberty.

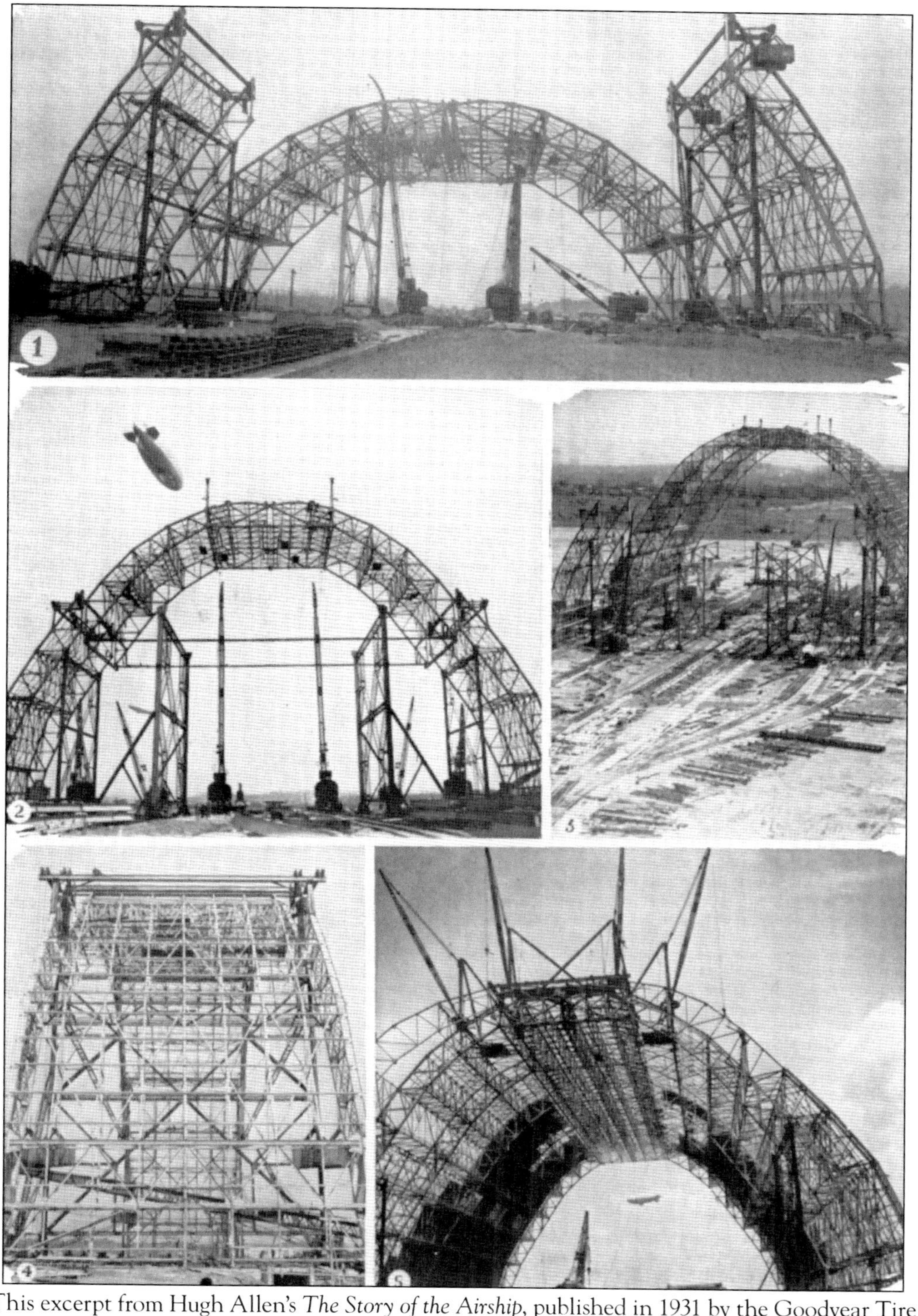

This excerpt from Hugh Allen's *The Story of the Airship*, published in 1931 by the Goodyear Tire & Rubber Company, tells in photographic sequence the construction of the airship dock's arch, center sections, and roof covering. (Author's collection.)

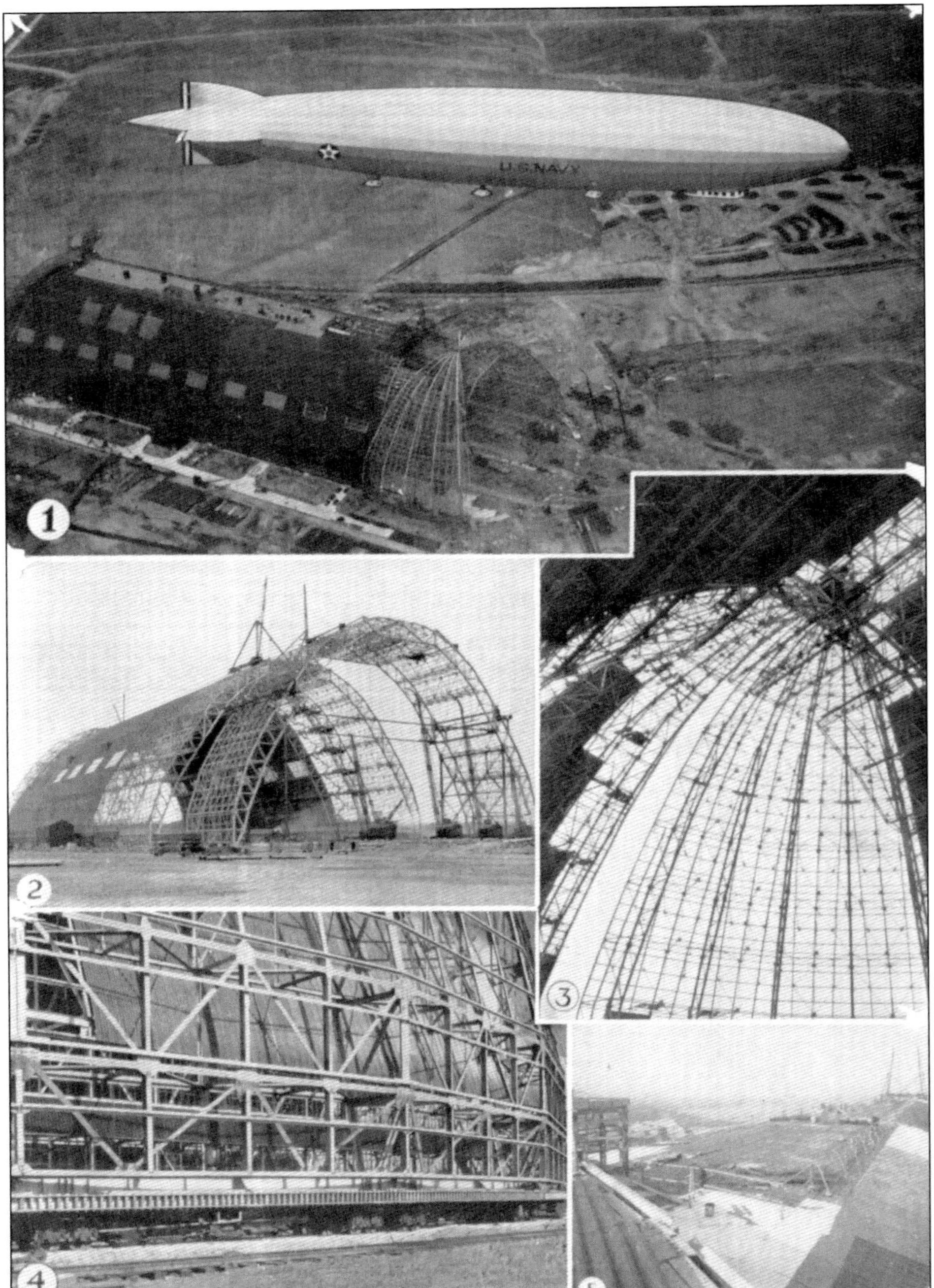

This excerpt from Hugh Allen's *The Story of the Airship* illustrates a number of items. The top photograph (1) shows the US Navy airship *Los Angeles* flying over the dock at the ring-laying ceremonies in November 1929. (2) The framework of the doors are plainly visible. (3) This is a ground view of progress on the airdock. (4) This is an internal view of the door framework. (5) Here, the doors of the dock, weighing 1,200 tons a pair, are mounted on standard railway tracks. (Author's collection.)

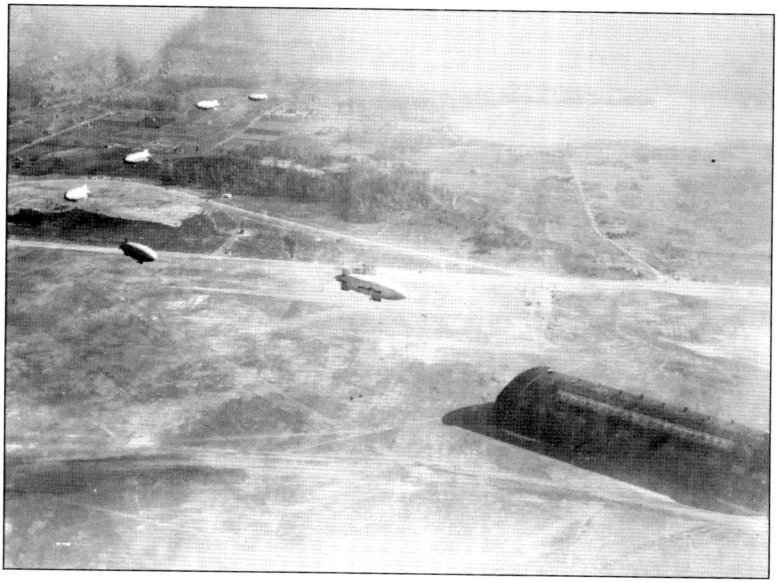

Smaller Goodyear Tire & Rubber Company airships pass in review over the newly completed Goodyear Zeppelin Airship Factory around November 1929.

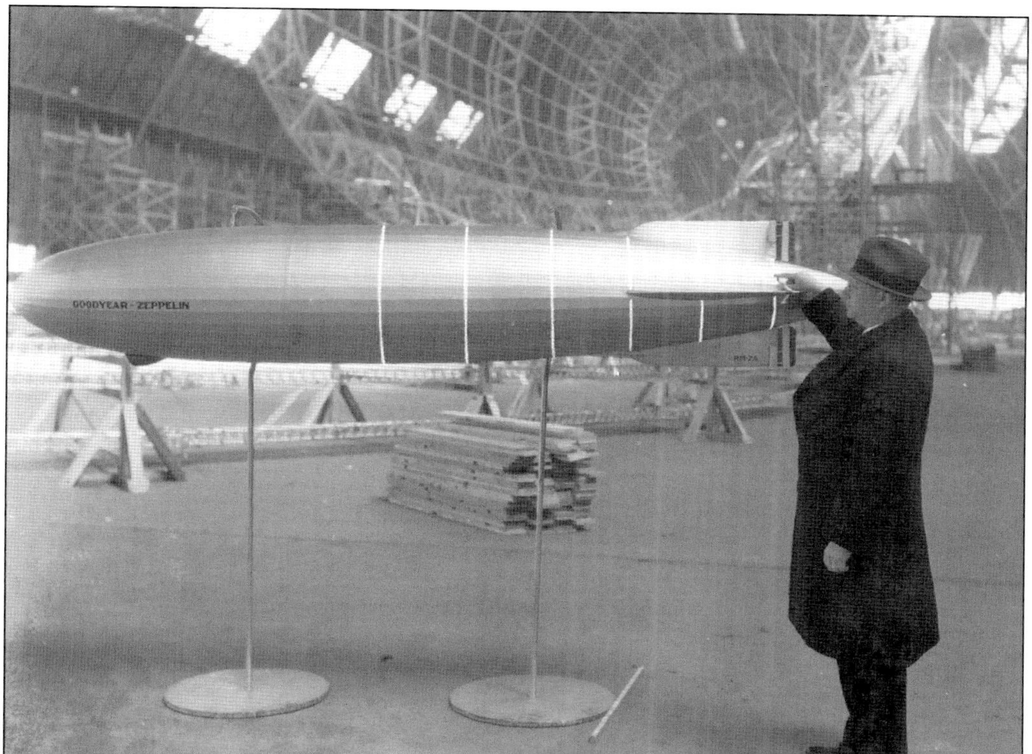

The Goodyear Zeppelin Company's director of engineering and design, Dr. Karl Arnstein, stands before a mock-up of the zeppelins of the future. In the late 1920s and early 1930s, Goodyear envisioned a world in which "great silver cruisers of the air" would rule the skies in use as intercontinental transportation. Work on the giant airship *Akron* (ZRS-4) can be seen in the background.

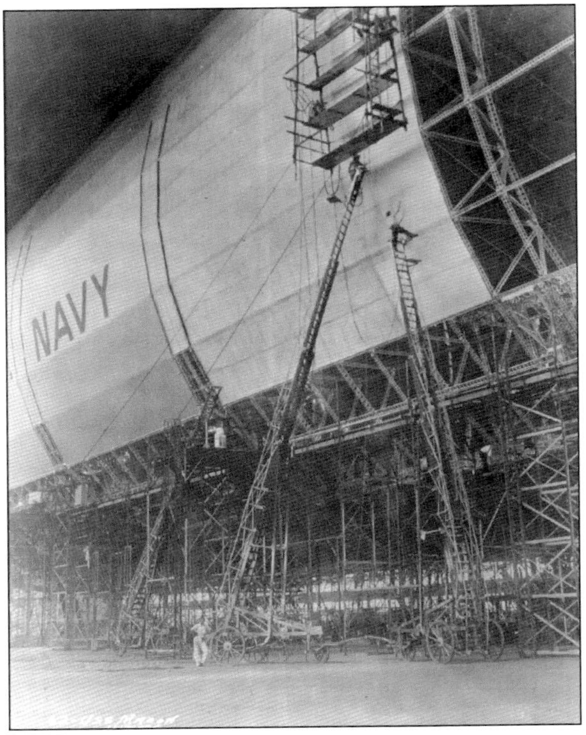

Workers are applying the outer skin coverings to the airship USS *Akron*. Airship laborers worked at heights in excess of 140 feet above the ground. Note the positions of the men on the mobile ladders and the location of the scaffolding. It appears that the best job is holding the ladder.

This 1932 photograph of the construction of USS *Macon* (ZRS-5), twin sister to the *Akron*, clearly shows the assembly of the tail section. The *Akron* and *Macon* would both crash while in service with the US Navy. Their tail sections would be a center of controversy as a possible cause.

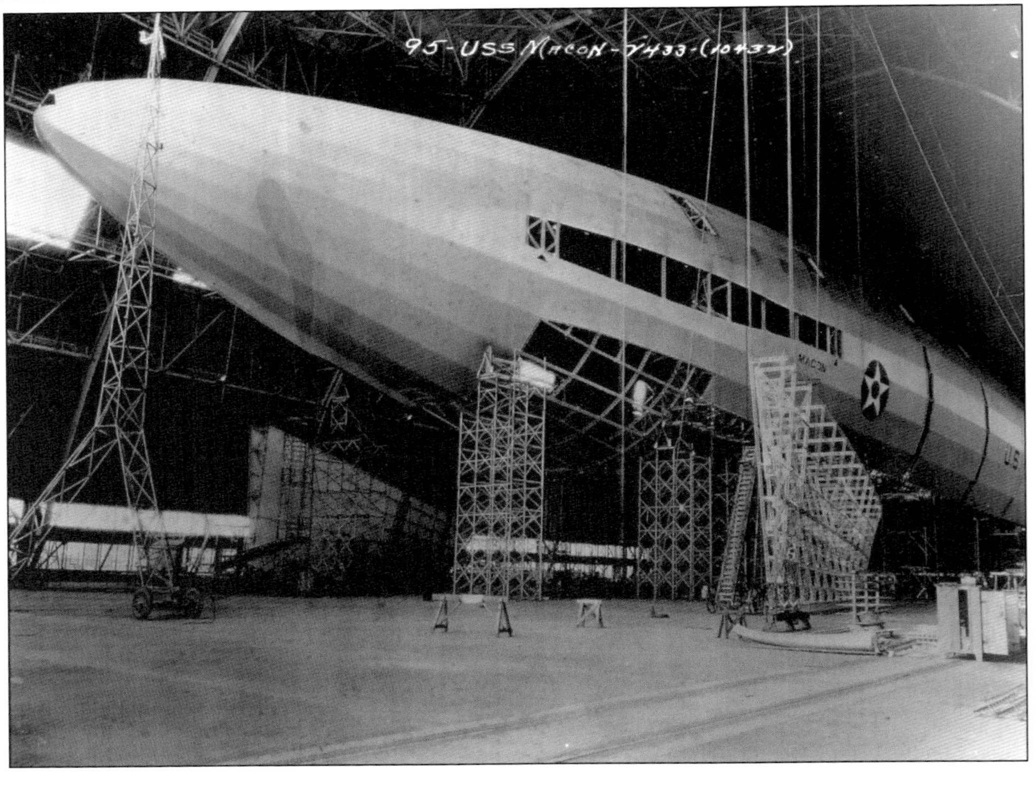

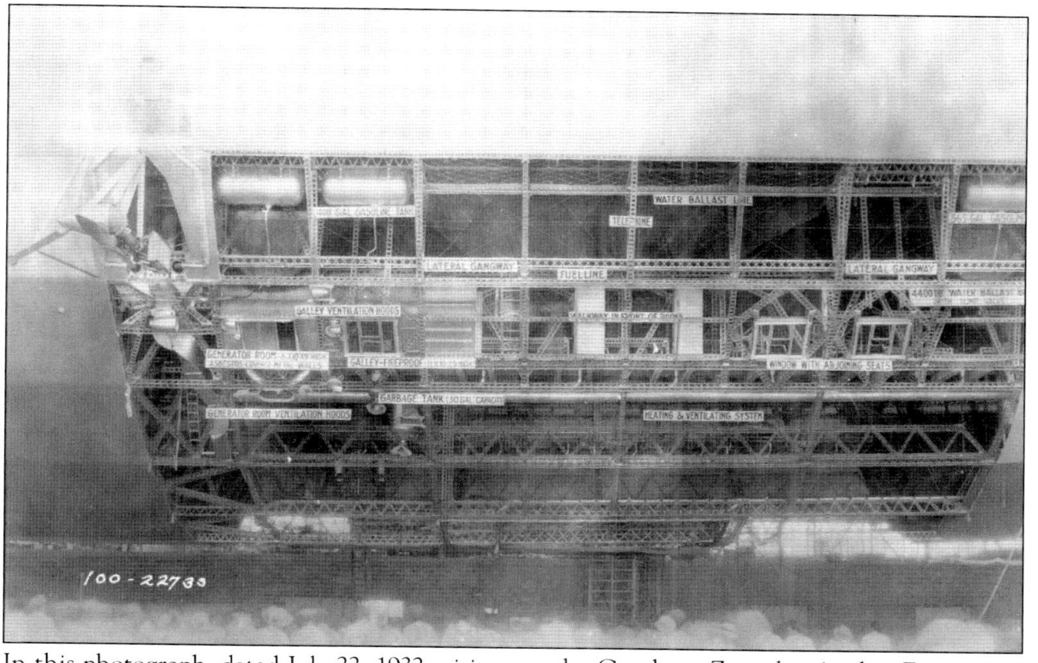

In this photograph, dated July 22, 1932, visitors to the Goodyear Zeppelin Airship Factory are given a look at the internal systems of the USS *Macon*. The outer covering has not yet been applied to this section. During construction of both the USS *Akron* and USS *Macon*, the public was welcomed into the facility to witness the progress and to purchase souvenirs.

Workers assemble the many duralumin girders that will eventually form the USS *Akron*. The newly formed Goodyear Zeppelin Company hired primarily local workers. Construction of the airship began in 1930, the beginning of the Great Depression. For most of these workers, it would be their last job for perhaps years.

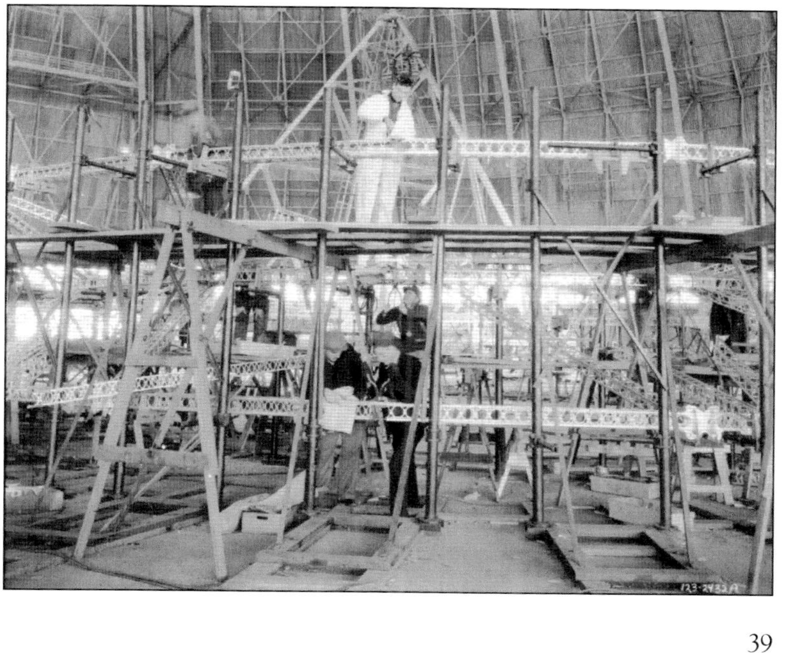

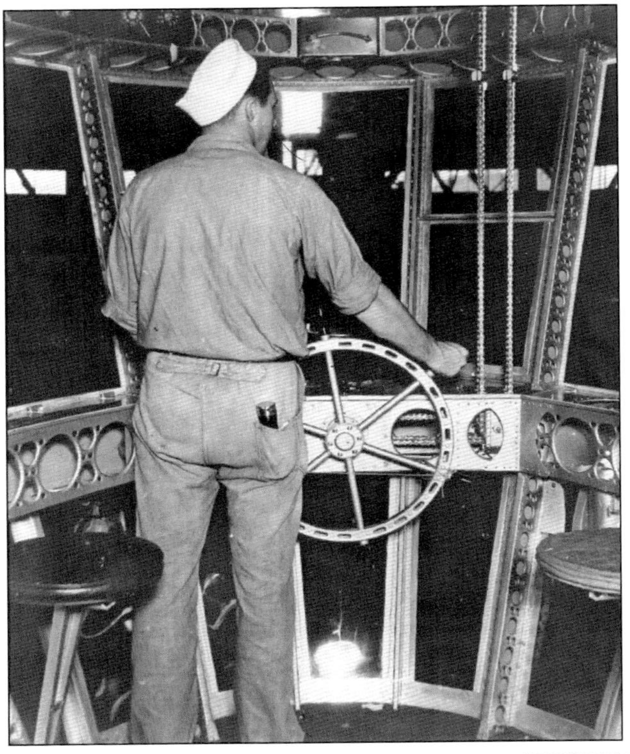

In this undated photograph, a crewman aboard the USS *Macon* mans the wheel on the navigation bridge while the airship is inside the Goodyear Zeppelin Airship Factory. Both the *Akron* and *Macon* had an auxiliary control car located at the leading edge of the bottom fin that could be used in emergency situations.

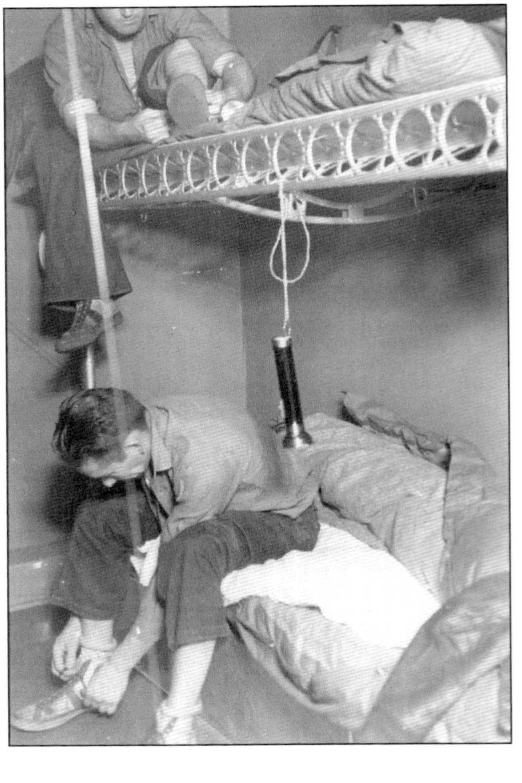

The sleeping quarters for the crewmen aboard the USS *Akron* and USS *Macon* were kept to bare necessity in the interest of weight reduction. These bunks are constructed of the same lightweight Duralumin girders as the frames of the airships.

This unidentified sailor is in the kitchen of the USS *Akron*. The aluminum stove was capable of serving a crew of 50 men on a 10-day cruise. It was designed and built by Tappan Stove Company in Mansfield, Ohio. On April 4, 1933, the *Akron* encountered a storm over the New Jersey coast and crashed, tail first, into the sea. Only 3 of the 76 men on board survived the accident.

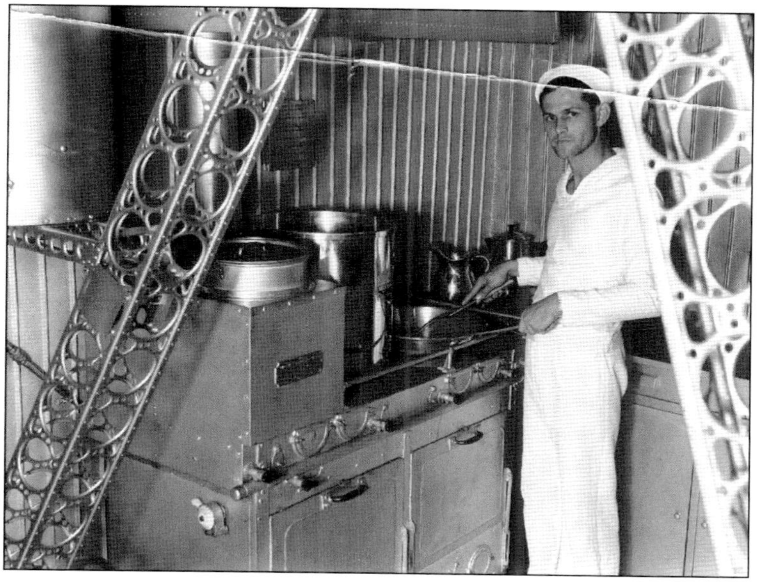

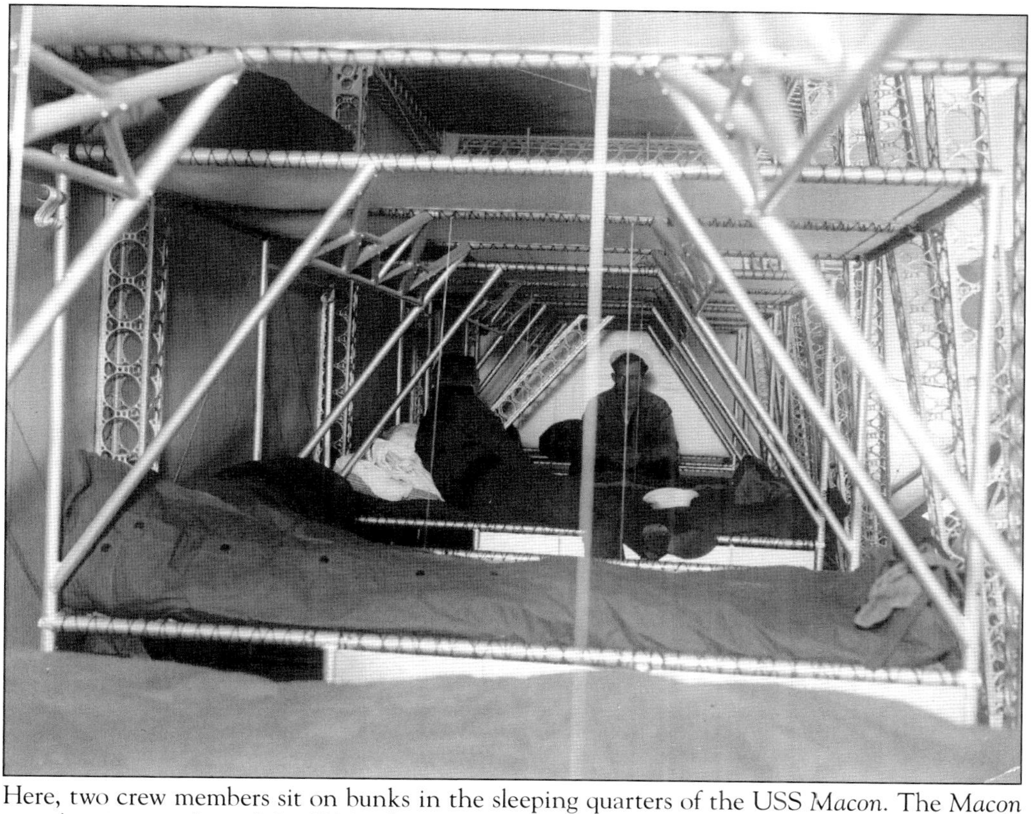

Here, two crew members sit on bunks in the sleeping quarters of the USS *Macon*. The *Macon* was the sister airship of the USS *Akron*. Both zeppelins carried a flight crew of 78. Note that these sailors are on the bottom bunk. Every operational section of the airship was designed as if on board a ship. Note the sailor's sea bags in the foreground.

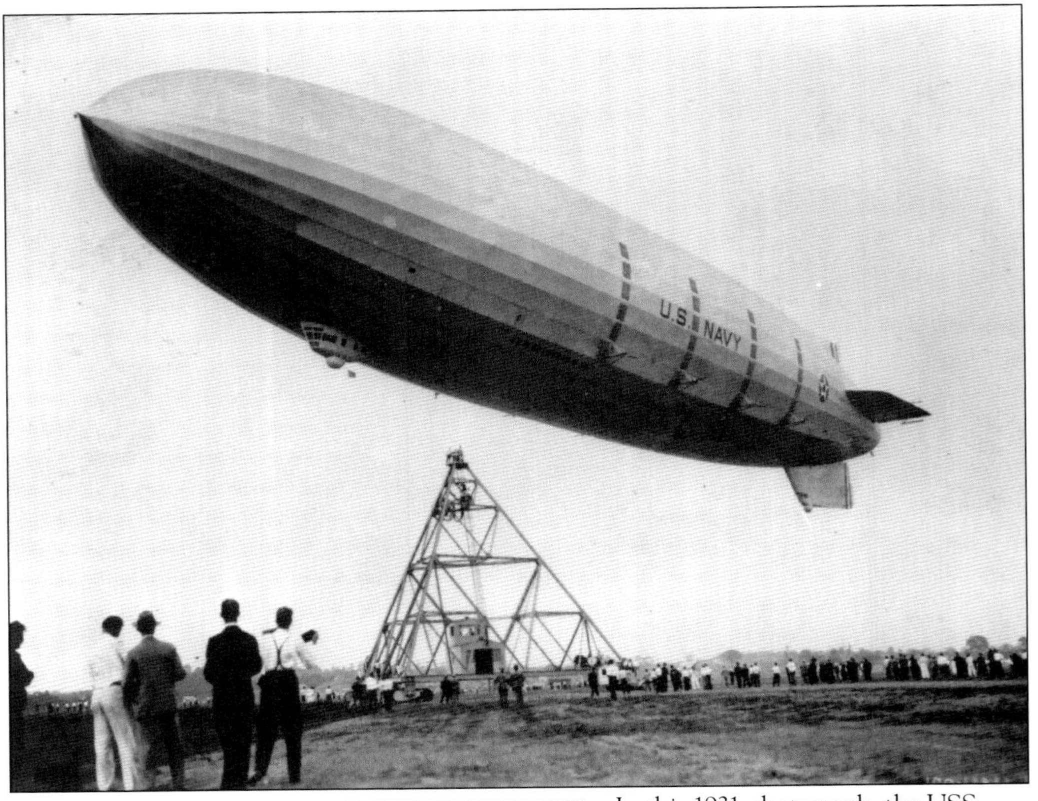

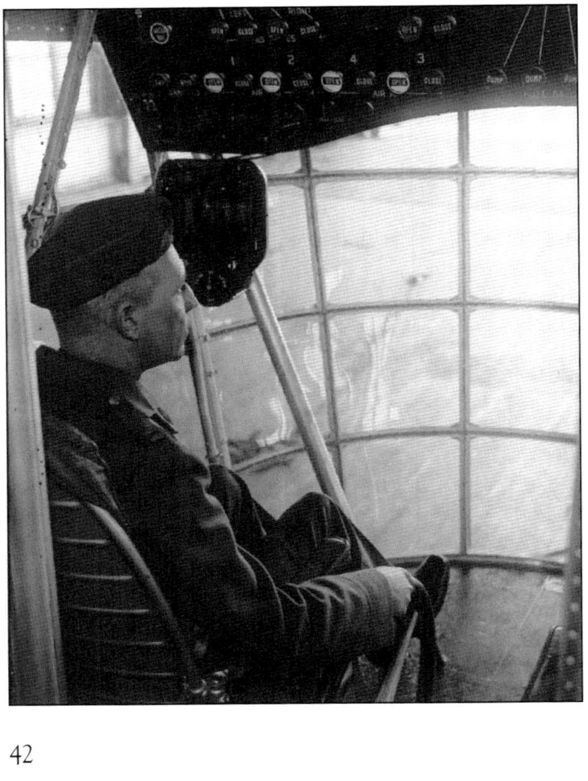

In this 1931 photograph, the USS *Akron* passes slowly overhead. The mobile mooring mast, known as "The Iron Horse," is in the foreground. No matter where the *Akron* sailed, it drew large crowds, as evidenced here by the activity on the ground. Note the lower tail fin set at left rudder. The rudder man's gondola station is in full view.

Capt. Clarence Lober is seen inside the cockpit of the zeppelin USS *Akron* in 1931. Elevator control was accomplished through the wheel on the captain's right. Rudder control was executed through voice or telegraph commands transmitted to the rudder man, stationed in the lower tail fin, approximately 785 feet in the rear.

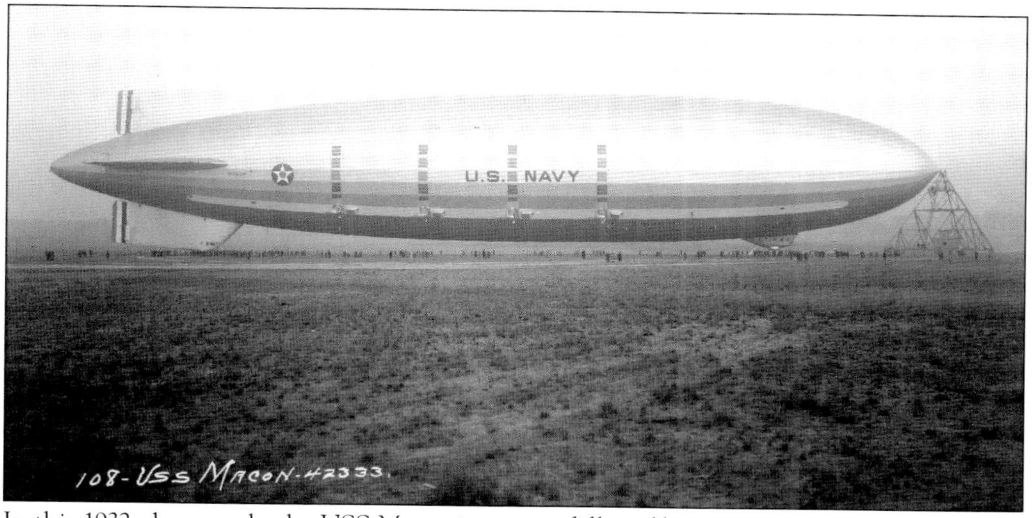

In this 1932 photograph, the USS *Macon* is seen in full profile, moored to its mast outside the Goodyear Zeppelin Airship Factory. Note the proportions of the airship compared to the size of the people on the ground. This airship had a total weight of 582,000 pounds, all suspended in flight by 6.5 million cubic feet of helium. Propelled by eight engines, the *Macon*'s maximum speed was 84 miles per hour.

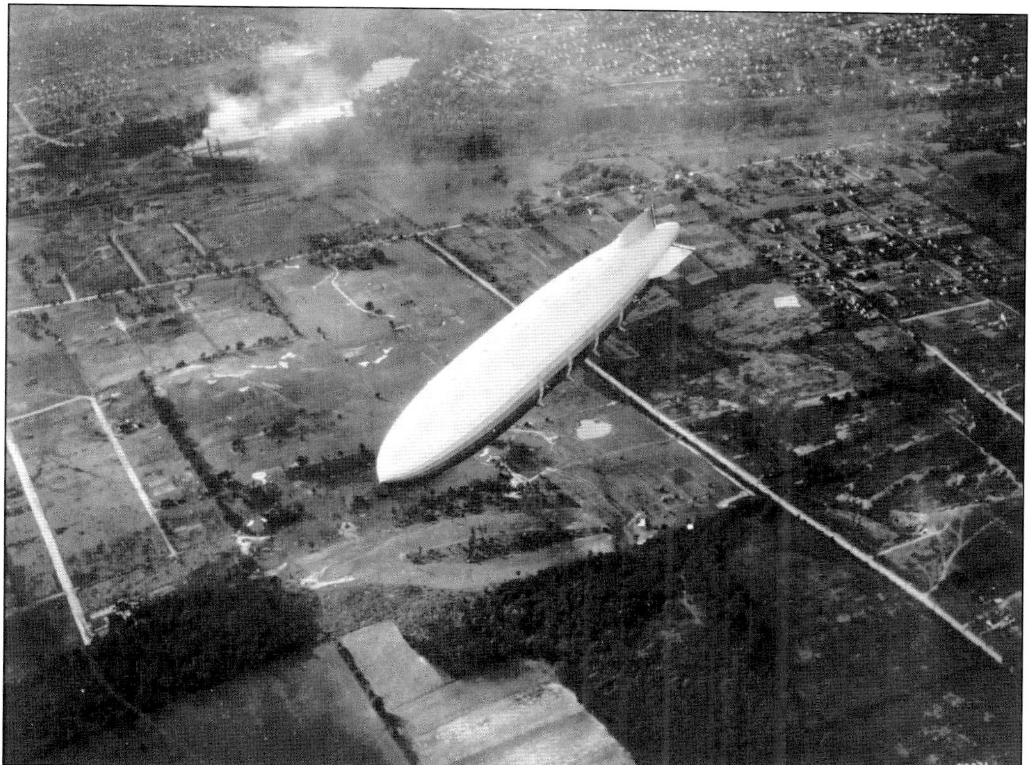

This 1932 aerial photograph shows the USS *Macon* sailing majestically over Akron and the Goodyear Tire & Rubber Company. Plant one and the Little Cuyahoga River can be seen through the ever-present smoke of an industrial boomtown.

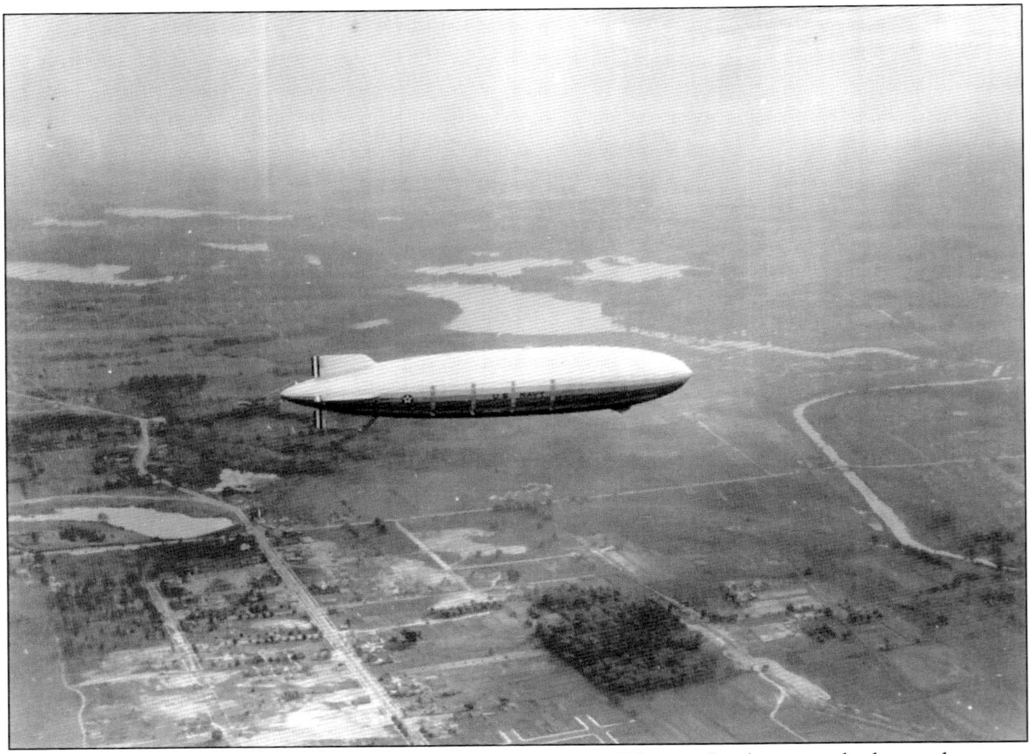

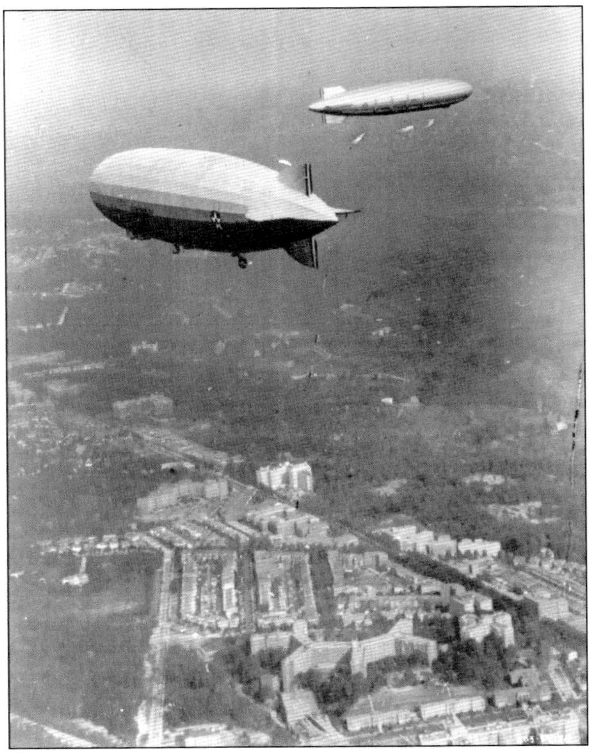

This early photograph shows the USS *Akron* heading out over the countryside. This is a clear view of the upper and lower fin outer structure, which would become a central point of discussion in analyzing the fatal crash that would claim the lives of 76 of her crew.

Because of cost restrictions imposed on the military by Congress in the early years of the Great Depression, the USS *Akron* and the USS *Macon* were sent on extensive public relations tours. In this rare photograph, both airships are seen together, dropping packages over an unidentified city.

The USS *Macon* approaches the Akron Municipal Airport. The *Macon* was the sister zeppelin of the USS *Akron*. Both airships had tragic ends. The USS *Macon* encountered a storm off Point Sur, California, and was brought down into the sea. All but two of her crew were rescued.

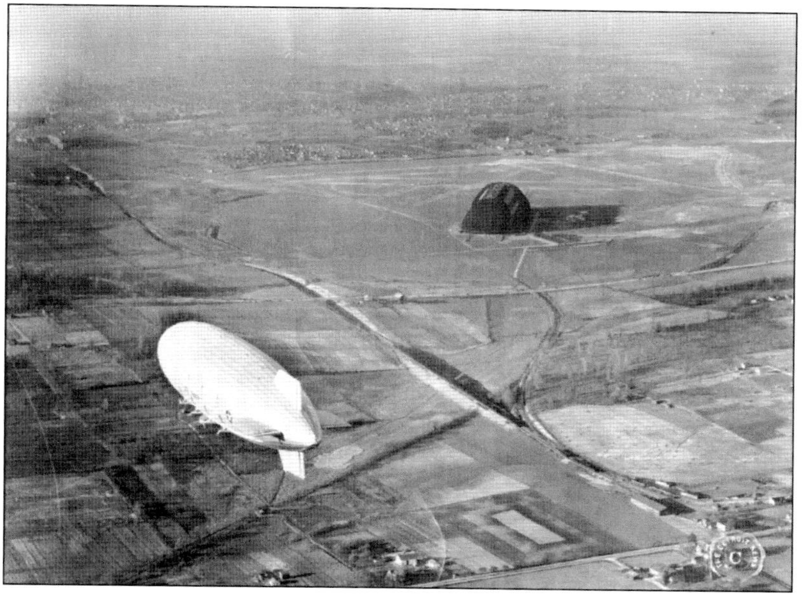

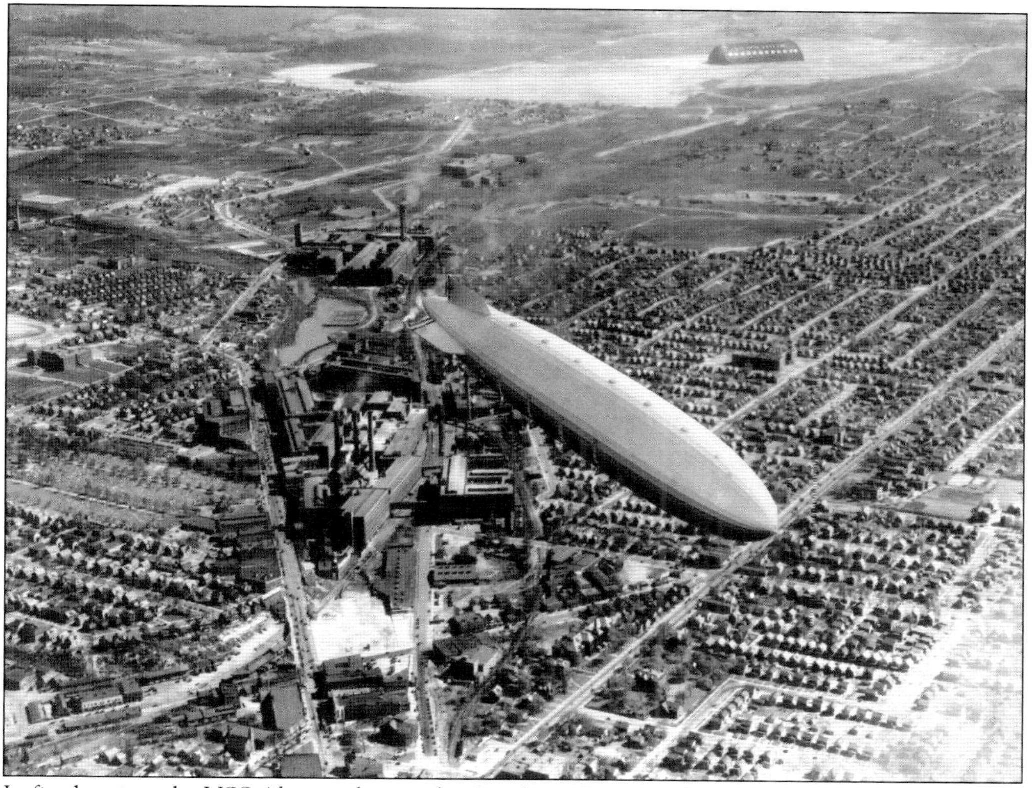

In final review, the USS *Akron* sails over the Goodyear Tire & Rubber Company en route to active service with the US Navy at Lakehurst, New Jersey. The Goodyear Zeppelin Airship Factory can be seen in the upper right. The Akron Municipal Airport, still under construction, is in the upper left. The newly constructed terminal building is visible to the left of the airdock.

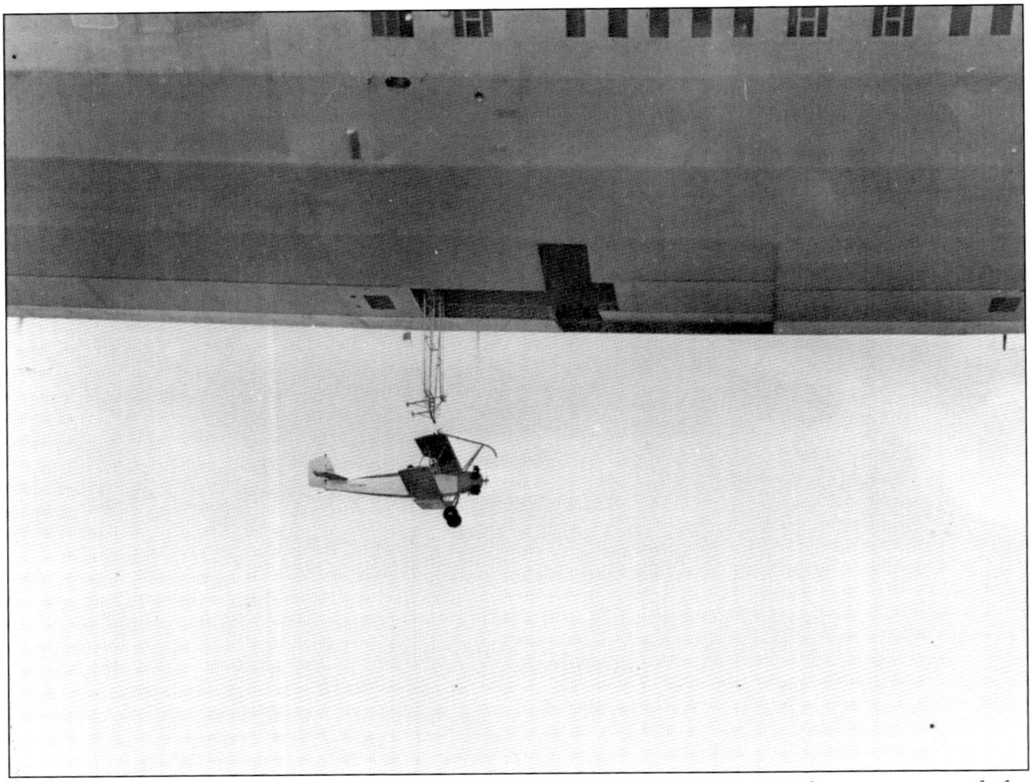

A truly unique feature of the giant airships was the concept of carrying their own aircraft for scouting purposes and defense. This photograph, taken of the aircraft from the USS *Akron*'s air group, clearly shows the delicate and difficult maneuver known as "hooking on." Records were unavailable as to the number of takeoffs and landings practiced while in flight. (Courtesy of the Naval History and Heritage Command.)

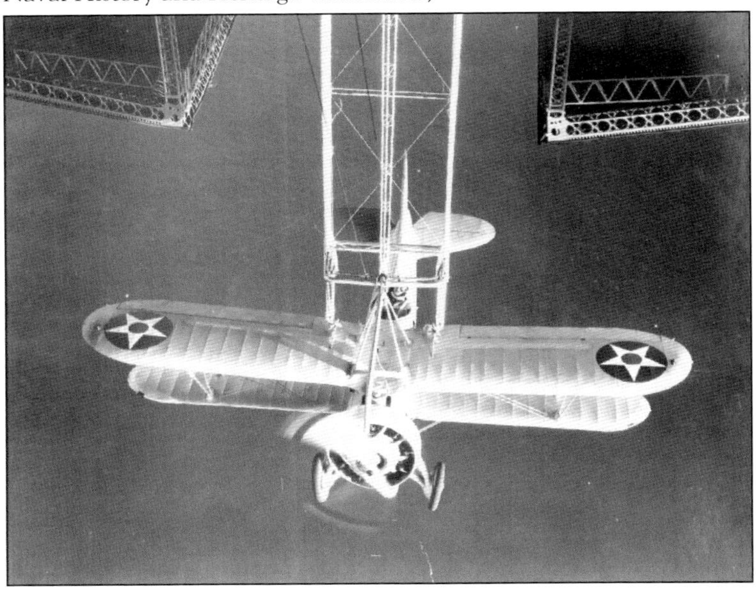

A closer view of what the USS *Macon*'s air group called "belly bumping" clearly shows the precision required for such a maneuver. Note the relatively small size of the Curtiss FX9 fighter and the precision engineering required to hoist the aircraft aboard. A look beyond the little fighter shows how an aborted landing could go very badly. (Courtesy of the Naval History and Heritage Command.)

This memorial stamp was made in honor of those lost in the USS *Akron* crash. It reads: "In Memoriam To The Lives Lost In The Akron Disaster. Memorial Day 1933. Lakewood Stamp Society—Lakewood, N.J." On the evening of April 3, 1933, the *Akron* cast off from the mooring mast to operate along the coast of New England, assisting in the calibration of radio direction finder stations. Rear Adm. William Moffett was on board, along with his aide. The airship encountered a heavy thunderstorm and broke up over the stormy Atlantic Ocean, killing 73 of its 76 crew members, including Moffett. This loss was followed by the crash of the USS *Macon* off the coast of Point Sur, California, on February 12, 1935, which resulted in the deaths of two crewmen. These disasters ended the era of the leviathans of the air.

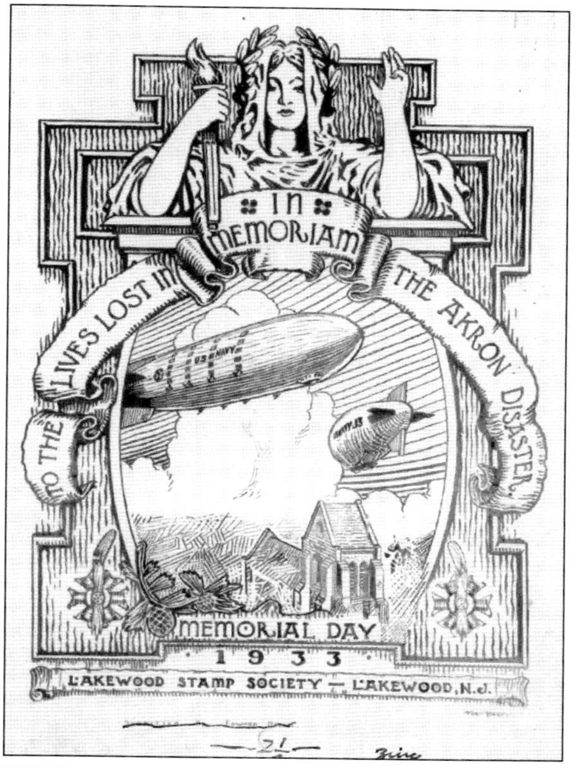

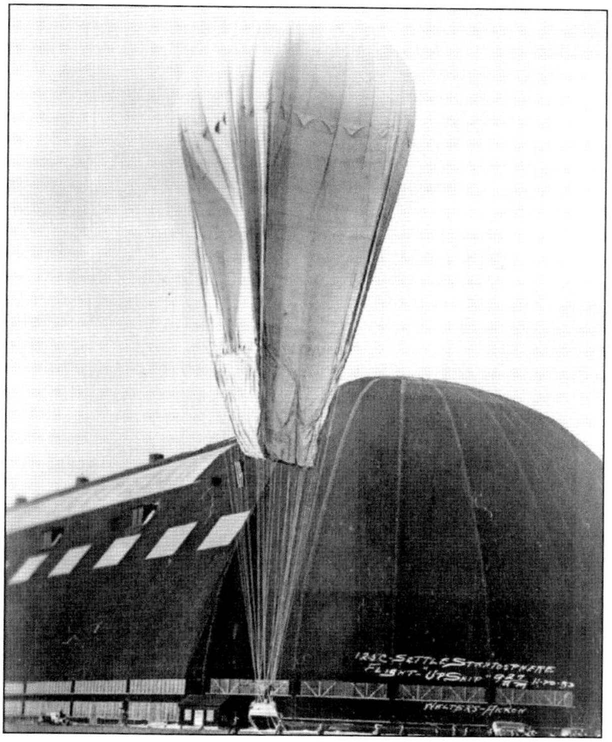

On November 20, 1933, the high-altitude balloon *Century of Progress*, piloted by Lt. Thomas G. "Tex" Settle and Marine major Chester L Fordney, lifts off from the Goodyear Zeppelin facilities in Akron, Ohio, in pursuit of a high-altitude record. The record was achieved by attaining an altitude of 61,237 feet.

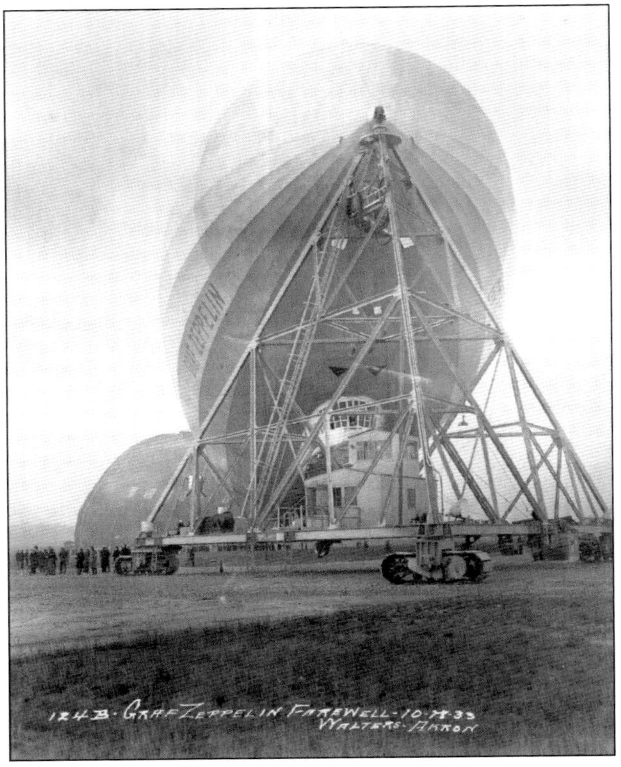

The German passenger airship *Graf Zeppelin* visits the Goodyear Zeppelin Airship Factory in Akron on its way back to Germany from an appearance at the Chicago Century of Progress Exposition in 1933. Note the size of the "Iron Horse" mobile mast.

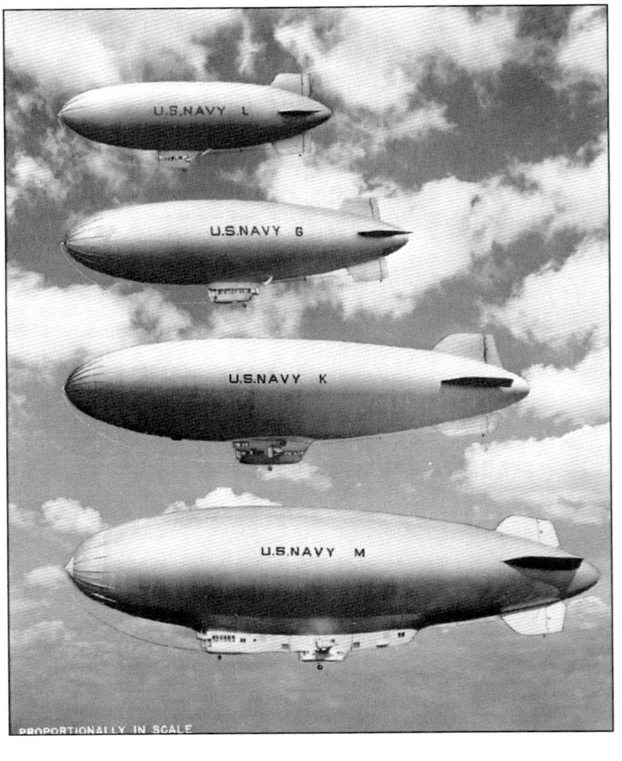

The age of the leviathans of the air ended with the loss of the USS *Macon* in February 1935. Akron and the Goodyear Tire & Rubber Company never lost their fascination with lighter-than-air flight. This photograph shows the new generation of lighter-than-air ships that took the place of their extraordinary predecessors.

Four

A Giant Aircraft Factory

In the winter of 1939–1940, the United States began developing plans should the country be drawn into war. Lighter-than-air flight become an integral part of those plans, as the US Navy examined its ability to defend the coasts and protect shipping lanes. Remembering the success of the airships in coastal defense during World War I, in June 1940, Congress, as part of a 10,000-airplane bill, included a request for 48 airships. In October 1940, the first contract for 48 K-type airships was awarded to the Goodyear Aircraft Corporation, a subsidiary of the Goodyear Tire & Rubber Company. The K-type airships had a helium capacity of 412,000 cubic feet, were 253 feet long, and were 80 feet high.

At that time, the Goodyear Aircraft Corporation was in its infancy, with only 36 men on its payroll, building aircraft parts for the Martin B26 "Marauder" medium bomber. By the end of the war, the company employed 33,500 workers and was producing 154 airships and 4,006 Corsair fighter aircraft. The company also produced wheels, brakes, and various aircraft components, including the following: airframes for 575 Boeing B29 Superfortresses, 165 Consolidated B24 "Liberator" bombers, 5,800 Martin B26 "Marauder" medium bombers, 3,000 Grumman TBF torpedo bombers, 900 Lockheed P38 "Lightning" fighter aircraft, 300 Curtiss Aircraft P40 "Warhawk" fighter aircraft, 900 Northrop "Black Widow" night fighter aircraft, 1,400 Martin PBM "Mariner" flying boats, 3,000 Grumman "Hellcat" fighter aircraft, 600 Grumman "Tigercat" fighter aircraft, 235 Consolidated "Coronado" long-range flying boats, 600 Lockheed "Ventura" medium-range patrol aircraft, and 125 helicopters. During the war years, the Goodyear Aircraft Corporation employed more workers than did all of the rubber factories in Akron during the Great Depression.

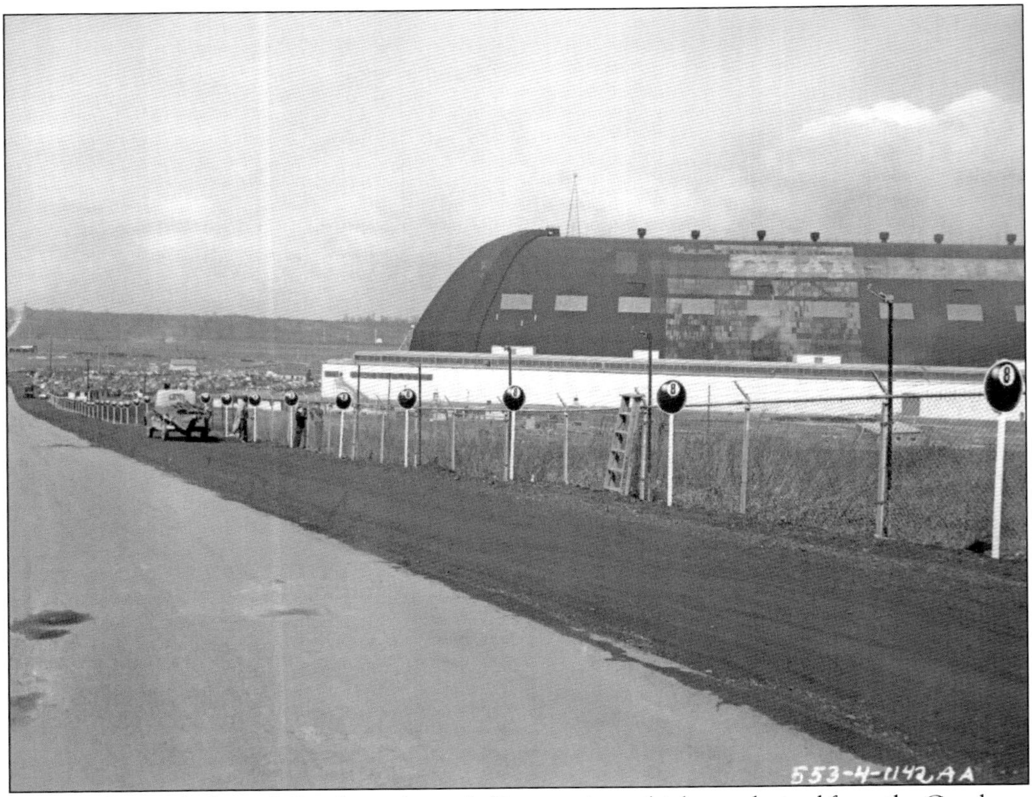

In 1939, the newly formed Goodyear Aircraft Corporation, which was derived from the Goodyear Zeppelin Corporation, had approximately 30 men on its payroll. In the last year of the war, 35,000 men and women were employed by Goodyear Aircraft Corporation. The "eight-ball" signs were a slogan designed to keep employees aware of President Roosevelt's nationwide wartime goal of 60,000 airplanes a year, or roughly one airplane every eight minutes, thus putting the Axis behind the "eight ball."

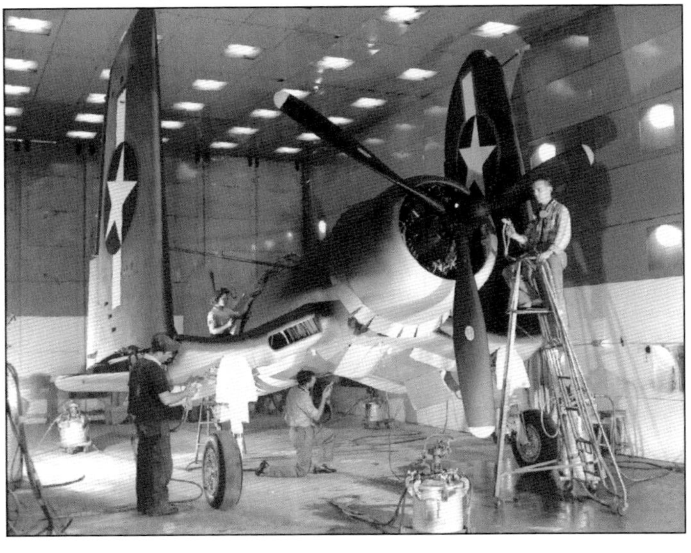

During the last three years of World War II, Goodyear Aircraft built approximately 4,000 FG-1D Corsair airplanes for the Navy. The Corsair had the most powerful engine and largest propeller of any fighter plane, and it could reach a speed of 400 miles per hour. This 1944 photograph shows the aircraft painting process. This plane's color scheme is regulation navy blue on top and light blue underneath, for aerial camouflage.

This 1944 photograph was taken at Goodyear's plant D, located adjacent to the airdock. This is an illustration of how industries adapted to other manufacturing techniques. Here, Corsair center sections are seen on the "broadway," which was a conveyor assembly similar to an automobile assembly.

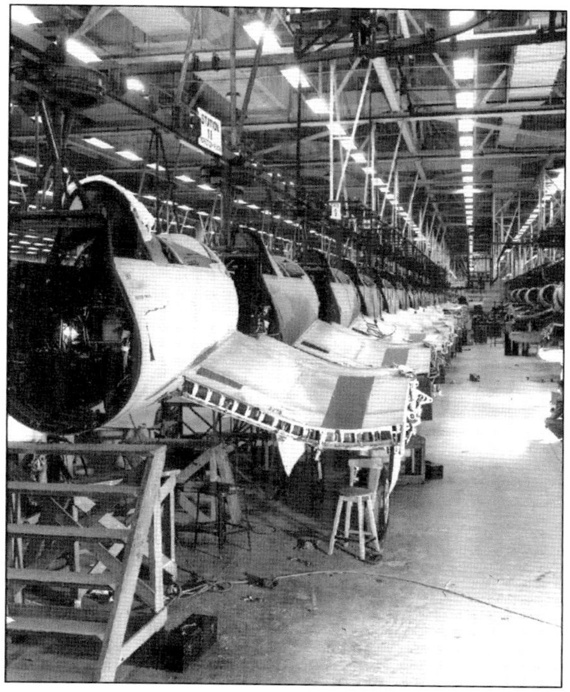

There were size restrictions on workers for certain types of jobs. This two-man team installs a fuel line behind the aircraft engine and forward of the cockpit. The worker inside the aircraft had to remove his shoes prior to entry, due to the tightly cramped work space.

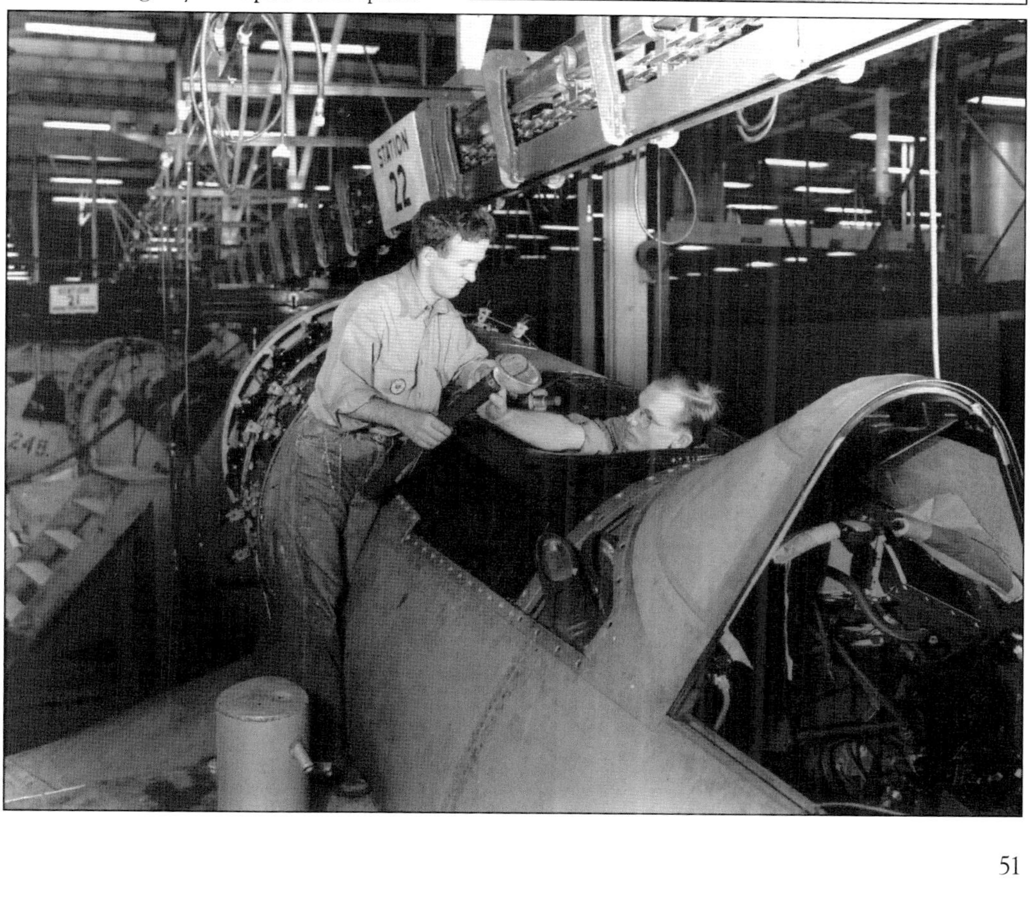

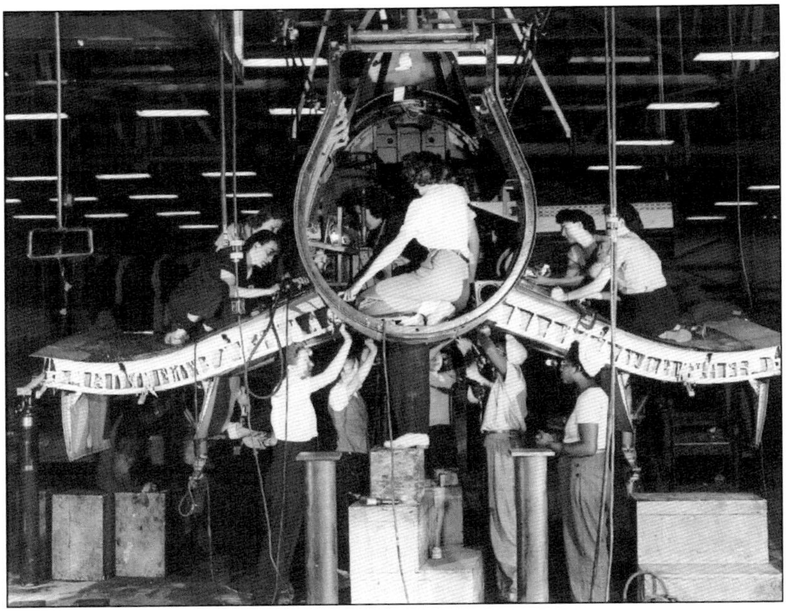

By the end of 1943, women made up the largest part of the Goodyear Aircraft workforce. These now-famous "Rosie the Riveters" made a remarkable transition from 1940s housewives to skilled aircraft workers capable of producing frontline fighter aircraft, airships, assemblies, parts, life rafts, life vests, self-sealing fuel tanks, and a host of other valuable goods for the war effort.

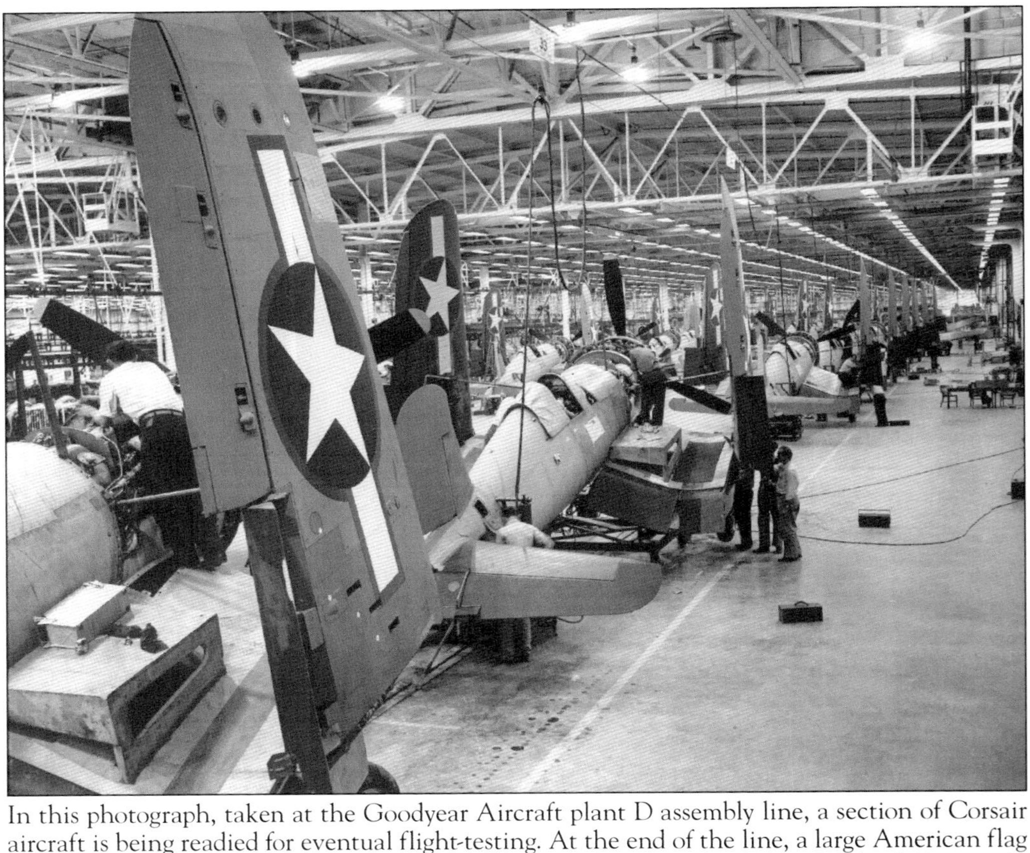

In this photograph, taken at the Goodyear Aircraft plant D assembly line, a section of Corsair aircraft is being readied for eventual flight-testing. At the end of the line, a large American flag can be seen on the hangar doors. Completed aircraft were rolled off the line to be flight-tested.

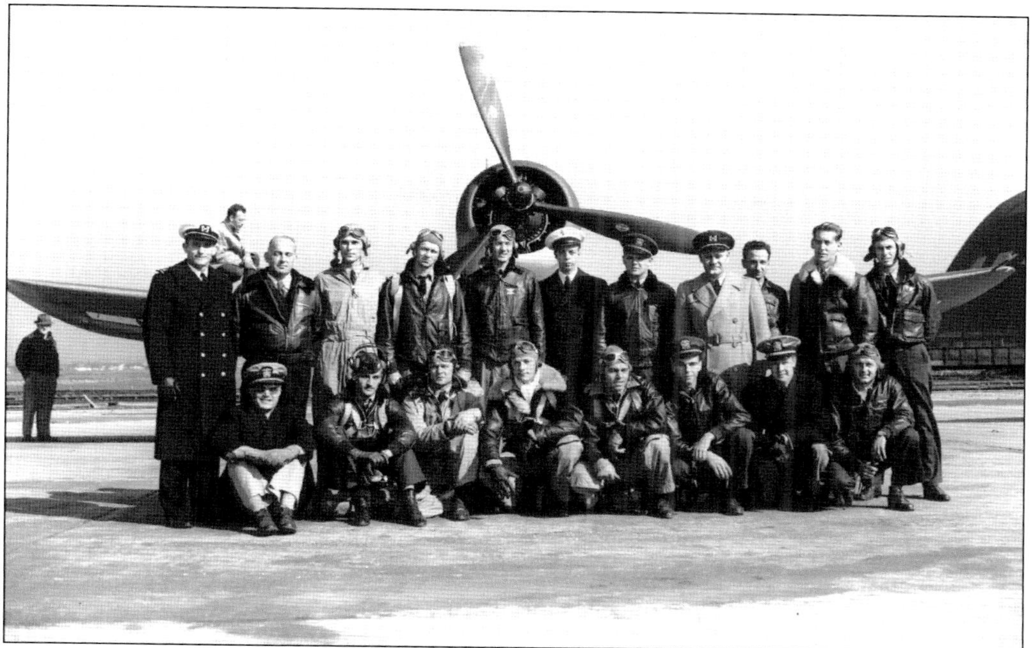

The Goodyear Aircraft Corporation flight department, organized in July 1942, poses in front of a Goodyear-built Corsair. This department of 25 pilots and mechanics would service and flight-test 4,008 Corsair aircraft from 1943 to 1945 with the loss of only two pilots and three aircraft.

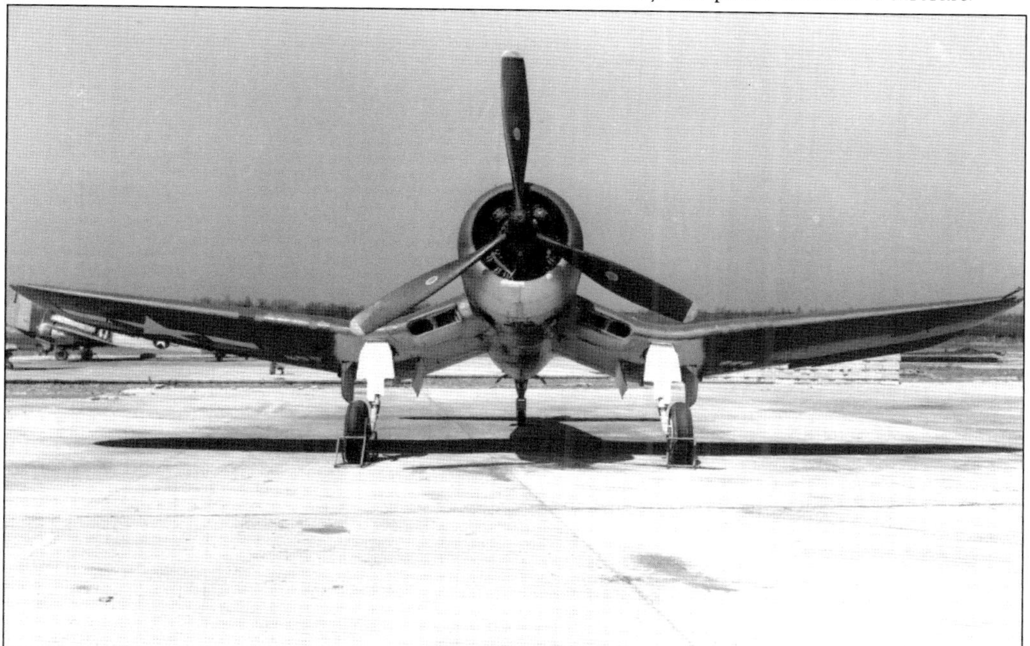

The FG-1 Corsair had a wingspan of 41 feet, a length of 33 feet, and a height of 15 feet. Powered by a Pratt and Whitney 2,800-horsepower "Double Wasp" aircraft engine, it could reach speeds of over 400 miles per hour in level flight. The gull-wing design kept the 16-foot-long propellers from striking the ground.

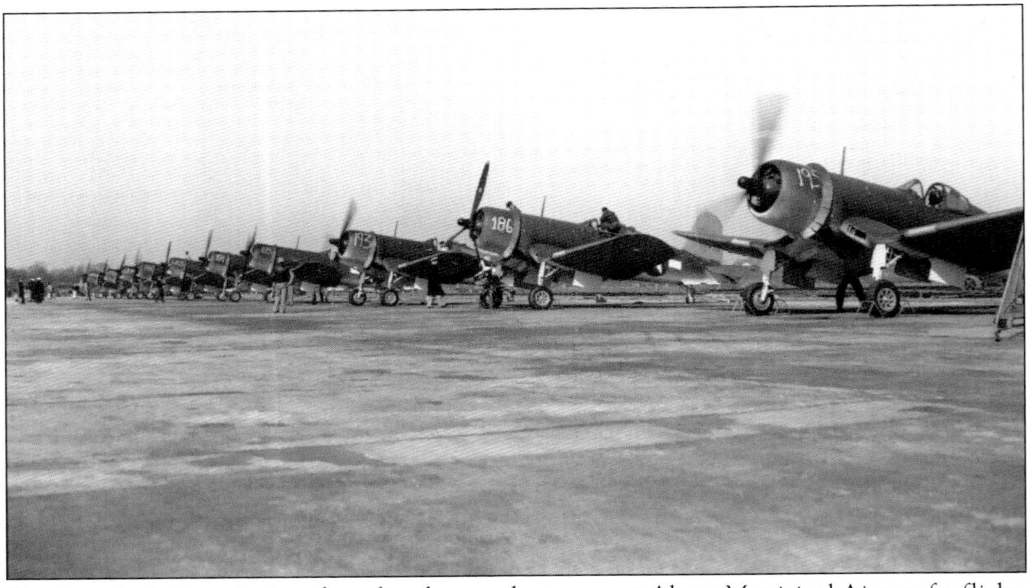

Goodyear-built Corsair aircraft are lined up on the tarmac at Akron Municipal Airport for flight-testing. The planes are being warmed by the mechanics. Note the number system on the aircraft nacelles and the test pilot at center walking nonchalantly toward his aircraft.

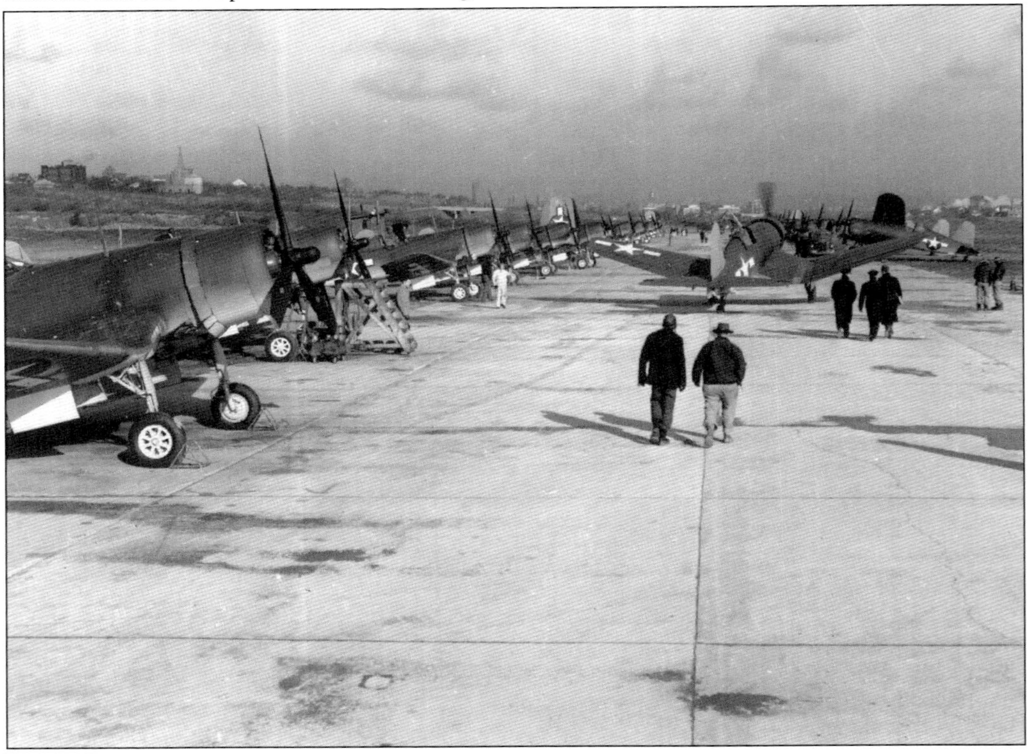

This is another view of Goodyear-built Corsairs. Test pilots, mechanics, ground crews, and inspection personnel were all involved in flight-testing. The number of individuals gathered around a moving aircraft bears testimony to the sense of urgency in producing these aircraft.

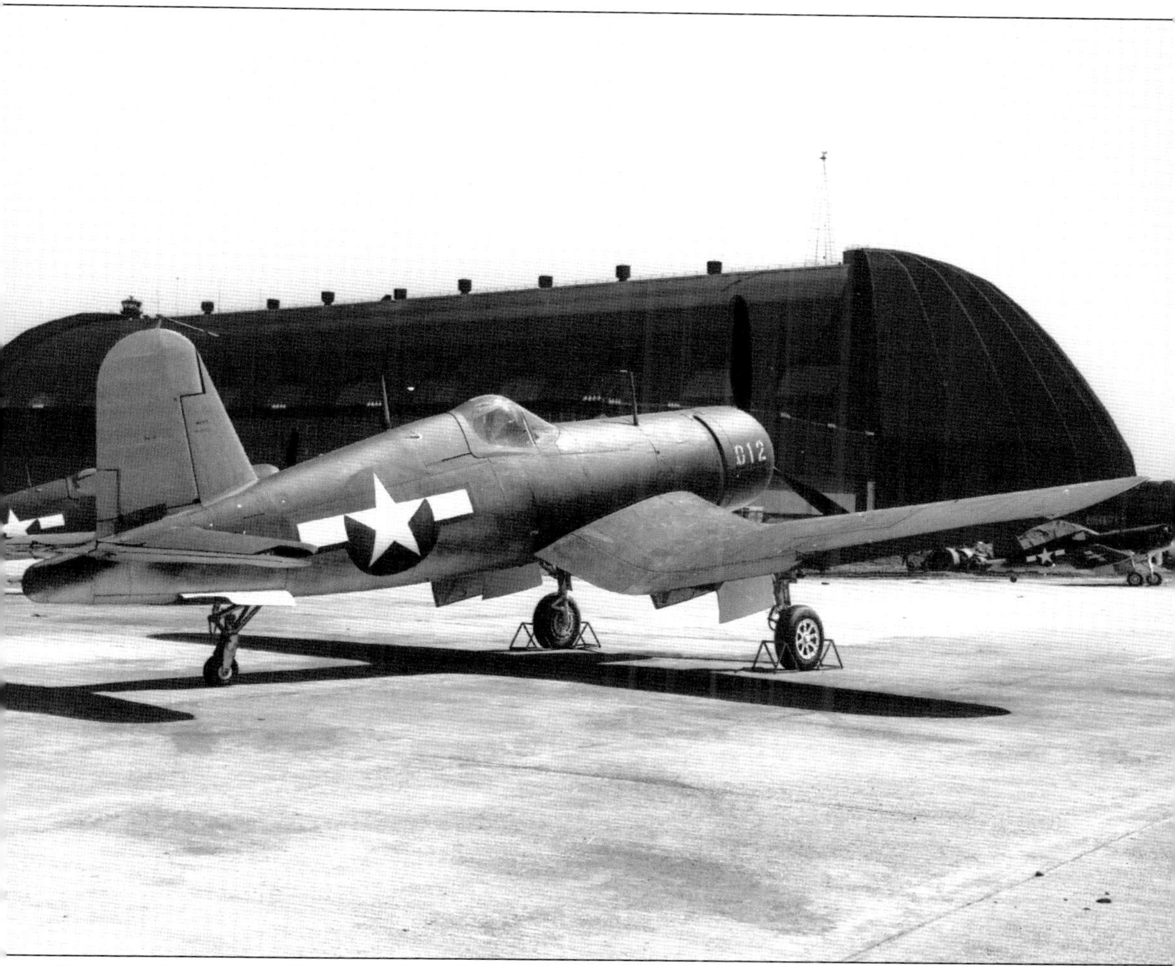

Posing in front of the Goodyear Zeppelin Airship Factory, this FG-1 Corsair sits in stark contrast to the hangar that was built on a dream of lighter-than-air international commercial flight just 14 years earlier. The dreams of commercial airship travel never materialized, but Akron never stopped looking to the skies. The knowledge gained from those early years enabled later aviation professionals to build a product never before dreamed of for national defense.

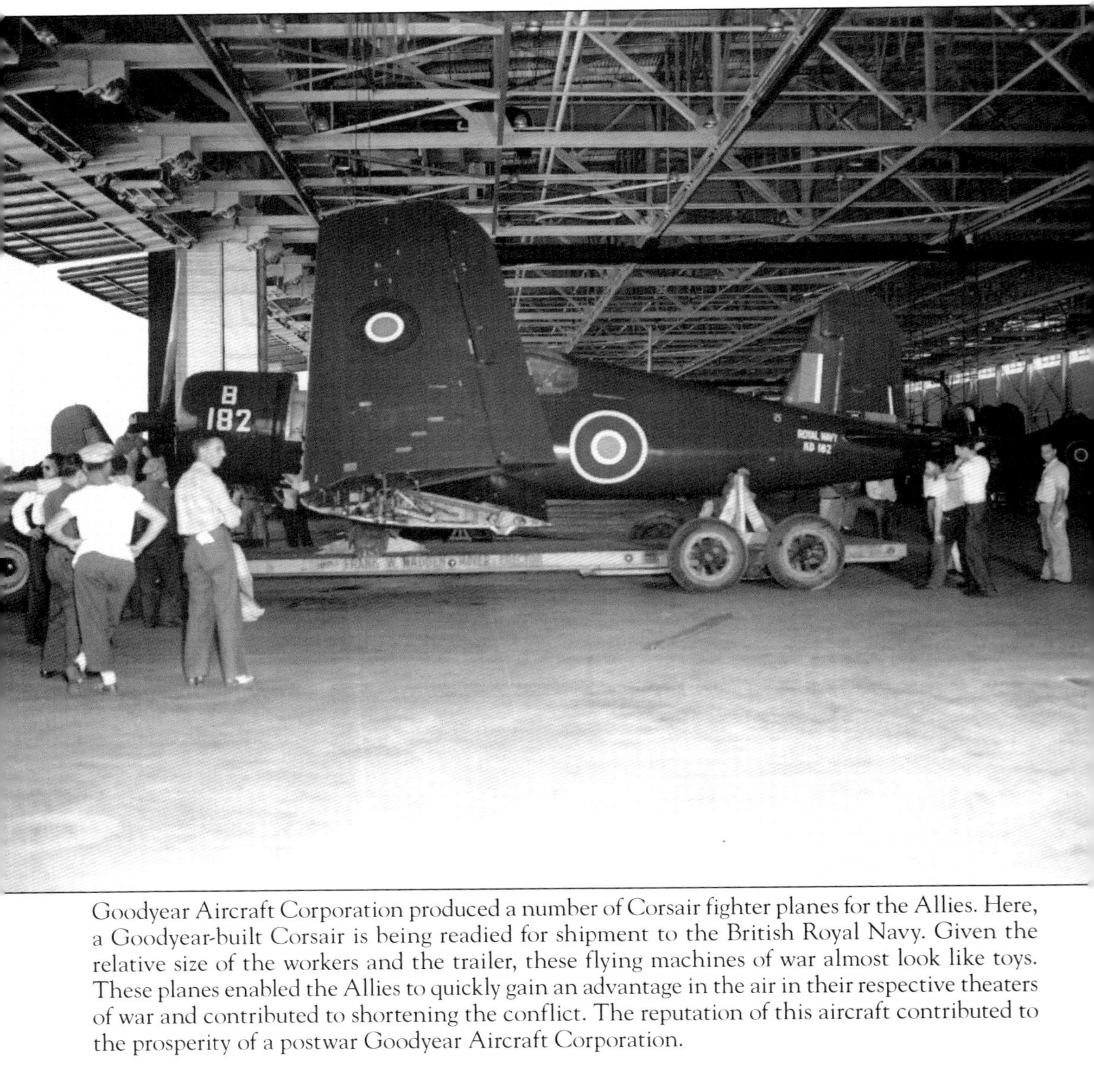

Goodyear Aircraft Corporation produced a number of Corsair fighter planes for the Allies. Here, a Goodyear-built Corsair is being readied for shipment to the British Royal Navy. Given the relative size of the workers and the trailer, these flying machines of war almost look like toys. These planes enabled the Allies to quickly gain an advantage in the air in their respective theaters of war and contributed to shortening the conflict. The reputation of this aircraft contributed to the prosperity of a postwar Goodyear Aircraft Corporation.

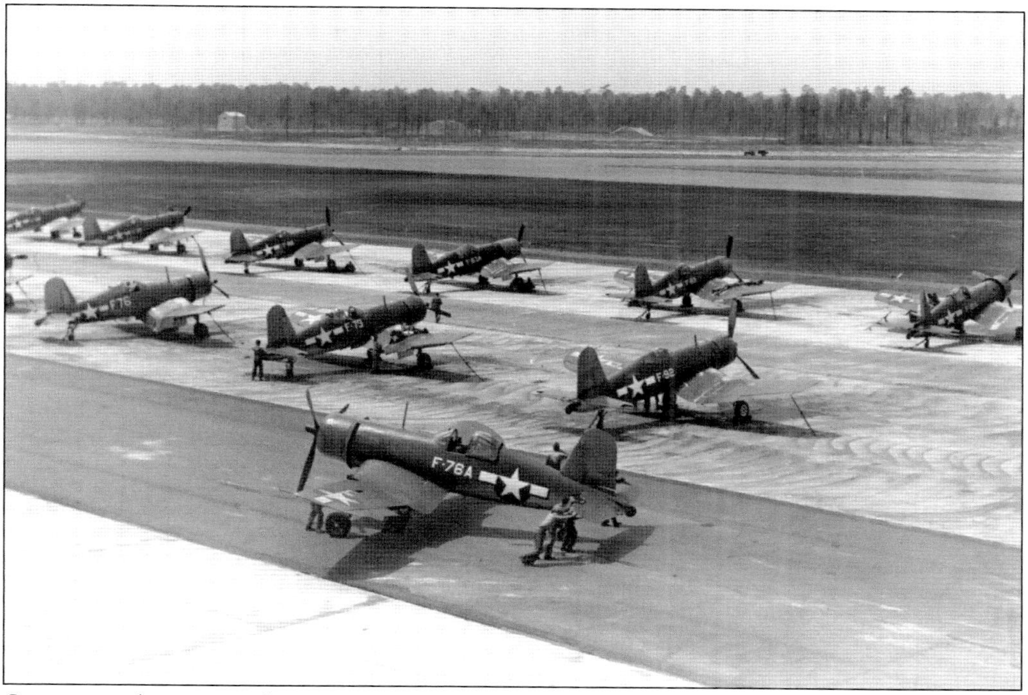

Corsairs are being taxied and readied for flight-testing. Goodyear Aircraft Corporation received the coveted Navy E for excellence award for consistently meeting or exceeding production goals and for excellent engineering and workmanship.

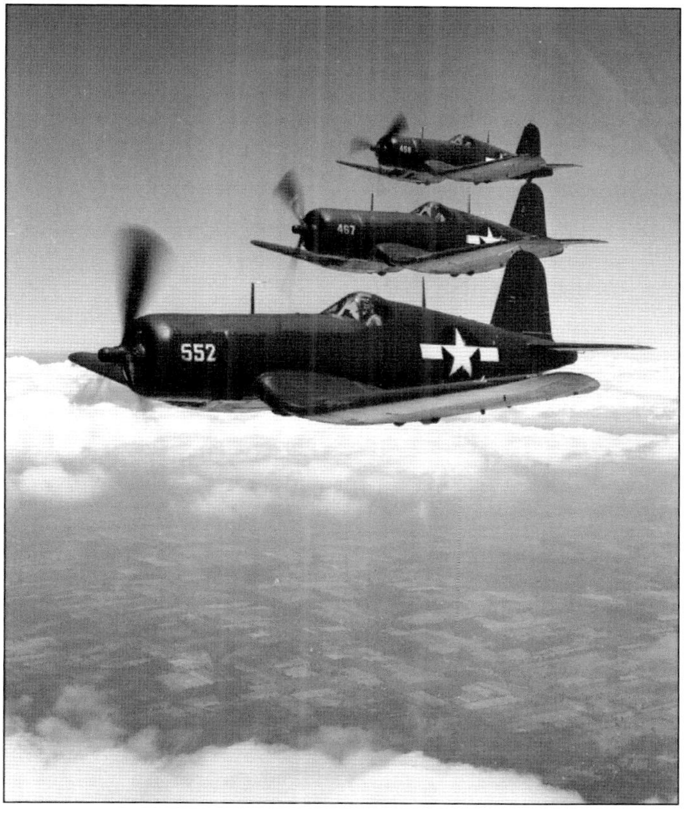

Here, three corsairs fly in formation as they head to active duty with the fleet. The Corsair would become the mainstay of US Navy fighter aircraft from 1943 to 1953. It would also become the catalyst for one of the most inspiring stories of the Korean War, fictionalized in James Michener's *The Bridges at Toko-Ri*.

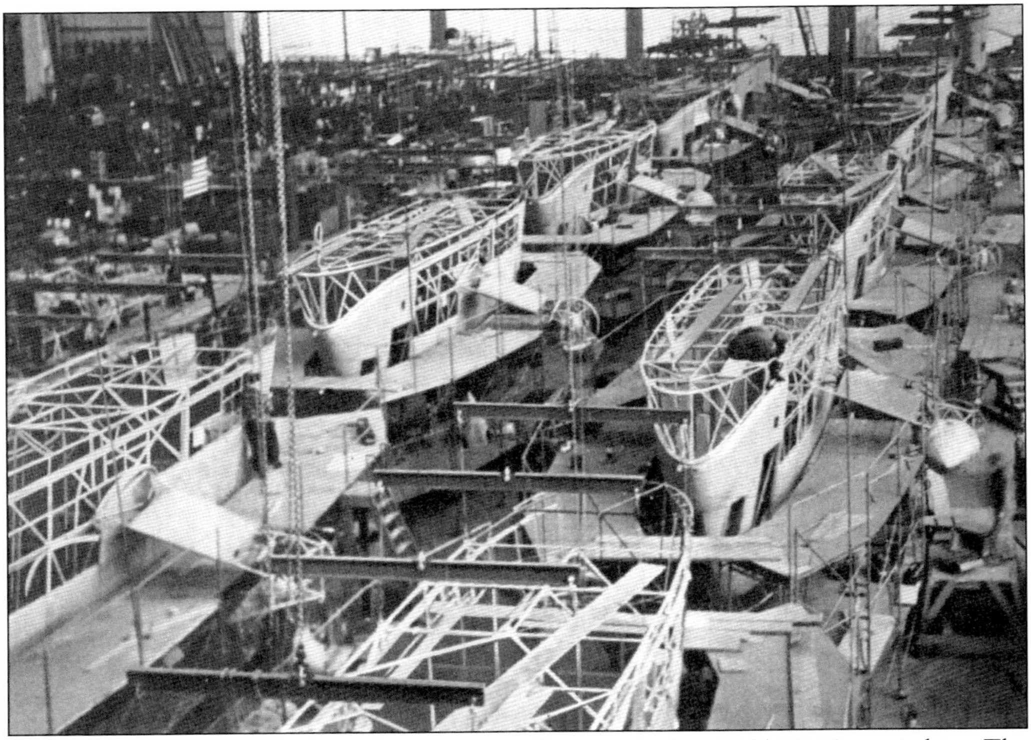

These photographs clearly show the enormous effort required to build US Navy airships. The photograph above shows airship gondola production. The photograph below shows airship final assembly at Wingfoot Lake Airship Facility. These images are taken from the Goodyear Tire & Rubber Company's 1943 book *Trail Blazing in the Skies*, written by Shafto Dene. (Author's collection.)

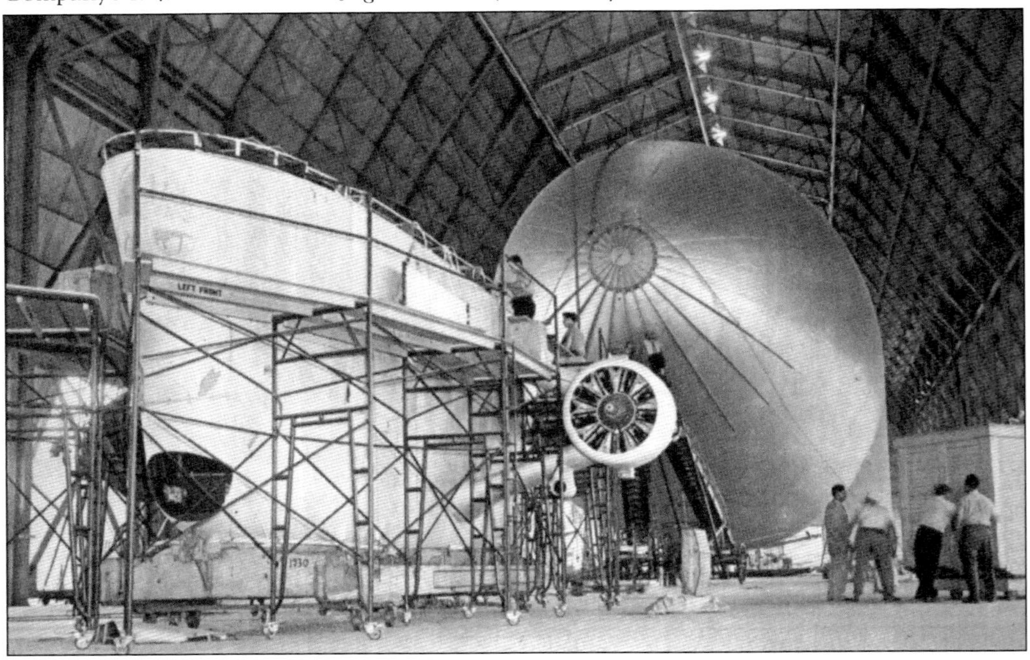

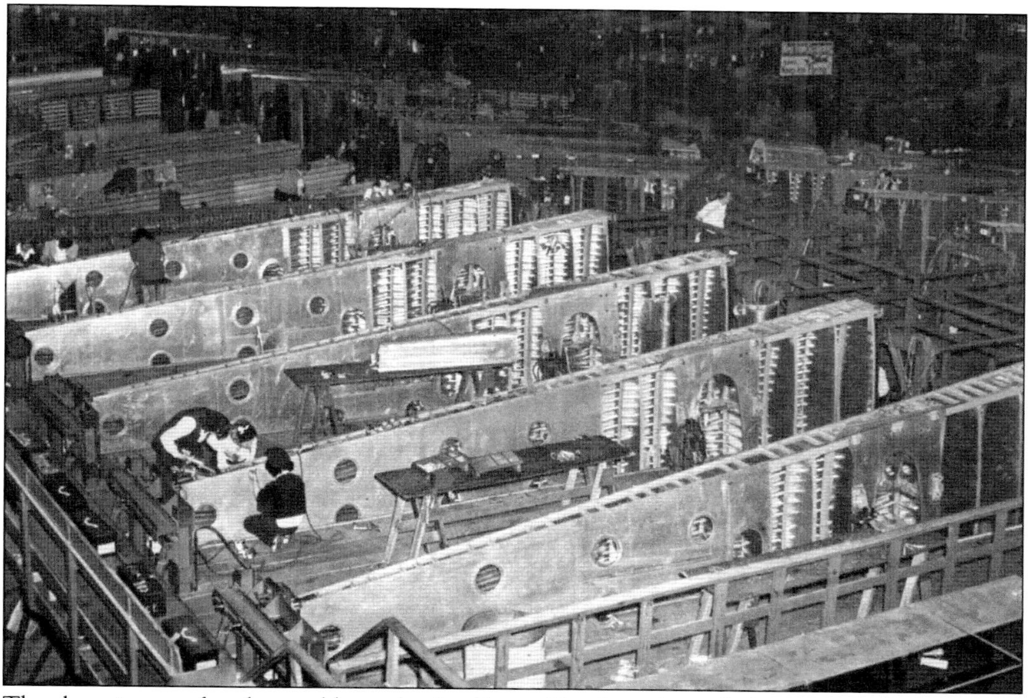

The above image of a subassembly production line at Goodyear Aircraft Corporation shows the vast area required for one operation in airplane mass production. The women are shown "bucking" and "riveting." The woman in black is holding a " bucking bar" while the women on the opposite side of the wing rib rivet with the use of an air-powered rivet gun. Below, Martin B-26 wings are nearly ready for final assembly. These images were seen in the Goodyear Tire & Rubber Company's 1943 book *Trail Blazing in the Skies*, written by Shafto Dene. (Both, author's collection.)

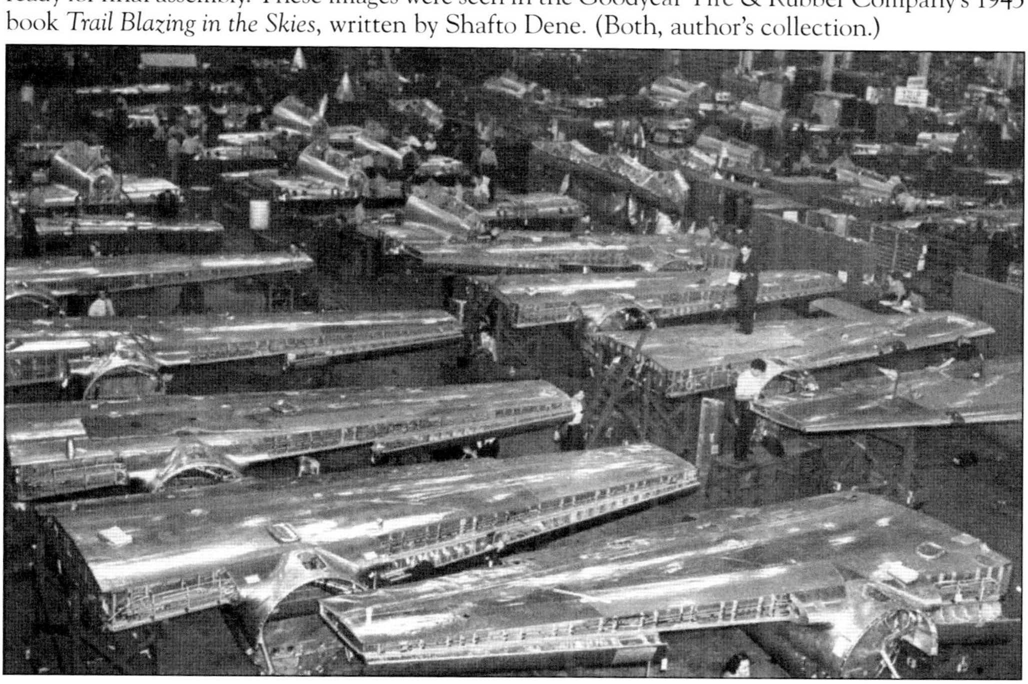

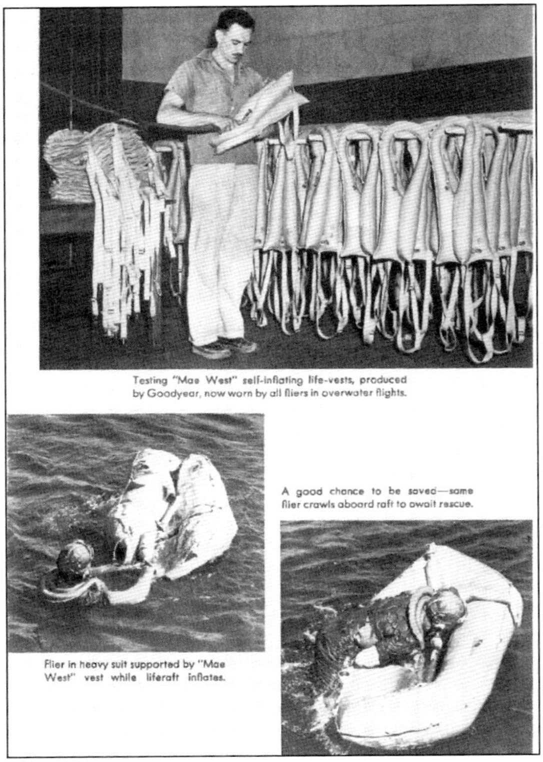

These three photographs show testing of the "Mae West" life vest, named after the famous actress. The vest was worn by all fliers on overwater flights. The two photographs at bottom demonstrate the combination of the "Mae West" and a small life raft. Goodyear Tire & Rubber Company's 1943 book *Trail Blazing in the Skies*, written by Shafto Dene, also showcased these images. (Author's collection.)

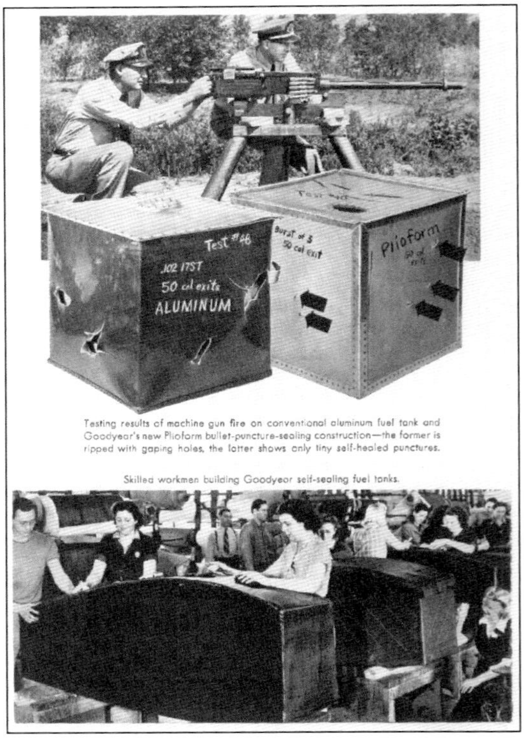

One of the most important advancements in World War II was the development of self-sealing aircraft fuel tanks. In the photograph at top, men test the results of machine-gun fire on a conventional aluminum fuel tank and Goodyear's Plioform bullet-puncture sealing construction. The bottom photograph shows tank construction. Note the supervisors in the background. These images were seen in the Goodyear Tire & Rubber Company's 1943 book *Trail Blazing in the Skies*, written by Shafto Dene. (Author's collection.)

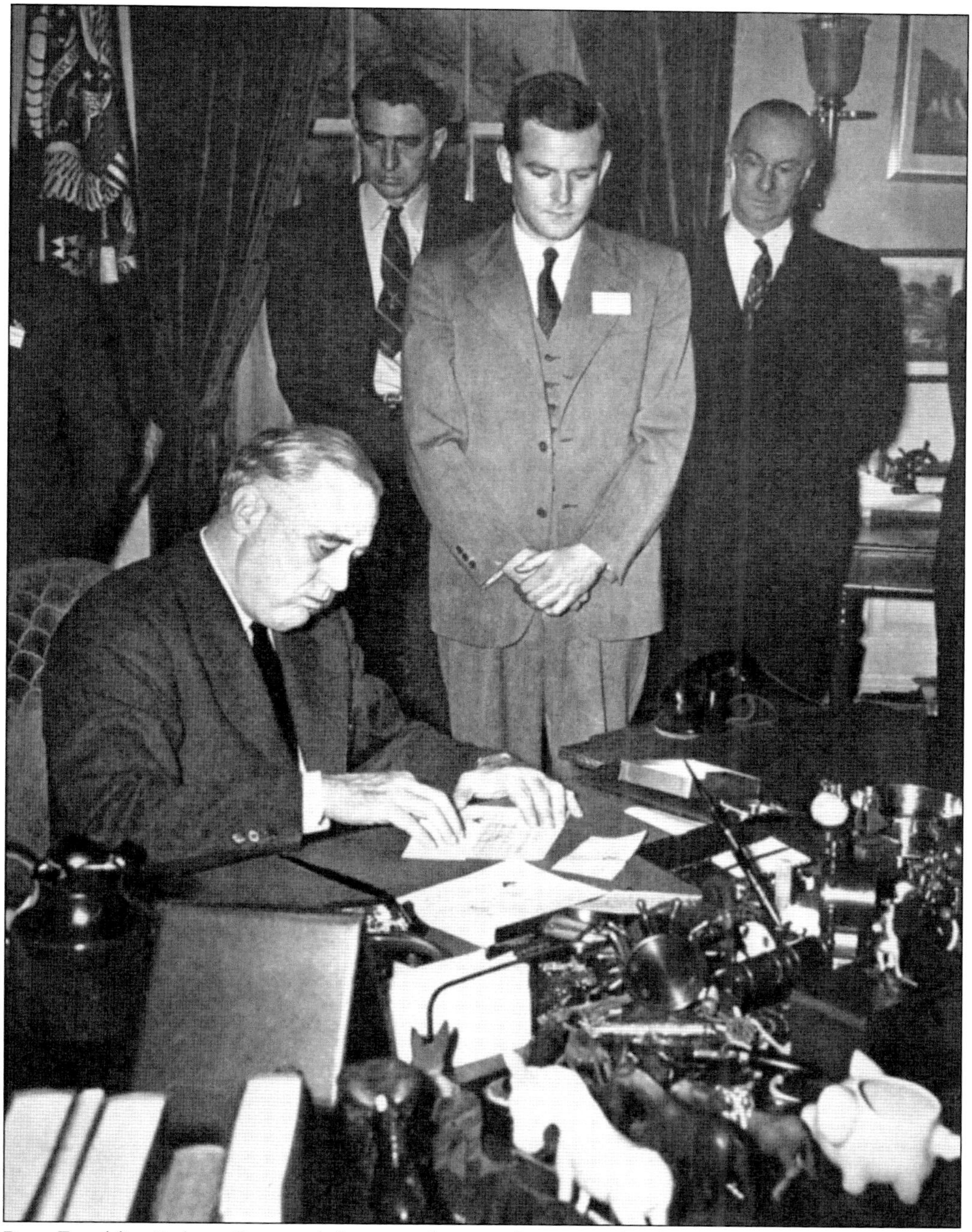

Pres. Franklin Delano Roosevelt bestows the rare Citation of Individual Production Merit, the highest civilian award, upon Goodyear research chemist James A. Merrill (center). The award was in recognition of the work done by Merrill and his associates in developing the self-sealing fuel tank, which became and still is standard equipment on all aircraft.

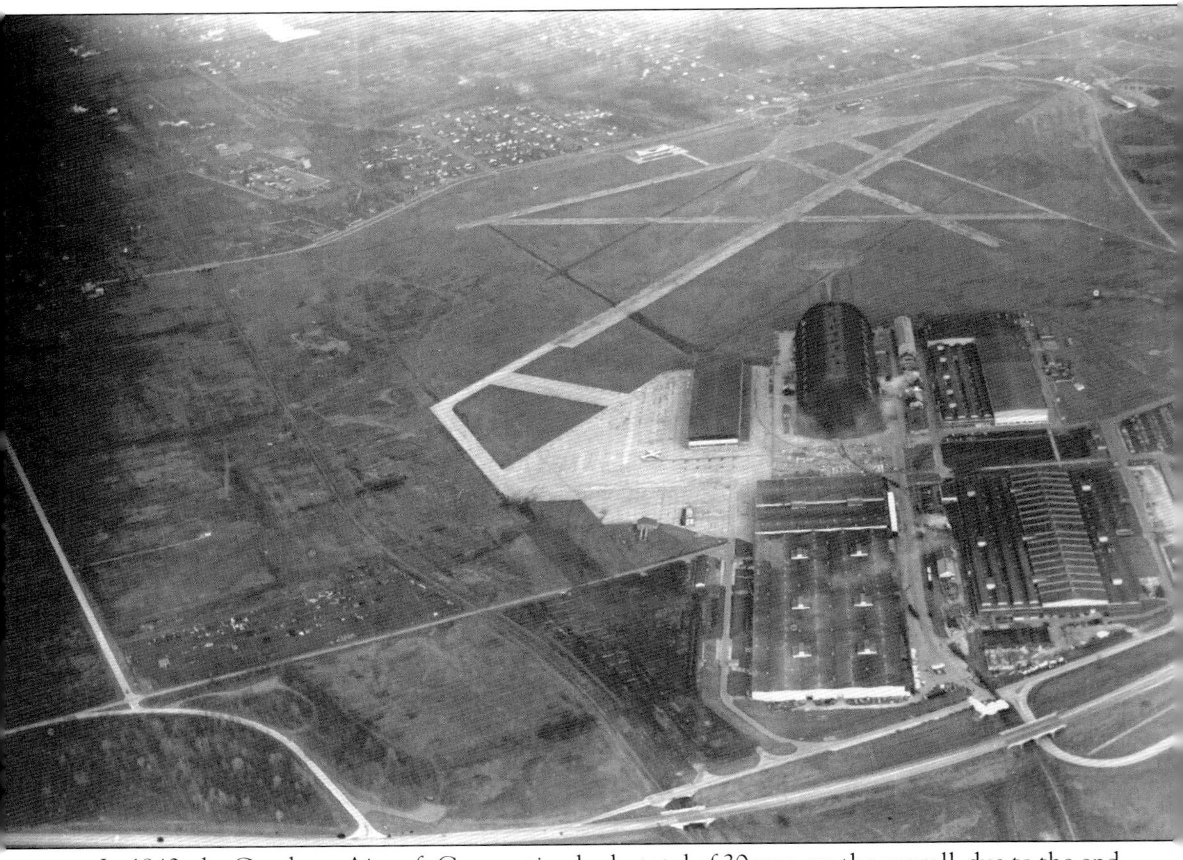

In 1940, the Goodyear Aircraft Corporation had a total of 30 men on the payroll, due to the end of the rigid airships, the ravages of the Depression, and the resulting lack of aviation-related orders. By the end of World War II, Goodyear Aircraft had a payroll in excess of 32,000 employees and became the Akron area's largest employer. The company would go on to produce 4,008 Corsairs, 156 blimps, aircraft assemblies for the Martin B26, the B29 Superfortress, and myriad other frontline aircraft. The incredible story of Goodyear Aircraft is not in the product, but in the people who became highly skilled craftsmen and women in the demanding world of aviation.

Five

Mr. Fulton and His Flying Field

Bain E. "Shorty" Fulton is the one man whose persistence, planning, and hard work was more responsible than any other for the creation and development of the Akron Municipal Airport. Bain Fulton was born on January 5, 1892, on a farm west of Kenton, Ohio. Fulton left high school to travel the Southwest and Old Mexico. While on this trip, he undertook some prep school work, along with classes in auto sales, racing, mechanics and engineering. He had a hitch at just about everything, including aviation, which proved the most interesting and alluring.

Arriving in Akron in 1916, Fulton worked for a period of time at both Goodyear's and Firestone's engineering departments and spent his spare time developing his flying field. Fulton purchased five lots and an old farmhouse at the Fulmer farm on Massillon Road. There, he designed and built an airplane that he flew to his hometown of Kenton on its first long flight.

Described as a "man with zip," Fulton began flying passengers out of his field in two decrepit aircraft in 1924. This was Akron's first airport. Almost immediately after opening his flying field, Fulton began pressing Akron officials for the development of a municipal airport. In 1928, with the combination of the Goodyear Zeppelin Company needing a location for its airship factory and Bain Fulton's energetic efforts, things began to happen, but not without opposition. Akron citizens were convinced that the idea of a municipal airport was purely to please Goodyear. Twice, Akron voters rejected bond issues to purchase the needed land. Then, Akron city councilmen, acting on their own, authorized four bond issues over a two-year period for a total of $1,838,000. Akron would get its airport.

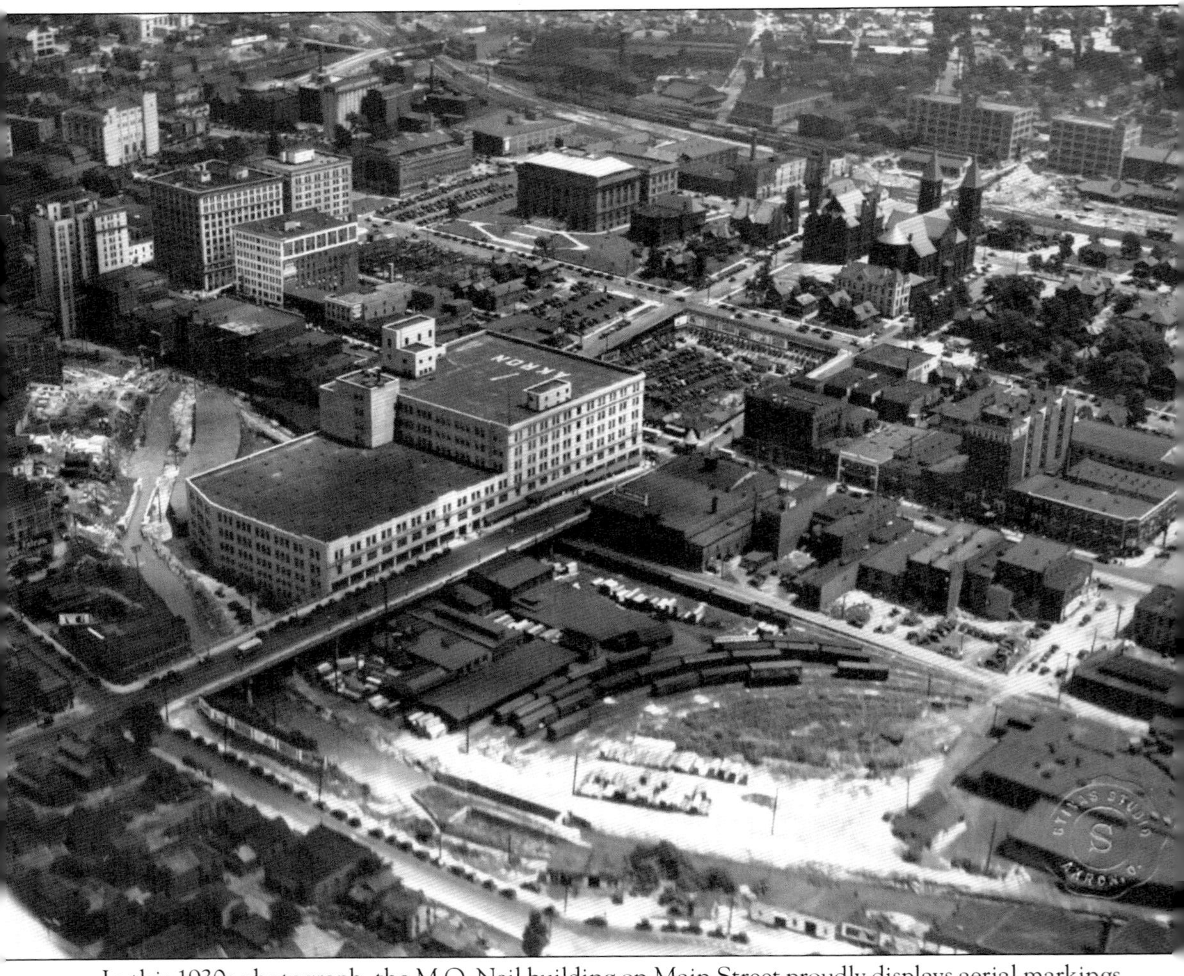

In this 1930s photograph, the M.O. Neil building on Main Street proudly displays aerial markings on its rooftop. Despite the Great Depression, Akron continued to look to the skies. Note the directional arrow above the lettering, directing aircraft to the airport.

This June 6, 1927, *Airway Bulletin* provides a description of Akron's first airport, Fulton Field. The field would eventually become the Akron Municipal Airport, due in large part to the building of the airdock and subsequent airships. Note the location of the obstacles and the short grass landing strips.

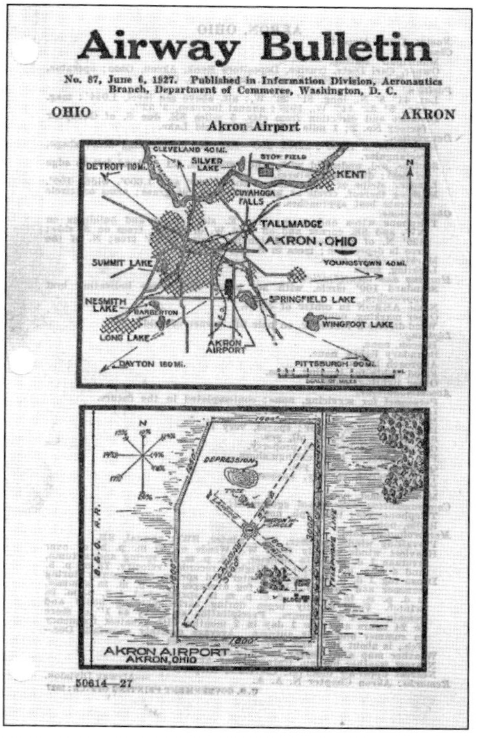

Airway Bulletin

No. 87, June 6, 1927. Published in Information Division, Aeronautics Branch, Department of Commerce, Washington, D. C.

OHIO AKRON

Akron Airport

50614—27

The creation of the Akron Municipal Airport can be largely attributed to the vision and perseverance of one man: Bain E. "Shorty" Fulton. He purchased land on the southern outskirts of the city and created Fulton Field, a grass landing strip with two runways. Standing in front of the new airport terminal, Fulton exudes confidence in spite of the mud.

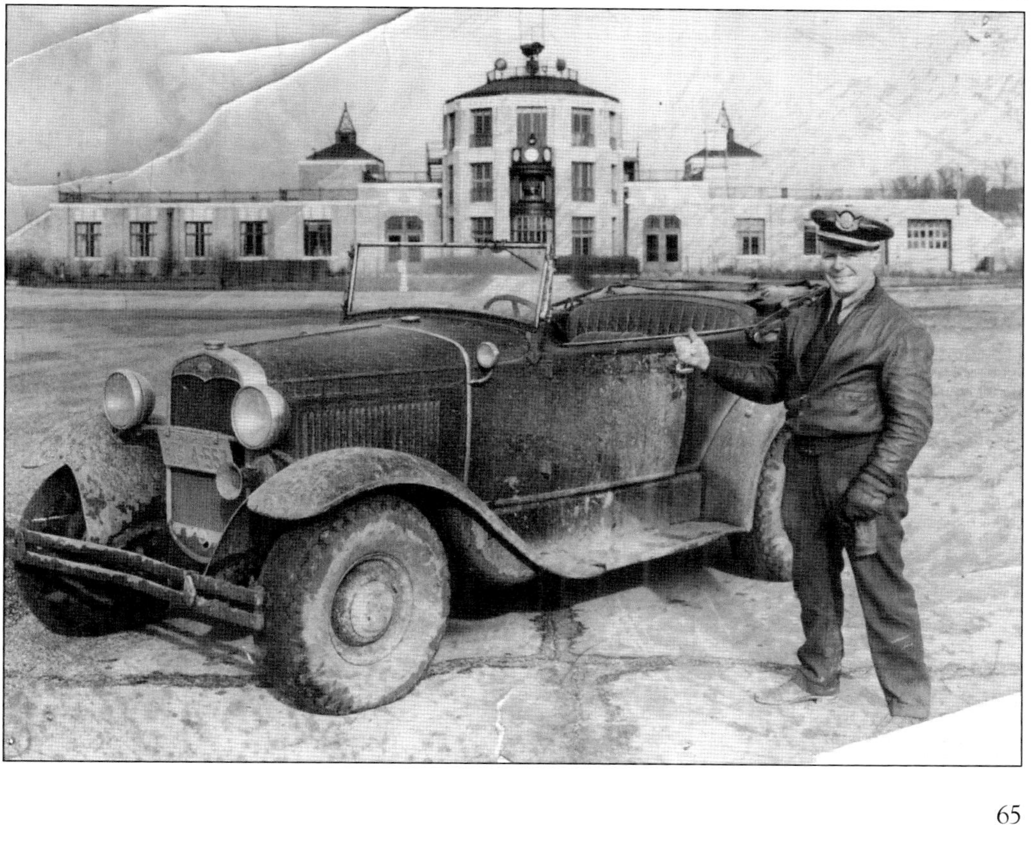

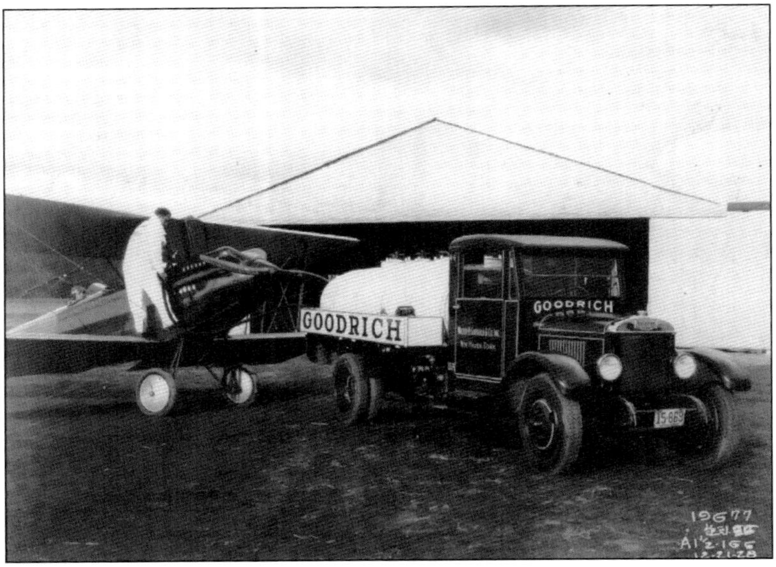

One of Fulton Field's first customers gasses up at the terminal building, which consisted of one hangar. Most Fulton Field users in the early years were barnstormers, occasional airmail flyers, and local aviation enthusiasts.

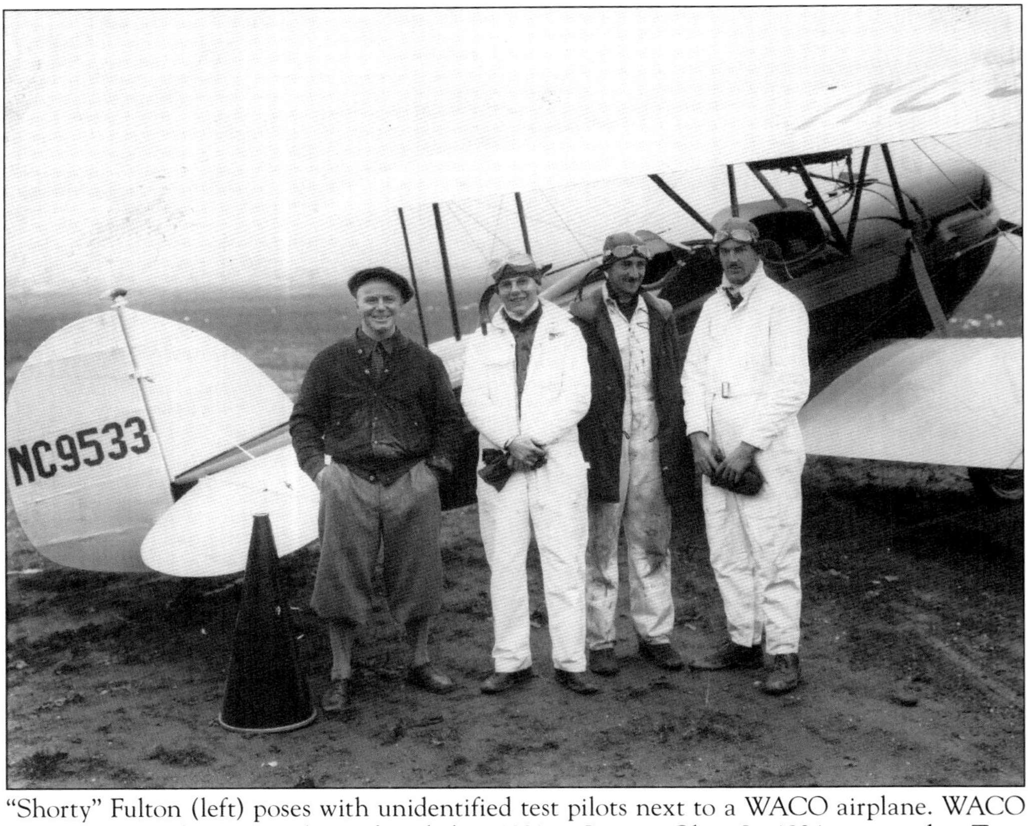

"Shorty" Fulton (left) poses with unidentified test pilots next to a WACO airplane. WACO (Weaver Aircraft Company) was founded in 1921 in Lorain, Ohio. In 1924, it moved to Troy, Ohio, and became the Advance Aircraft Company but kept the WACO logo. In 1929, the firm changed its name to the WACO Aircraft Company. It produced over 80 airplane models between 1919 and 1946.

Shown here is the Akron Municipal Airport Planning Board. "Shorty" Fulton is second from right. The other members of the board are, in unknown order, F.E. Swineford, director, Department of Public Service; E.A. Kemmler, highway engineer; C.F. Fisher, planning engineer; and L.B. Hiebel, assistant planning engineer.

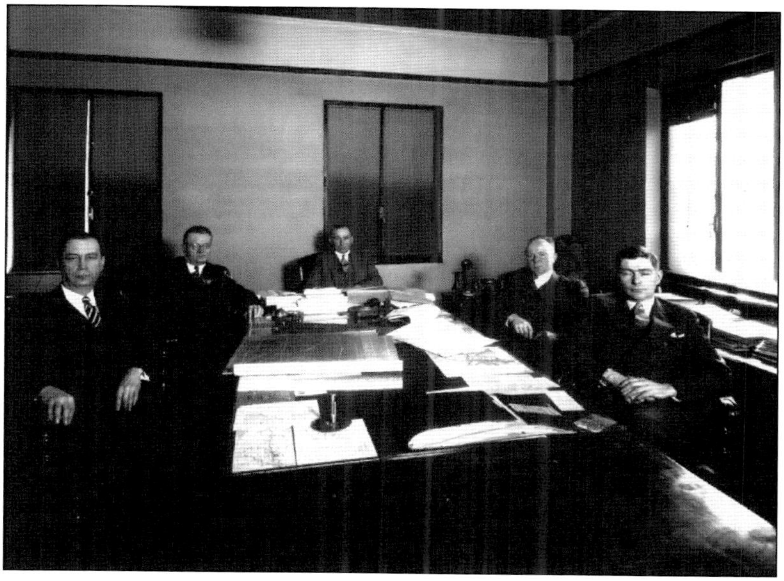

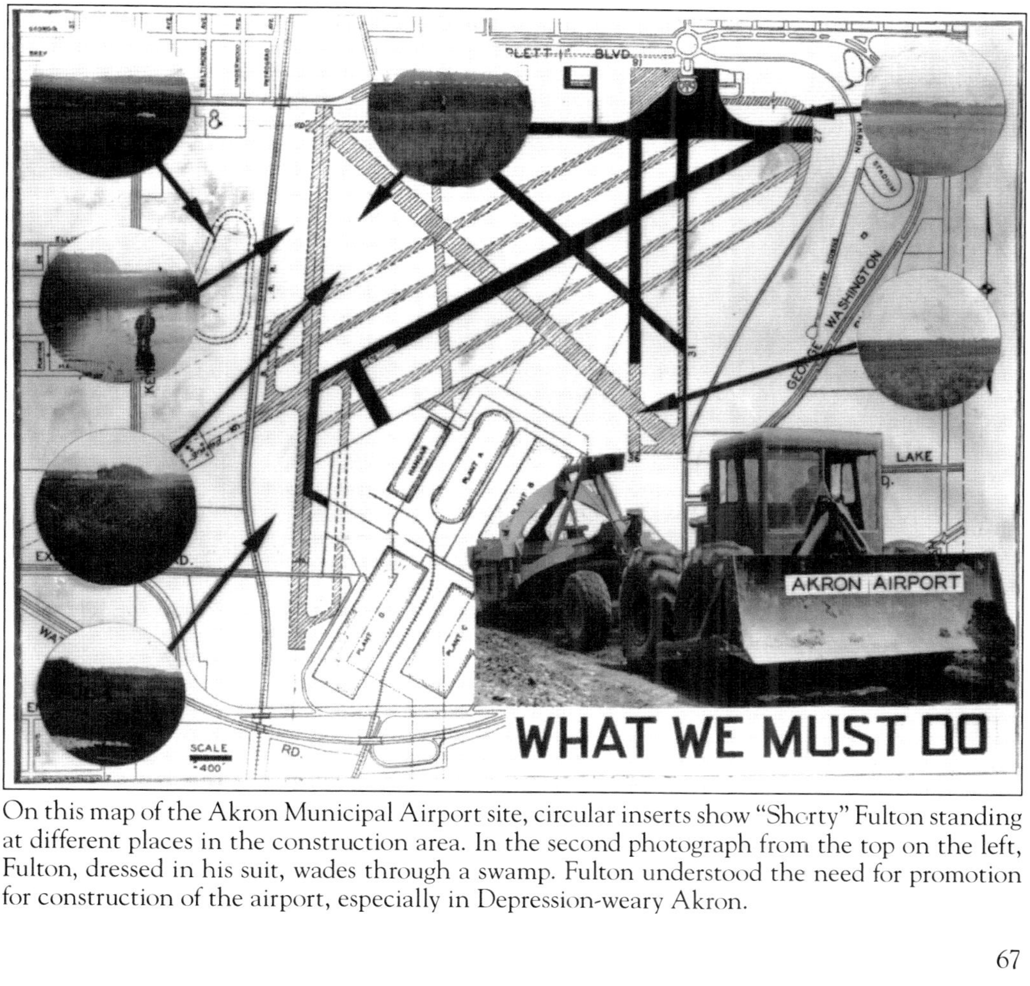

On this map of the Akron Municipal Airport site, circular inserts show "Shorty" Fulton standing at different places in the construction area. In the second photograph from the top on the left, Fulton, dressed in his suit, wades through a swamp. Fulton understood the need for promotion for construction of the airport, especially in Depression-weary Akron.

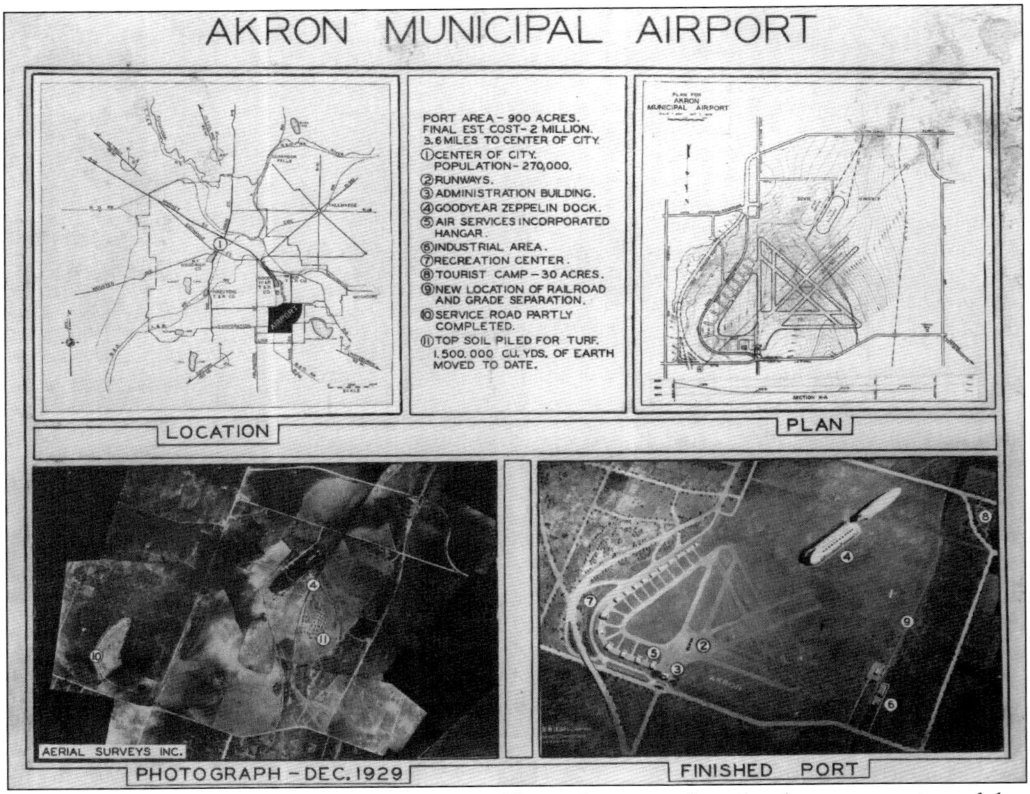

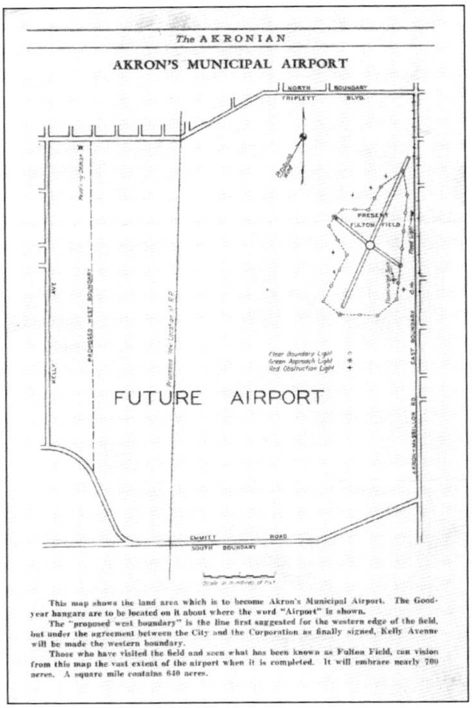
The AKRONIAN

AKRON'S MUNICIPAL AIRPORT

This map shows the land area which is to become Akron's Municipal Airport. The Goodyear hangars are to be located on it about where the word "Airport" is shown.

The "proposed west boundary" is the line first suggested for the western edge of the field, but under the agreement between the City and the Corporation as finally signed, Kelly Avenue will be made the western boundary.

Those who have visited the field and seen what has been known as Fulton Field, can vision from this map the vast extent of the airport when it is completed. It will embrace nearly 700 acres. A square mile contains 640 acres.

Shown here are plans for the construction of the Akron Municipal Airport. The map at upper left shows the location of the airport in Summit County. The map at upper right shows a detailed drawing of the airport complex. The aerial photograph at lower left, taken in December 1929, shows the progress of airport construction. The model at lower right shows how the airport will look when completed.

Page two of the October-November 1928 issue of the *Akronian*, the Akron Chamber of Commerce newsletter, describes the proposed Akron Municipal Airport. Note the size of Fulton Field in comparison to the new airport.

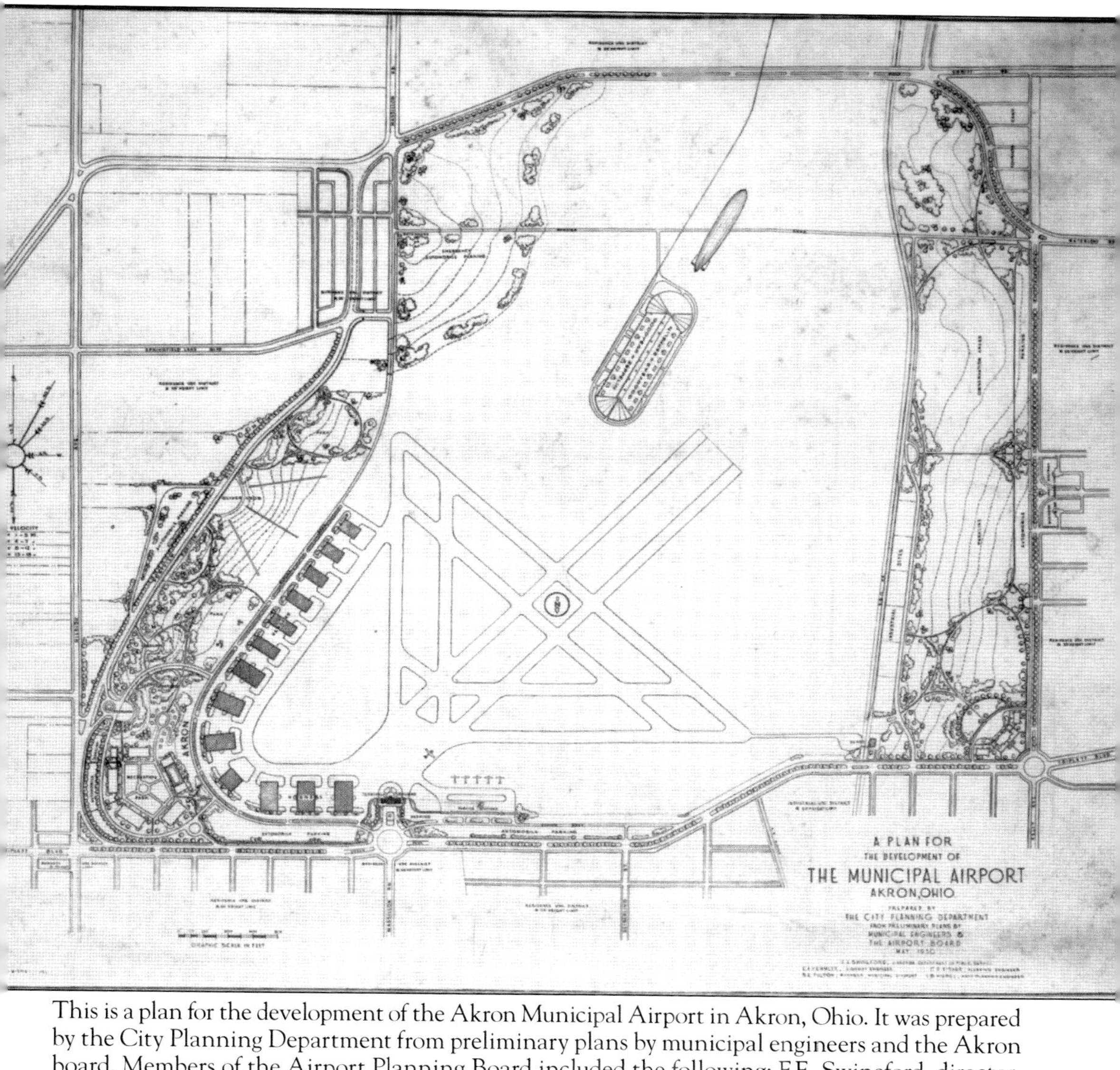

This is a plan for the development of the Akron Municipal Airport in Akron, Ohio. It was prepared by the City Planning Department from preliminary plans by municipal engineers and the Akron board. Members of the Airport Planning Board included the following: F.E. Swineford, director, Department of Public Service; E.A. Kemmler, highway engineer; C.F. Fisher, planning engineer; B.E. Fulton, manager, Akron Municipal Airport; and L.B. Hiebel, assistant planning engineer. Note the glider hill to the east.

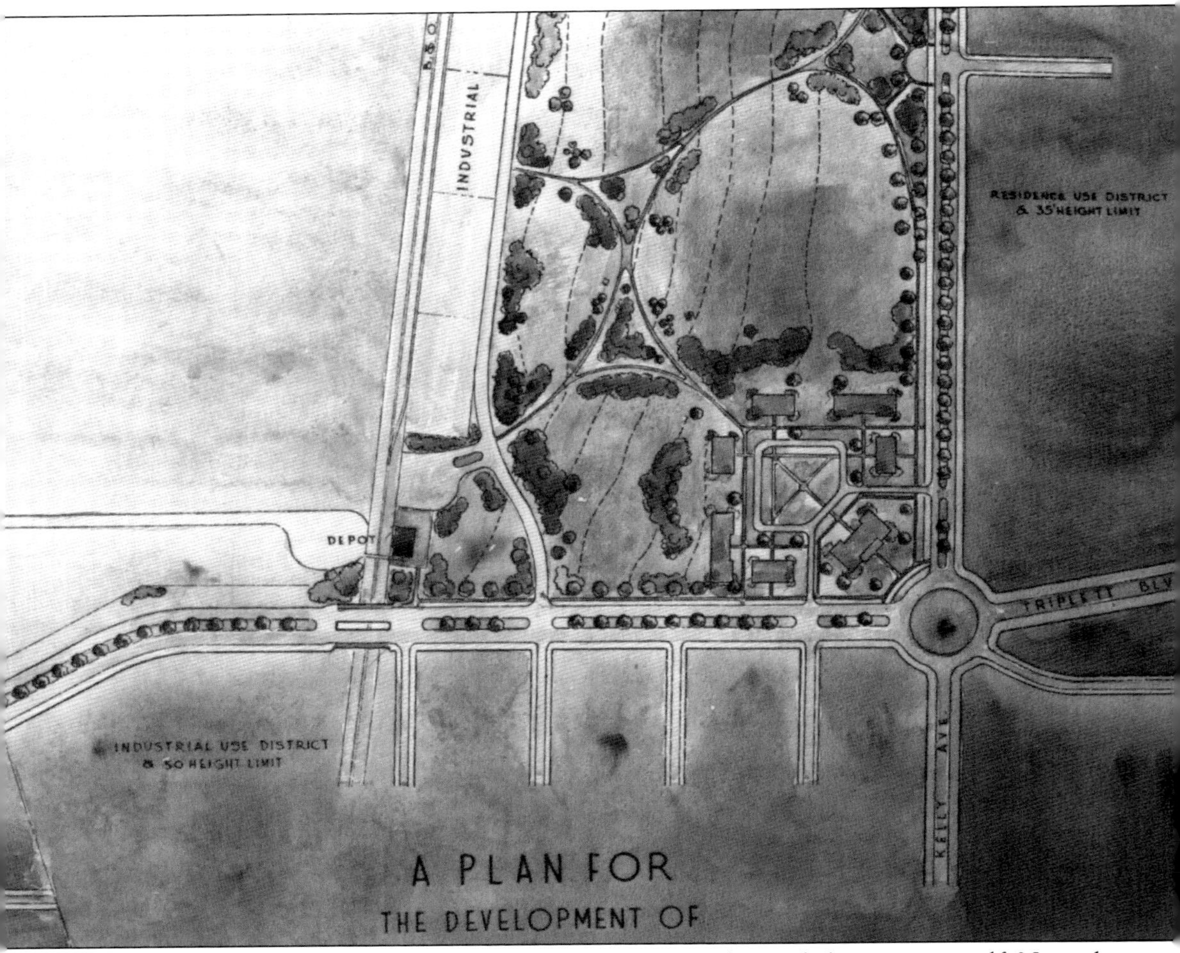

This rendering shows the scope of planning necessary beyond the airport itself. Note the beautification project along Triplett Boulevard. Kelley Avenue would be renamed Massillon Road. This layout remains virtually the same today.

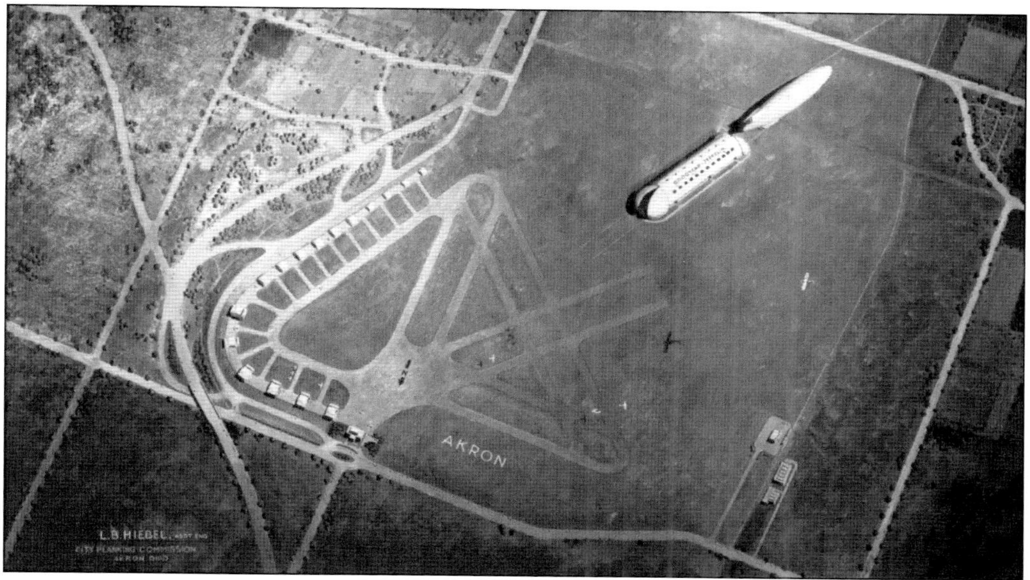

This model depicted the final plan for the Goodyear Zeppelin Airship Factory and Akron Municipal Airport. In 10 years, with the outbreak of World War II, the airport would look completely different.

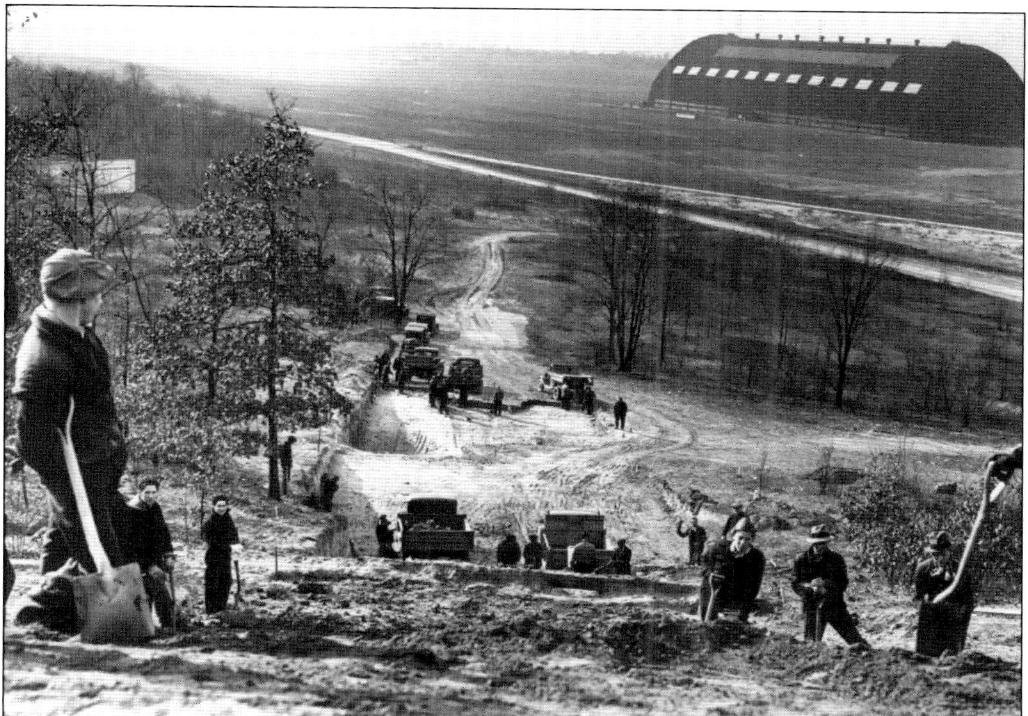

This c. 1931 photograph shows workers on the airport construction project. It is estimated that nearly 1,500 men worked at the airport from 1929 until completion. The majority of these workers were a part of Works Progress Administration (WPA) projects.

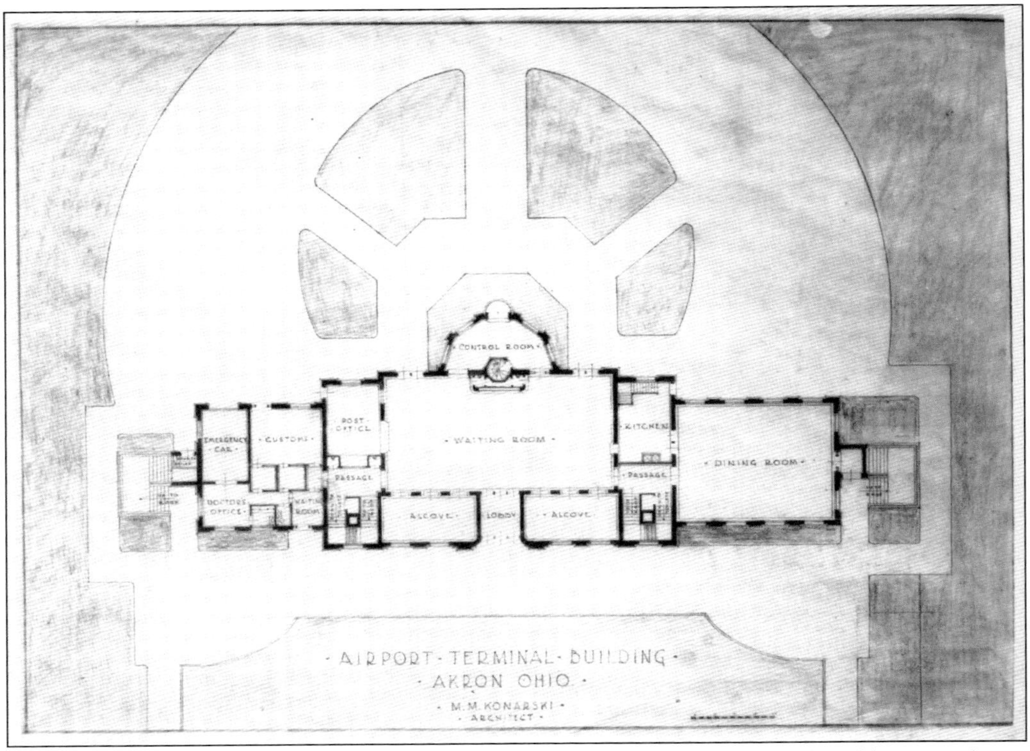

This is an architectural drawing of the Akron Municipal Airport terminal building in Akron, Ohio. The airport was created and managed by Bain E. "Shorty" Fulton.

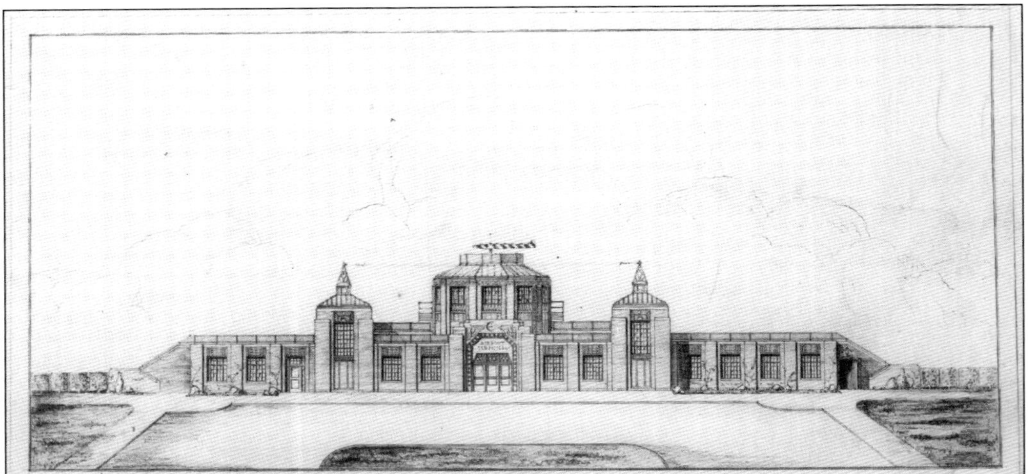

This is an architectural drawing of the front exterior of the terminal building at the Akron Municipal Airport. The terminal was uniquely designed to represent the future in 1930s America. The classic Art Deco exterior and interior facades were studied as excellent architectural examples of the day.

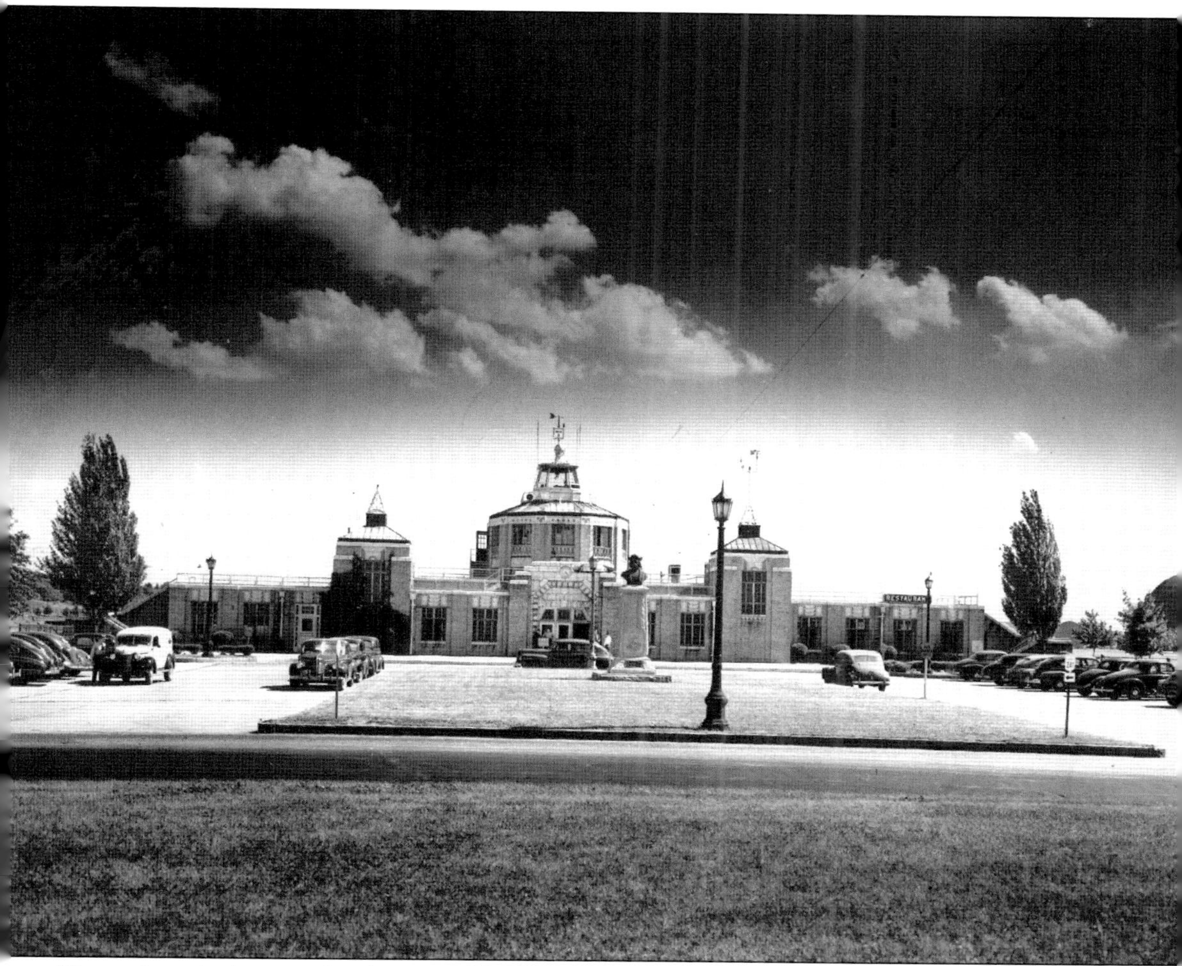

Shown here is the completed terminal building of the Akron Municipal Airport. Designed by M.M. Konarski, architect for the Akron Public Schools, the airport terminal quickly became the centerpiece for the field. The building was designed in the classic Art Deco motif and retains much of that original flavor today.

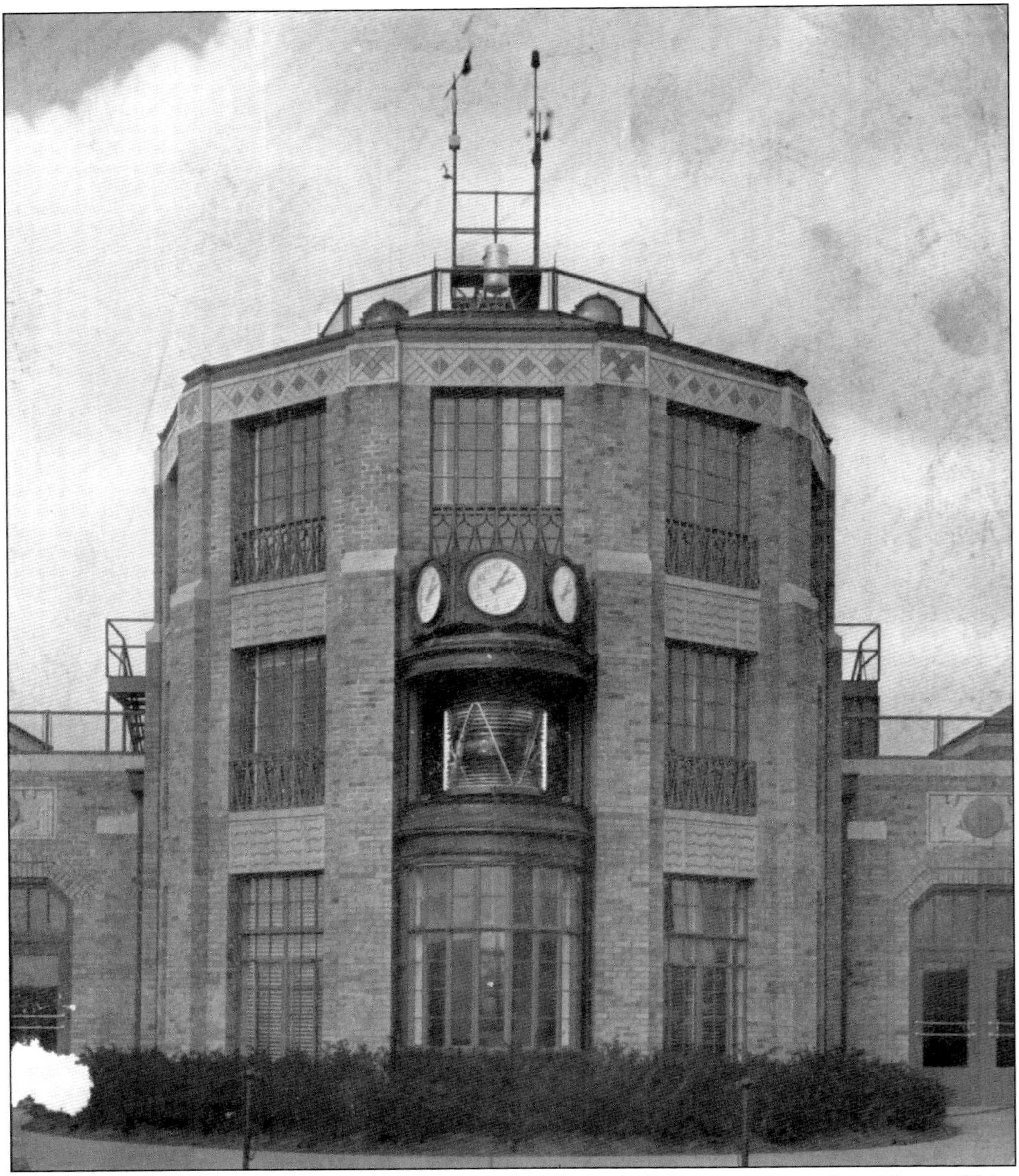

This is a close-up of the clock tower on the Akron Municipal Airport terminal in Akron, Ohio. The tower and the beacon became iconic symbols of the airport. The landing beacon was used to bathe the loading and unloading areas in light and to guide taxiing aircraft to the terminal.

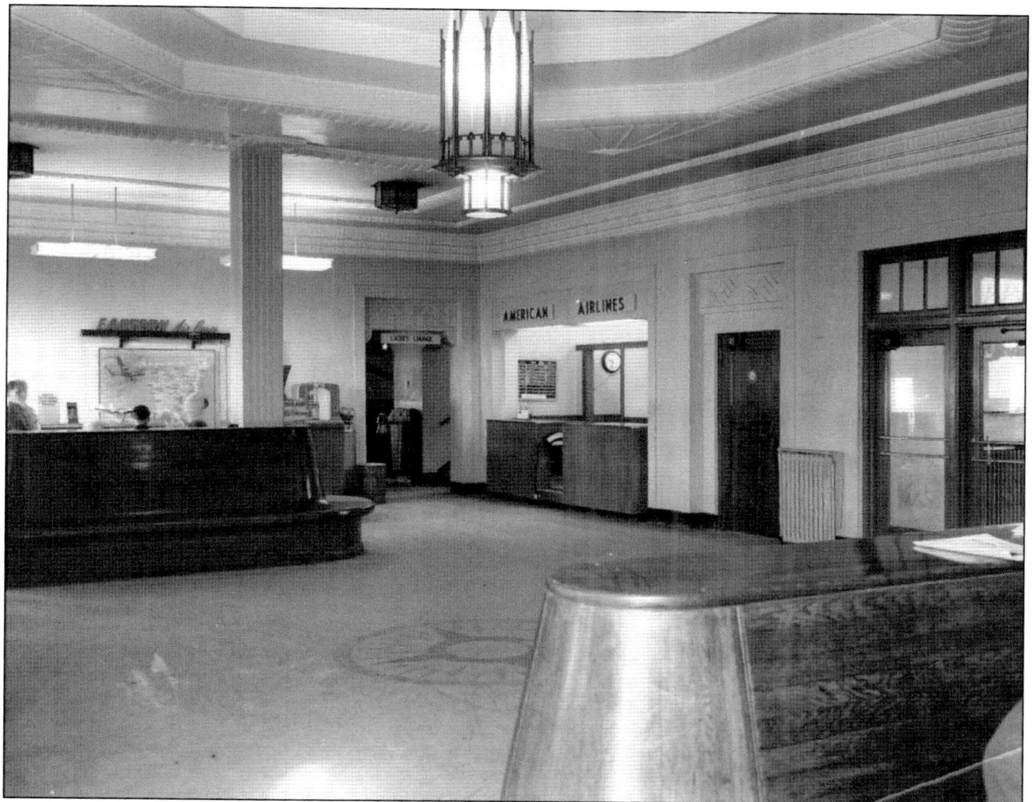

This is the Akron Municipal Airport lobby. The Eastern Airlines check-in desk is on the left. The entrance to the ladies' lounge is in the background at center. The American Airlines check-in desk is at right of center. The Akron Municipal Airport was created and managed by Bain E. "Shorty" Fulton.

This is another view of the Akron Municipal Airport lobby. Note the Eastern Airlines and American Airlines ticket offices. They are a far cry from airline counters today. Located underneath the ladies' lounge is a machine for purchasing life insurance prior to departure.

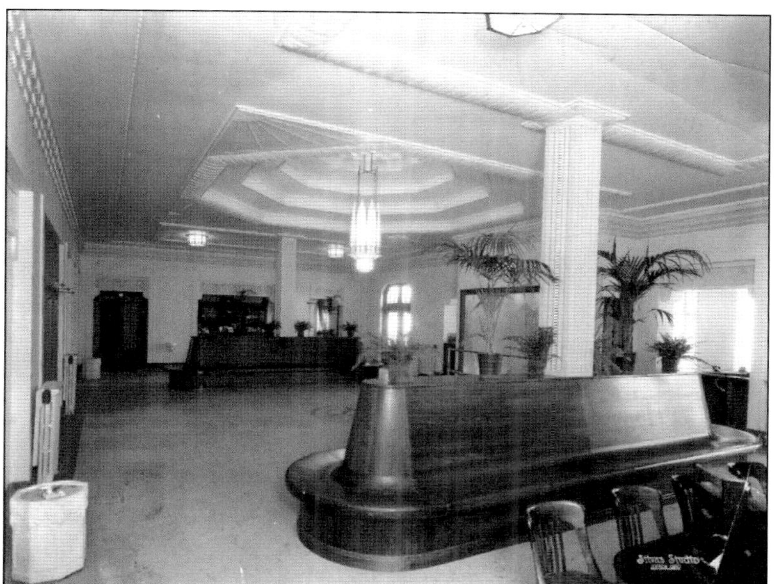

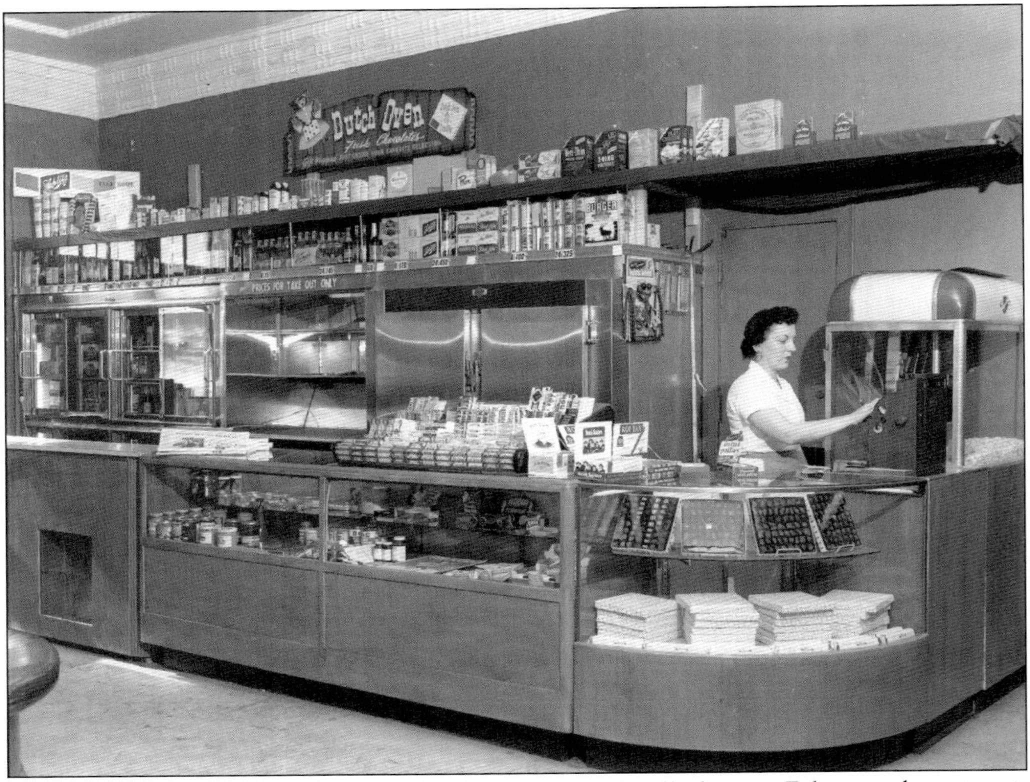

The snack bar at the Akron Municipal Airport became locally famous. Fulton made certain it was fully stocked and immaculate. Note the chocolate display, offering items for the business traveler to bring home.

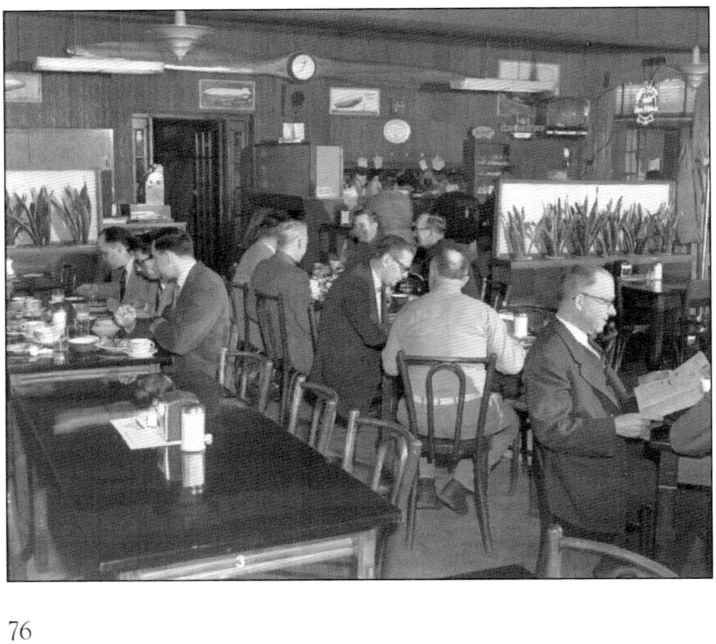

The inn at the Akron Municipal Airport became the gathering spot for local businessmen. "Shorty" Fulton can be seen in the center of the photograph, with his back to the camera, speaking to *Akron Beacon Journal* sportswriter Jim Schlemmer, seen here in his trademark dark suit and horn-rimmed glasses. Schlemmer would become an Akron legend in his own right as a proponent—along with Fulton—for the creation of the All American Soap Box Derby.

Shown here is the front cover of the menu from the Akron Municipal Airport. The Pad's menu not only described the food served at the restaurant, but also gave a brief history of the airport, Goodyear Zeppelin Airship Factory, Rubber Bowl, and Derby Downs.

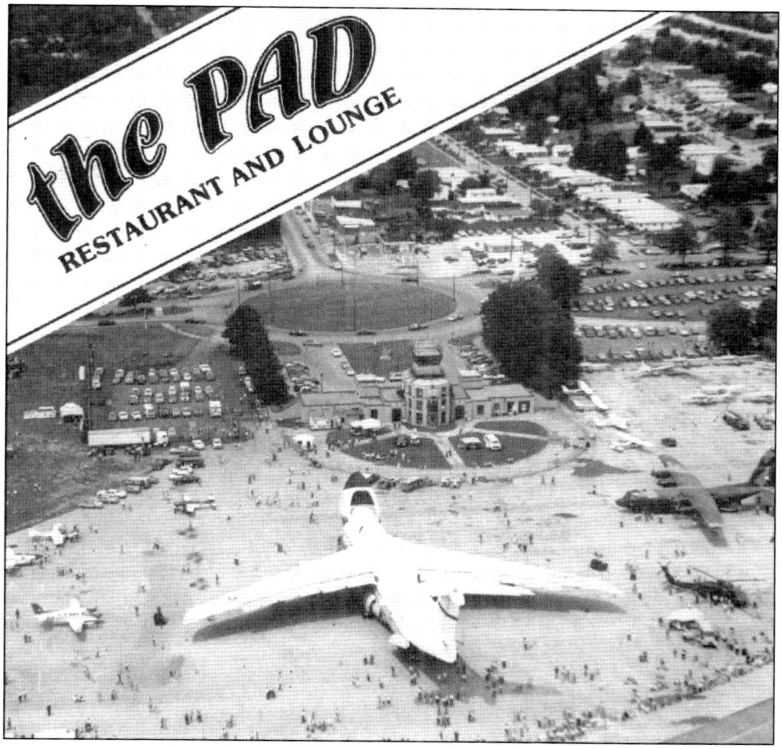

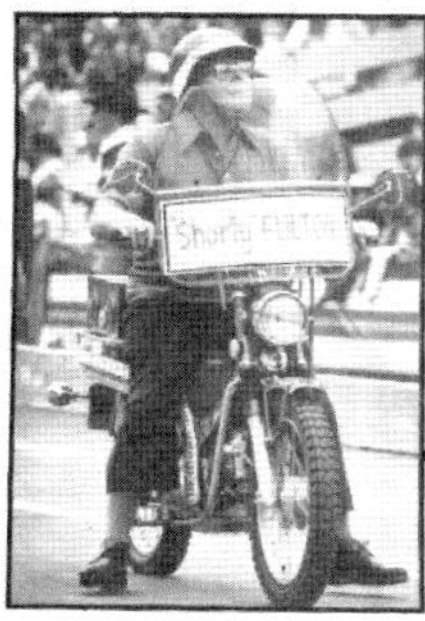

B.E. "Shorty" Fulton once was described as Akron's *champion* long distance dreamer. He was a highly spirited aviation enthusiast. Shorty let nothing get in the way of his vision of "Extraordinary Municipal Air Center and Recreational Wonderland". Akron developed the first municipal airport in the United States designed to accommodate both heavier-than-air and lighter-than-air craft. Shorty Fulton oversaw the operations of Akron Municipal Airport, later named Akron Fulton Airport, from 1928 to 1963.

1. THE CHAMP

GENEROUS SLICES OF TURKEY AND HAM ON TOAST, TOPPED WITH CHEDDAR CHEESE THEN BAKED W/SALAD 4.25

Goodyear's need to build a mammoth hanger coincided with the dreams of Shorty Fulton to get a municipal airport. The two were built in conjunction with one another.

The airdock...

- The largest building in the world without interior support
- As high as a 22 story building
- The dock was used as a production plant for airplanes in WWII

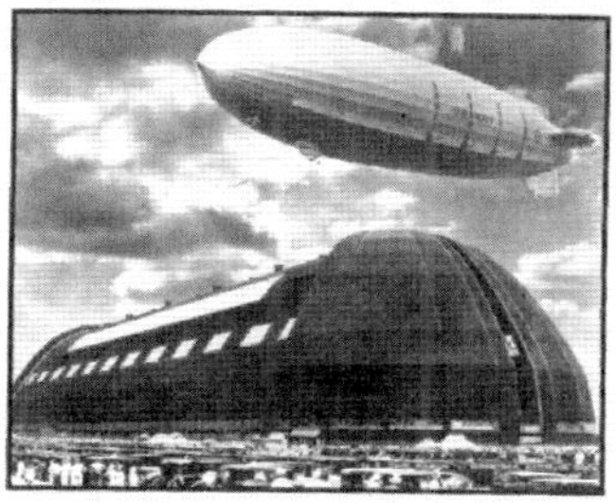

2. THE AIRDOCK

BREAST OF TURKEY, IMPORTED HAM, SWISS CHEESE, BACON ON TOASTED BUN................ 3.50

* ASK YOUR WAITRESS ABOUT OUR DAILY SPECIALS

The Pad menus were highly regarded for their photographic record of the airport. This page celebrates the airdock and "Shorty" Fulton. Note the food prices.

This menu page offers a rare look at Goodyear Aircraft Corporation's amphibious sport airplane, the Duck. Only three of these models were built, along with a slightly larger version known as the Drake. Although unsubstantiated, it was rumored that Donald Douglas of Douglas Aircraft pressured Goodyear into ceasing production, due to the Duck's potential popularity.

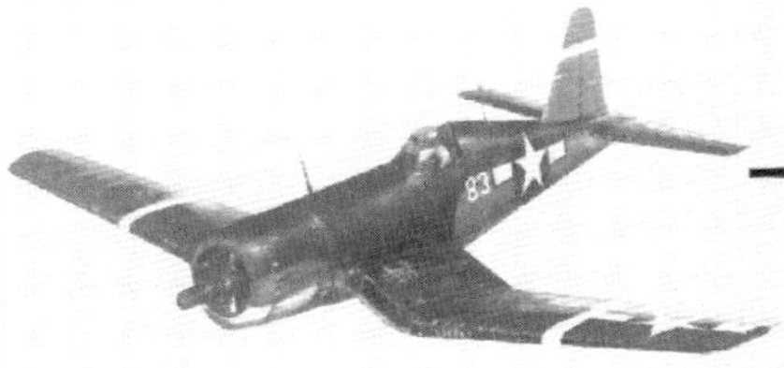

The Corsair FG-4 fighter plane was produced by Goodyear Aircraft for the Navy. 4,006 were built by the war's end.

3. THE CORSAIR COLD STACK

SERVED COLD AND STACKED HIGH ON A LOAF OF FRESH SOURDOUGH BREAD WITH CHIPS

HAM 2.35
TURKEY 2.75
ROAST BEEF 2.95
ADD 50¢ FOR SWISS OR AMERICAN CHEESE

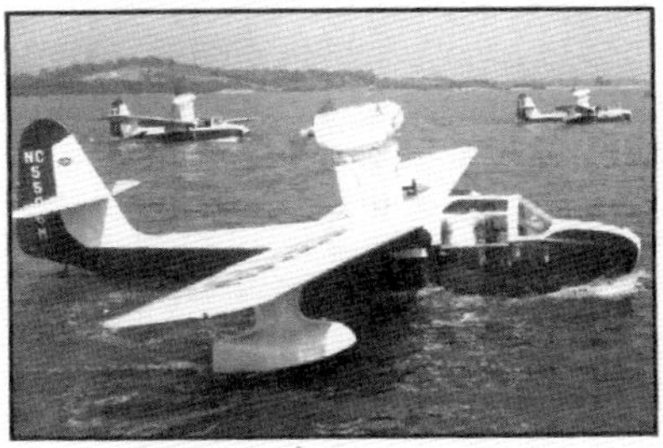

The Goodyear Duck, an amphibious aircraft, was skillfully crafted for a very short time after WWII when Goodyear considered entering the production aircraft industry.

4. THE VEGGY DUCK

FRESH VEGETABLES AND MUSHROOMS WITH CHEESE — BROILED ON PITA BREAD 2.95

This page offers a glimpse inside the airdock in which three Navy blimps are hangared. The blimp in the foreground appears to be a ZPG2W antisubmarine airship flown from around 1957 to 1962. The ZPG2W and ZPG3W would be the largest postwar airships ever built.

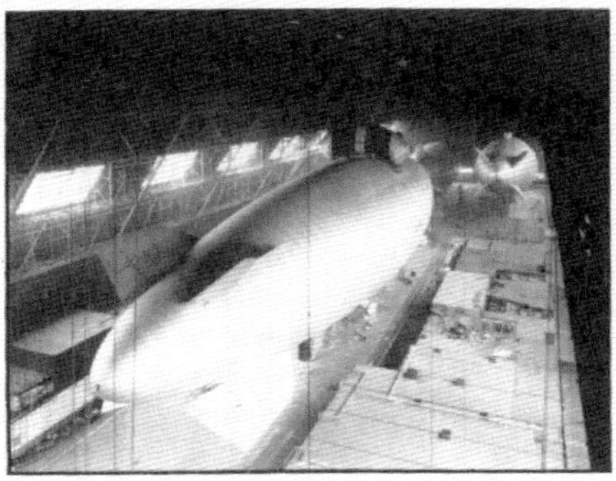

The zeppelin, *Akron*, made her maiden flight on Wednesday September 23, 1931. ZEPPELINS were rigid airships. They had metal frameworks within their envelopes to maintain their shape. The dream that the Rubber City would be the Zeppelin Capital of the world crashed with the crashes of the Akron-built zeppelins, the *Akron* and her sister ship, the *Macon*.

Non-rigid airships, or BLIMPS, were developed to a high degree of efficiency by Goodyear for the U.S. Navy during and after WWII. Used primarily for anti-submarine patrol during the war, airships escorted more than 89,000 ships in convoy without the loss of a single vessel. They can also be called dirigibles.

5. BLIMP BURGER

BROILED THE WAY YOU LIKE, AND SERVED WITH SLICED TOMATO, LETTUCE AND DILL PICKLE WEDGE AND CHIPS. ADD 50¢ PER ITEM: SWISS CHEESE, CHEDDAR CHEESE, AMERICAN CHEESE, BACON, MUSHROOMS 2.25

6. THE AKRON SALAD

ZEPPELIN SIZE SALAD. A MEAL IN ITSELF WITH CHEESES, HAM AND TURKEY. ADD 50¢ FOR FRESH MUSHROOMS 3.75

7. THE MACON SALAD

A MOUND OF CRAB STIX WITH EGG WEDGES, TOMATO AND OLIVES SERVED WITH IT'S OWN DRESSING 3.95

This page celebrates the world-famous Soap Box Derby Downs and Akron Rubber Bowl. Derby Downs is still in existence. The Akron Rubber Bowl, which opened in 1940, was closed around 2005.

8. THE ZEPPELIN

KIELBASA - HOT OR MILD ON PITA BREAD 3.75

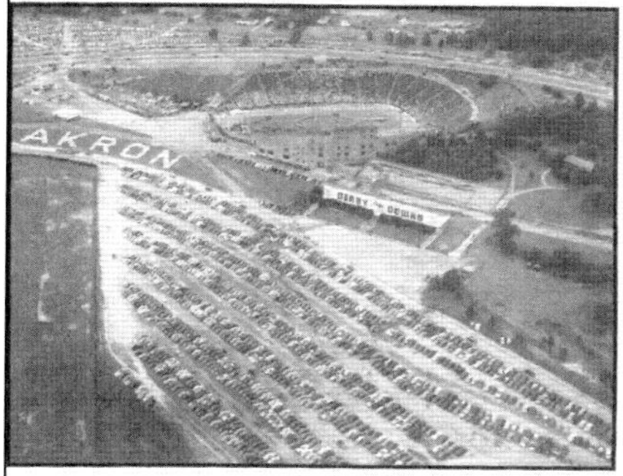

9. DERBY DOWNS TID BITS

TENDER, JUICY, BONELESS STRIPS OF CHICKEN BREAST, LIGHTLY BREADED AND DEEP FRIED. SERVED WITH FRENCH FRIES AND OUR OWN BBQ SAUCE 4.95

Excavation for the new Akron Municipal Airport left a huge hole in the side of a hill. Shorty Fulton and James Schlemmer, sports editor of the Beacon Journal, envisioned a sports arena in the excavated area. Again Shorty's vision became reality. The WPA put hundreds of men to work on the project. A sports facility seating over 35,000 was opened in 1940. The Akron Rubber Bowl is now owned by the University of Akron.

10. CHILI BOWL .... cup 95¢ bowl 1.75

11. SOUP OF THE DAY cup 75¢ bowl 1.25

12. THE AIRPORT GEORGE

FOR THE "STEAK AND POTATO MAN" LUNCHEON STEAK WITH FRENCH FRIES OR SALAD 5.25

(P.S. Is she out of the beauty shop yet?)

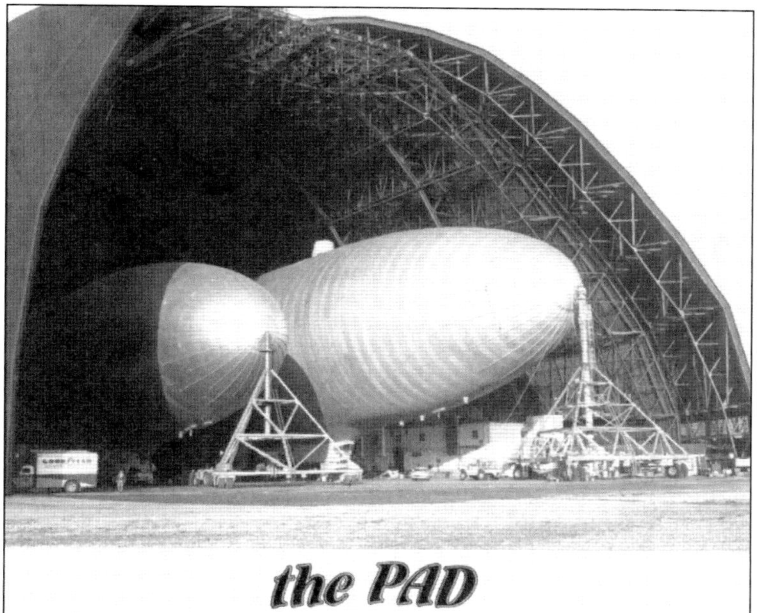

Akron Fulton Airport
1800 Triplett Blvd.
Akron, Ohio 44312
216-784-0079

*Largest Aircraft on the Front Cover is a C-5A Galaxy

This photograph offers a rare look at two ZPG2W airships ready to emerge from the airdock. The dome at the top of the airship is an early-warning radar. The ZPG2W and ZPG3W were to be the US Navy's versions of the US Air Force DEW line. Improved radar detection capabilities, combined with the July 6, 1960, crash of ZPG3W 144242, with the loss of 18 aircrew members, ended the naval airship program.

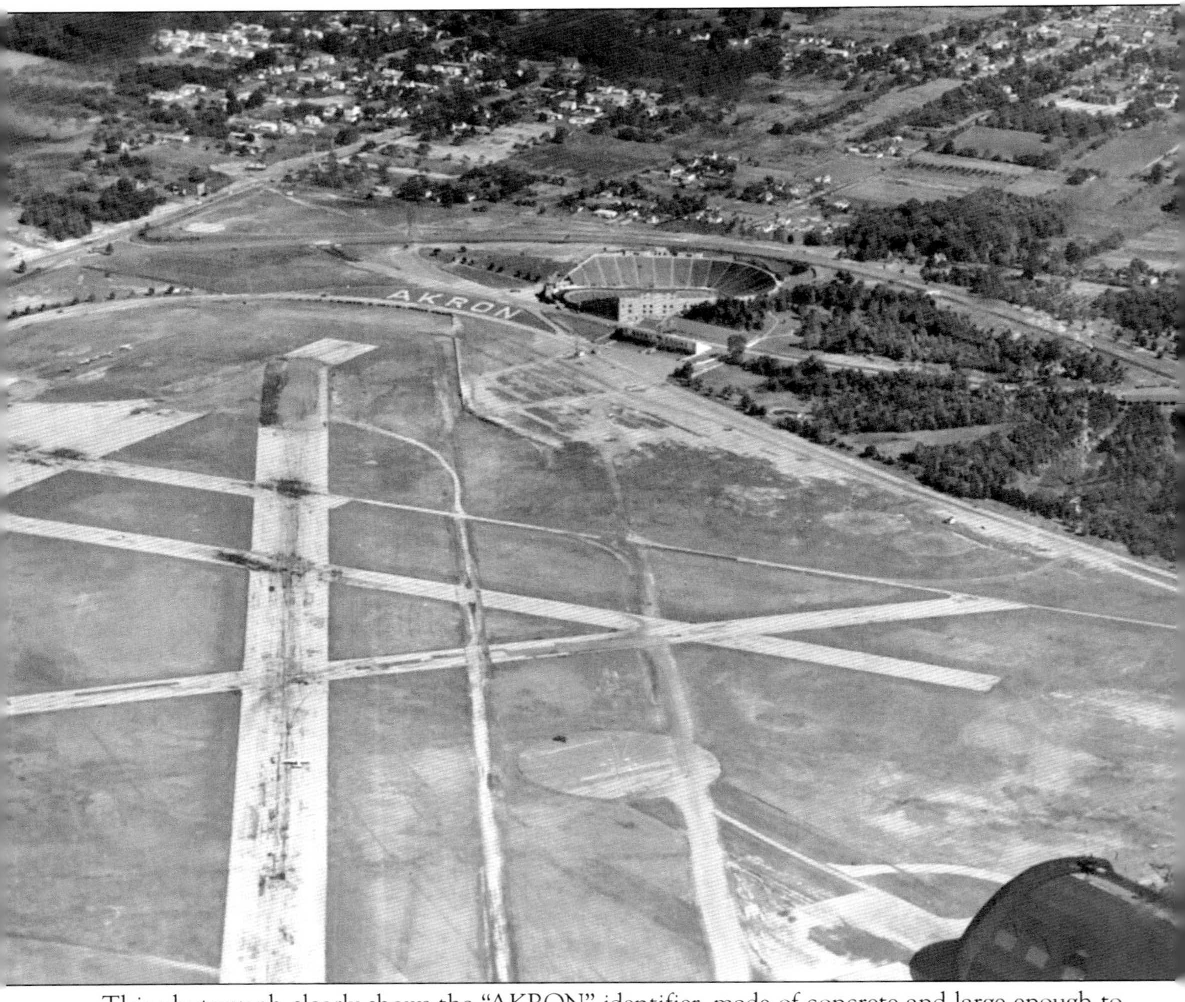

This photograph clearly shows the "AKRON" identifier, made of concrete and large enough to be read from the air. This identifier still exists today and remains a local icon, featured in print, photographs, paintings, and even screen-print T-shirts. The aerial sign was installed near the completion of the airport, around 1931.

This inside of a Christmas brochure features an aerial photograph of the Akron Municipal Airport. The front cover of the brochure reads, "Season's Greetings and Many Good Cross Countries." Shorty Fulton regularly sent Christmas cards, brochures, and posters featuring the Akron Municipal Airport. This insert clearly depicts the vision Fulton and the City of Akron had for the airport. Of particular interest is that this brochure was created during the worst period of the Depression.

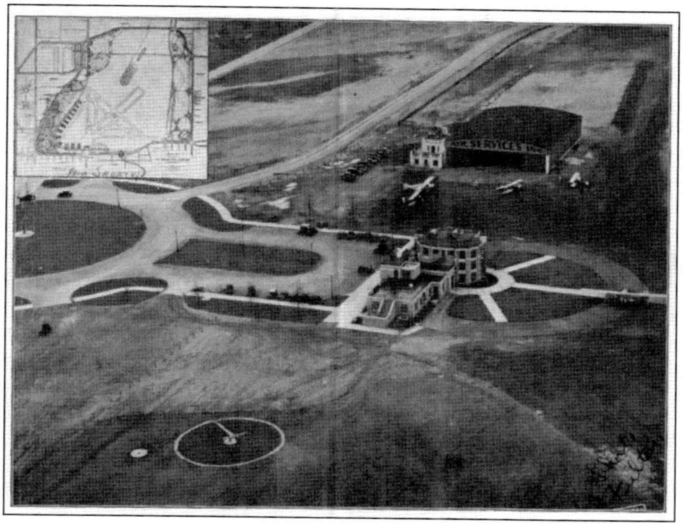

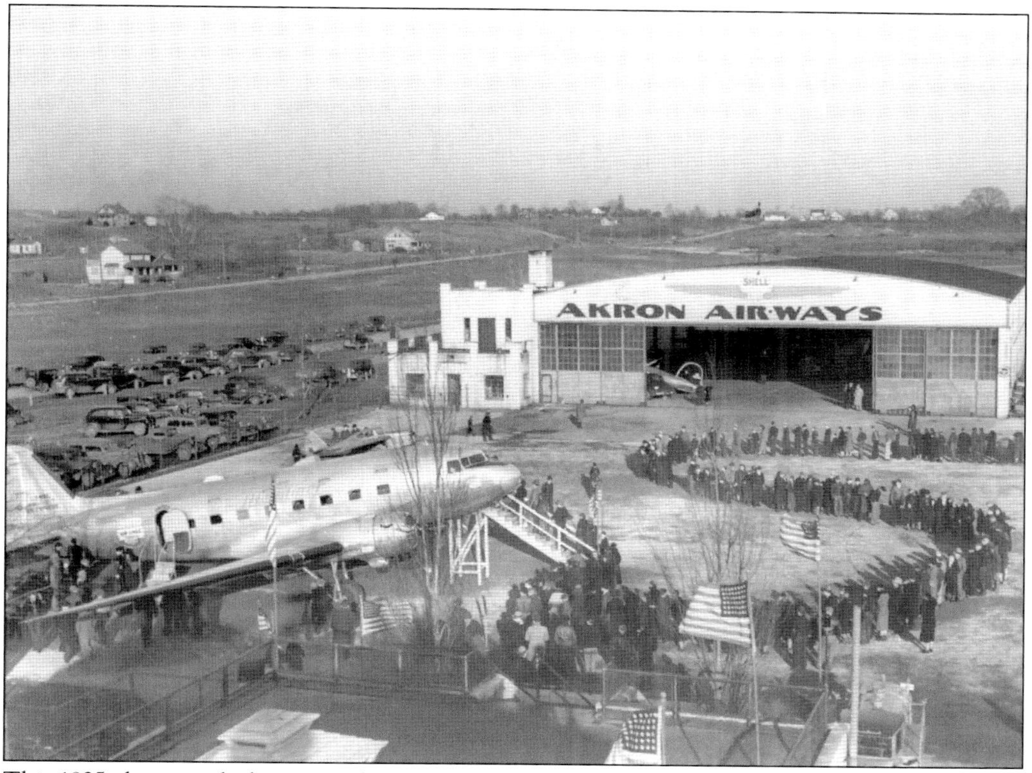

This 1935 photograph shows people touring a DC-2 or DC-3 United Airlines Mainliner. The tour was part of the ceremonies inaugurating flight service at the Akron Municipal Airport. The DC-3 was the first airliner to make a profit by carrying passengers only. It could be fitted as a sleeper for 14 passengers, or as a day plane seating 28.

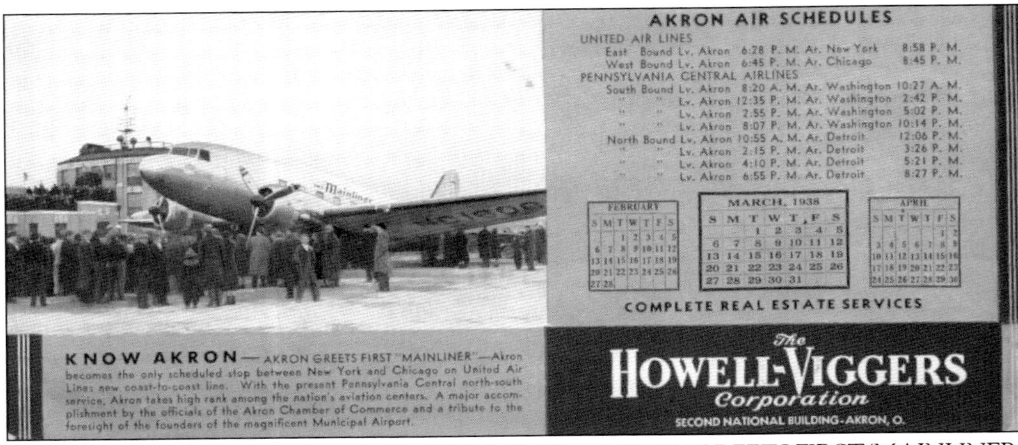

The caption of this photograph reads: "KNOW AKRON—AKRON GREETS FIRST 'MAINLINER.' Akron becomes the only scheduled stop between New York and Chicago on United Air Lines new coast-to-coast line. With the present Pennsylvania Central north-south service, Akron takes high rank among the nation's aviation centers. A major accomplishment by the officials of the Akron Chamber of Commerce and a tribute to the foresight of the founders of the magnificent Municipal Airport."

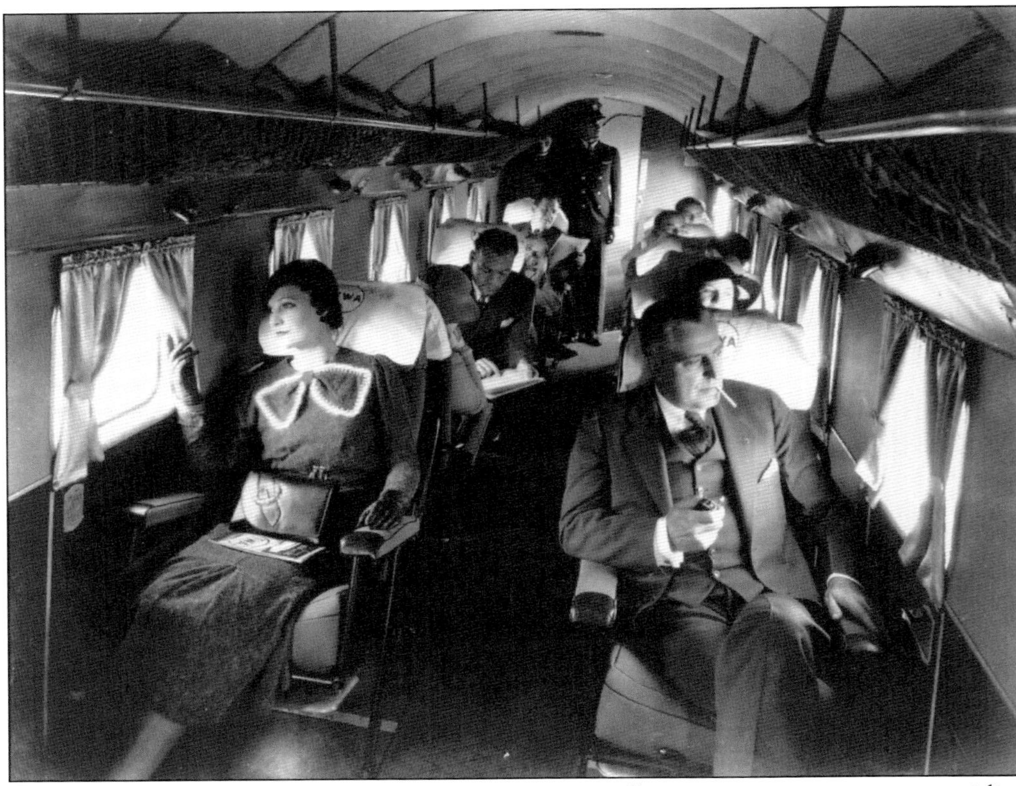

This photograph, taken aboard a TWA DC-3, gives an excellent presentation on passenger airline travel in the mid-1930s. Note the single seats and drawn curtains on the passenger windows. Maximum seating was 10 to 12 passengers.

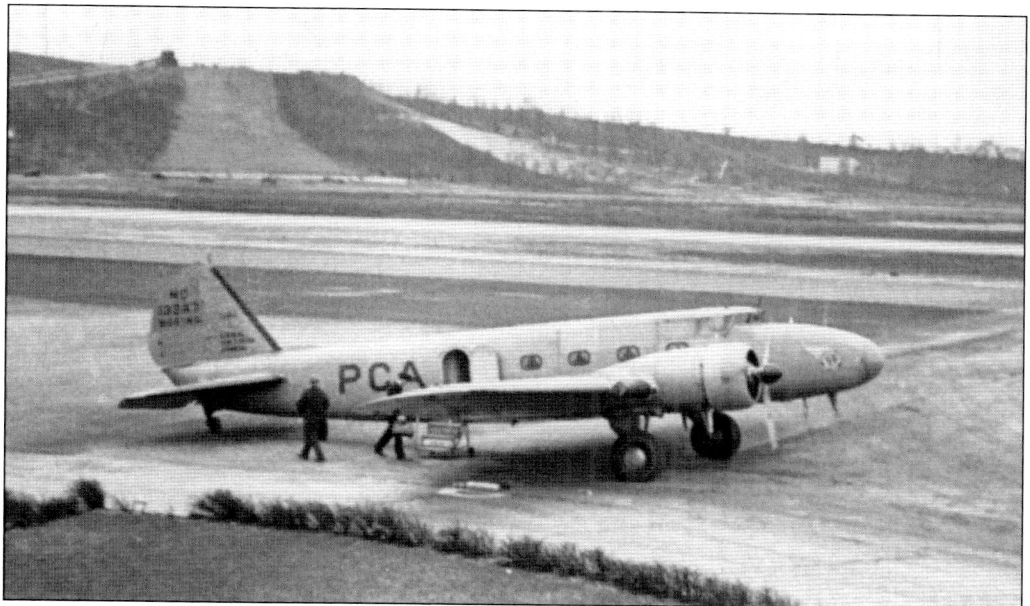

This Pennsylvania Central Airlines (PCA) Boeing B247 airliner awaits passenger loading at Akron Municipal Airport. Created on November 1, 1936, and originating out of Pittsburgh, PCA regularly scheduled flights out of Akron Municipal Airport until 1941.

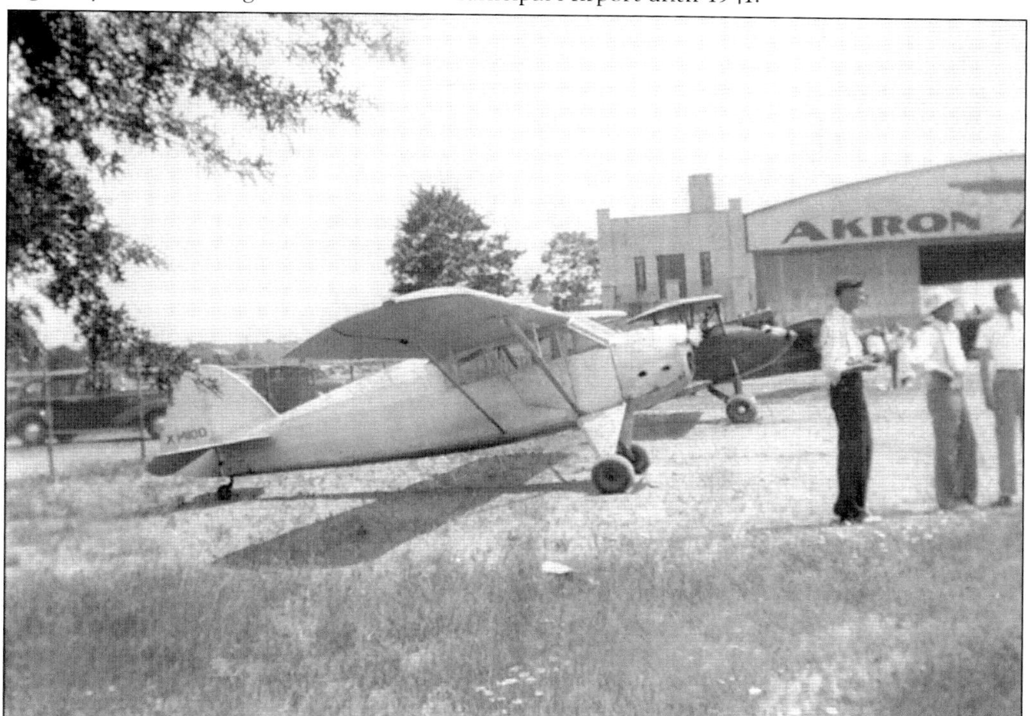

This is a Model A powered plane at the Akron Municipal Airport. During the 1930s, the airport was an attraction for new ideas in aviation. Aircraft like this one were not uncommon sights on the field.

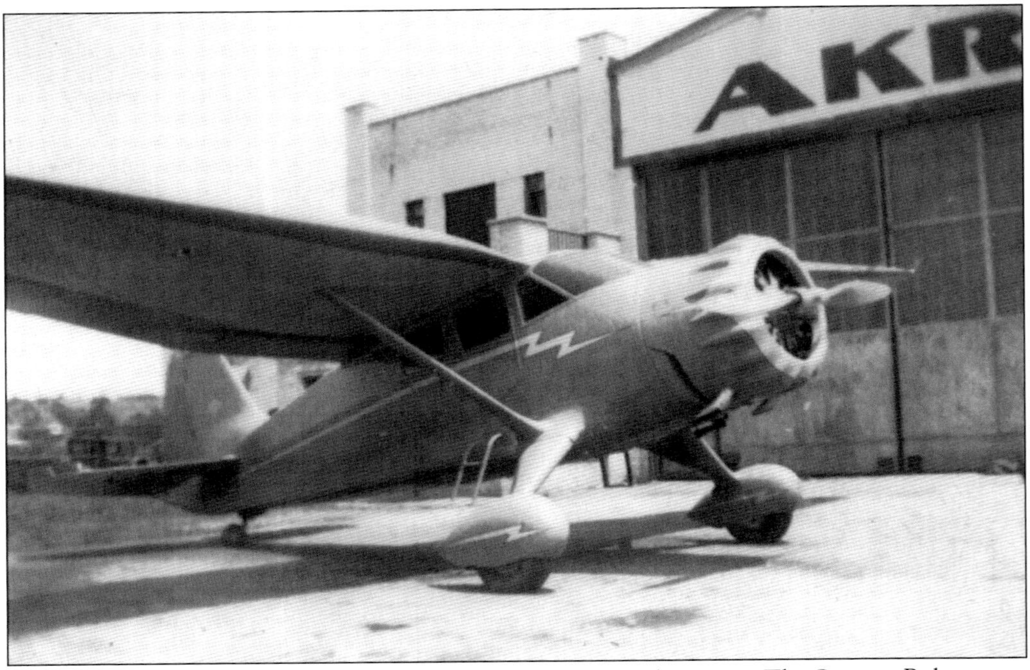

A Stinson Reliant plane rests quietly at the Akron Municipal Airport. The Stinson Reliant was perhaps the most common aircraft of the period. It was used extensively as a private, commercial, and military aircraft.

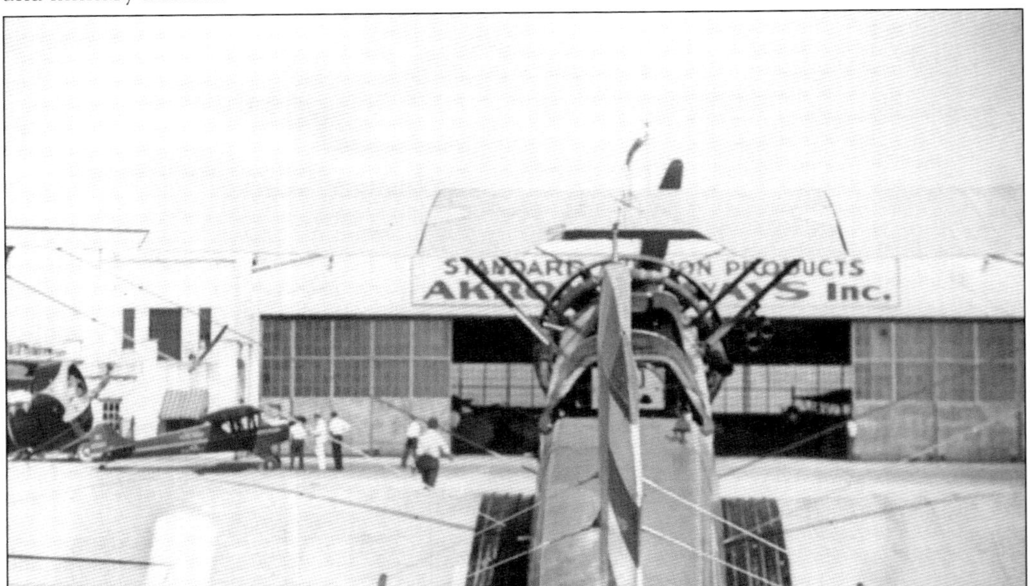

This unidentified plane sits at the Akron Municipal Airport in Akron, Ohio. The airport played host to a wide variety of aircraft and aircraft maintenance operations. Akron Airways was an early tenant beginning in the 1930s.

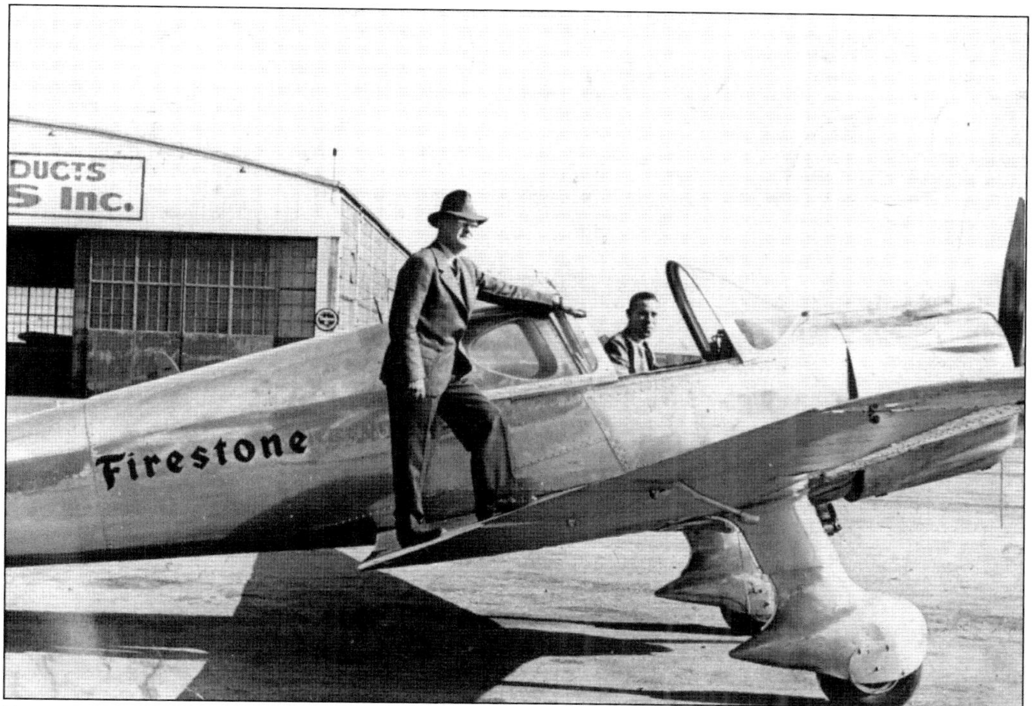

Firestone representatives are seen in a 1930s photograph boarding a company plane. Akron companies were among the first to recognize the value of corporate aircraft.

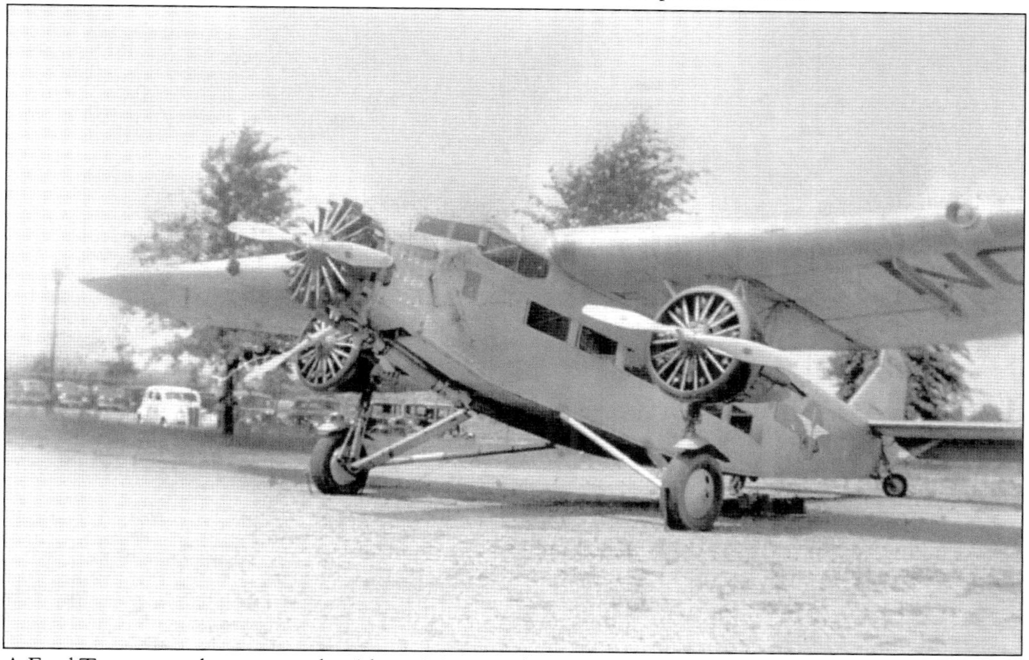

A Ford Transport plane sits at the Akron Municipal Airport in July 1937. Although unsubstantiated, it appears this could be an American Airlines aircraft. American operated out of Akron Municipal Airport until the late 1940s.

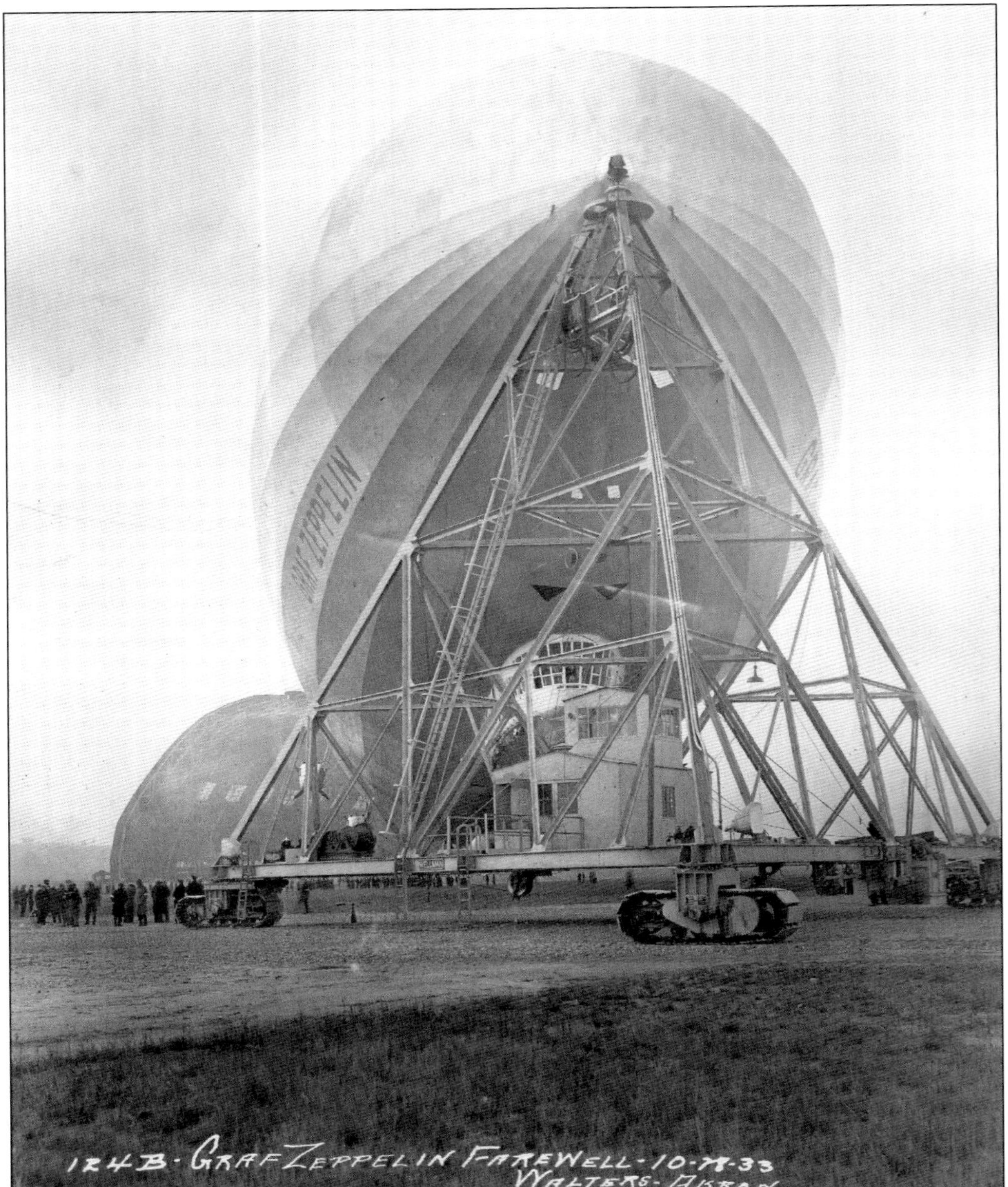

The German passenger airship *Graf Zeppelin* visits the Goodyear Zeppelin Airship Factory in Akron, Ohio, on its way back to Germany from an appearance at the Chicago Century of Progress Exposition in 1933. In 1930, the *Graf Zeppelin* set a record for flying around the world. Because of the ship's flight safety and performance record, proponents of "heavier than air" flight were becoming concerned that the zeppelin would replace the airplane in commercial travel. This prompted famed aviator Wiley Post and his navigator, Harold Gatty, to embark on a record-setting, eight-day flight around the world in the monoplane *Winnie Mae* in June 1931.

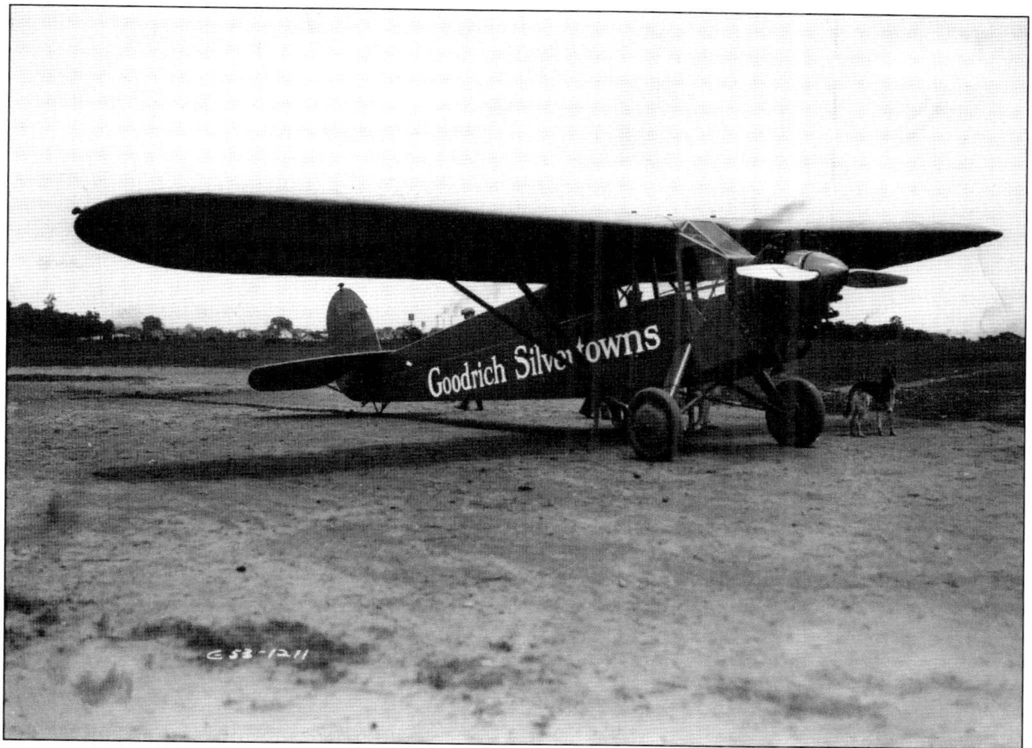

Local rubber companies were quick to take advantage of the airport and the use of aircraft. Pictured here is a 1928 Curtis-Robin aircraft sporting the message of the Goodrich Silvertown Tires.

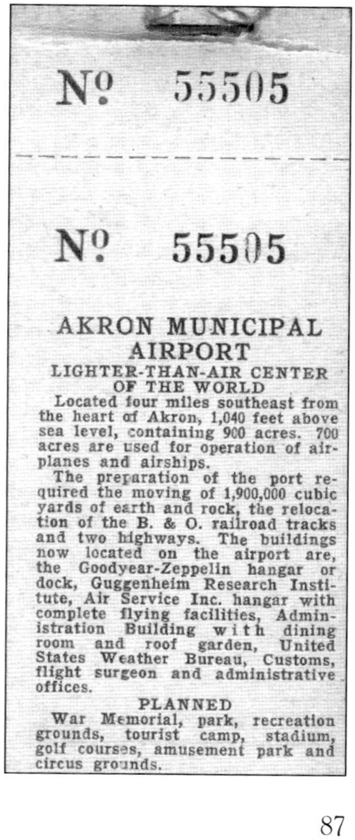

Nº 55505

Nº 55505

AKRON MUNICIPAL AIRPORT

LIGHTER-THAN-AIR CENTER OF THE WORLD

Located four miles southeast from the heart of Akron, 1,040 feet above sea level, containing 900 acres. 700 acres are used for operation of airplanes and airships.

The preparation of the port required the moving of 1,900,000 cubic yards of earth and rock, the relocation of the B. & O. railroad tracks and two highways. The buildings now located on the airport are, the Goodyear-Zeppelin hangar or dock, Guggenheim Research Institute, Air Service Inc. hangar with complete flying facilities, Administration Building with dining room and roof garden, United States Weather Bureau, Customs, flight surgeon and administrative offices.

PLANNED

War Memorial, park, recreation grounds, tourist camp, stadium, golf courses, amusement park and circus grounds.

Bain Fulton was a tireless promoter of Akron Municipal Airport. This early parking ticket takes great pains to remind patrons of the future that is to come and of the effort to reach the present. Fulton liked to promote Akron as the lighter-than-air center of the world. This was true until the tragic ends of the USS *Akron* and USS *Macon*.

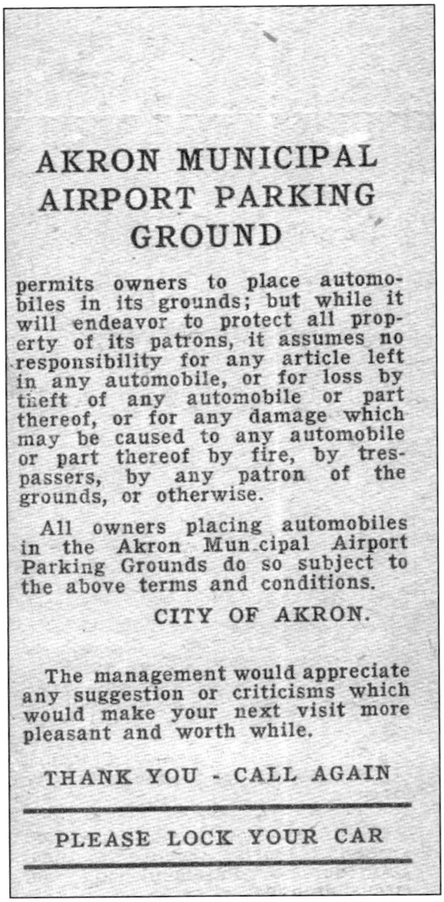

AKRON MUNICIPAL AIRPORT PARKING GROUND

permits owners to place automobiles in its grounds; but while it will endeavor to protect all property of its patrons, it assumes no responsibility for any article left in any automobile, or for loss by theft of any automobile or part thereof, or for any damage which may be caused to any automobile or part thereof by fire, by trespassers, by any patron of the grounds, or otherwise.

All owners placing automobiles in the Akron Municipal Airport Parking Grounds do so subject to the above terms and conditions.

CITY OF AKRON.

The management would appreciate any suggestion or criticisms which would make your next visit more pleasant and worth while.

THANK YOU - CALL AGAIN

PLEASE LOCK YOUR CAR

Some things never change, as witnessed by the disclaimer on the back of the ticket shown on the previous page. Fulton, in a monogram to the City of Akron, described attempts to remove the concrete stones on the "AKRON" identifier in the middle of the day.

The 1937 National Air Races, held in Cleveland, were extremely important to Akron aviation. Fulton was heavily involved with races that year, promoting Akron and his beloved airport. Shown here is the pass required for all the days of the event.

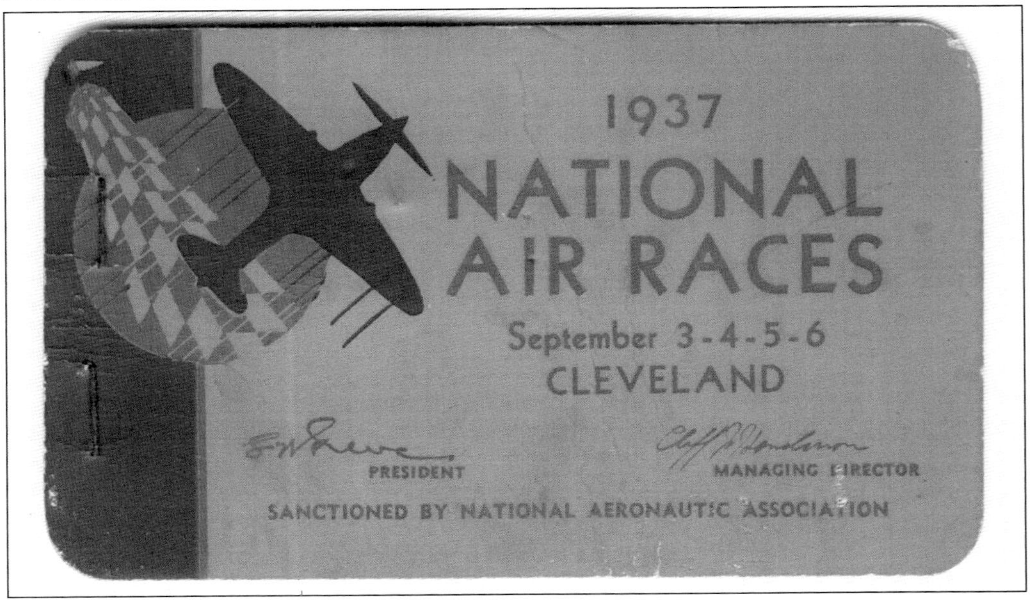

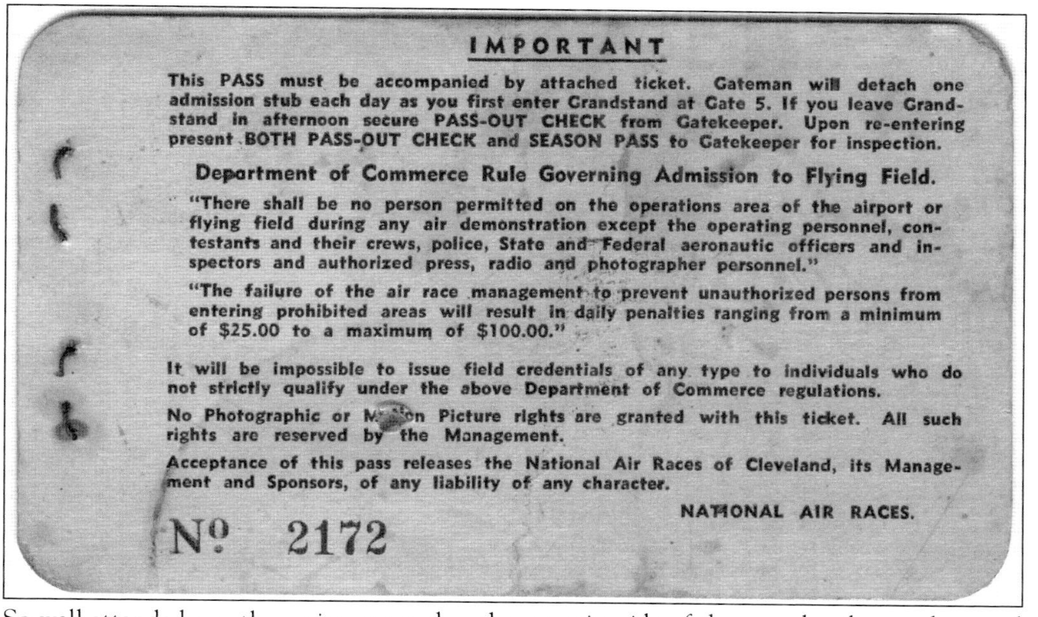

IMPORTANT

This PASS must be accompanied by attached ticket. Gateman will detach one admission stub each day as you first enter Grandstand at Gate 5. If you leave Grandstand in afternoon secure PASS-OUT CHECK from Gatekeeper. Upon re-entering present BOTH PASS-OUT CHECK and SEASON PASS to Gatekeeper for inspection.

Department of Commerce Rule Governing Admission to Flying Field.

"There shall be no person permitted on the operations area of the airport or flying field during any air demonstration except the operating personnel, contestants and their crews, police, State and Federal aeronautic officers and inspectors and authorized press, radio and photographer personnel."

"The failure of the air race management to prevent unauthorized persons from entering prohibited areas will result in daily penalties ranging from a minimum of $25.00 to a maximum of $100.00."

It will be impossible to issue field credentials of any type to individuals who do not strictly qualify under the above Department of Commerce regulations.

No Photographic or M[illegible]on Picture rights are granted with this ticket. All such rights are reserved by the Management.

Acceptance of this pass releases the National Air Races of Cleveland, its Management and Sponsors, of any liability of any character.

NATIONAL AIR RACES.

Nº 2172

So well attended was the racing event that the opposite side of the pass details crowd control measures. "The failure of the air race management to prevent unauthorized persons from entering prohibited areas will result in daily penalties ranging from a minimum of $25.00 to a maximum of $100.00."

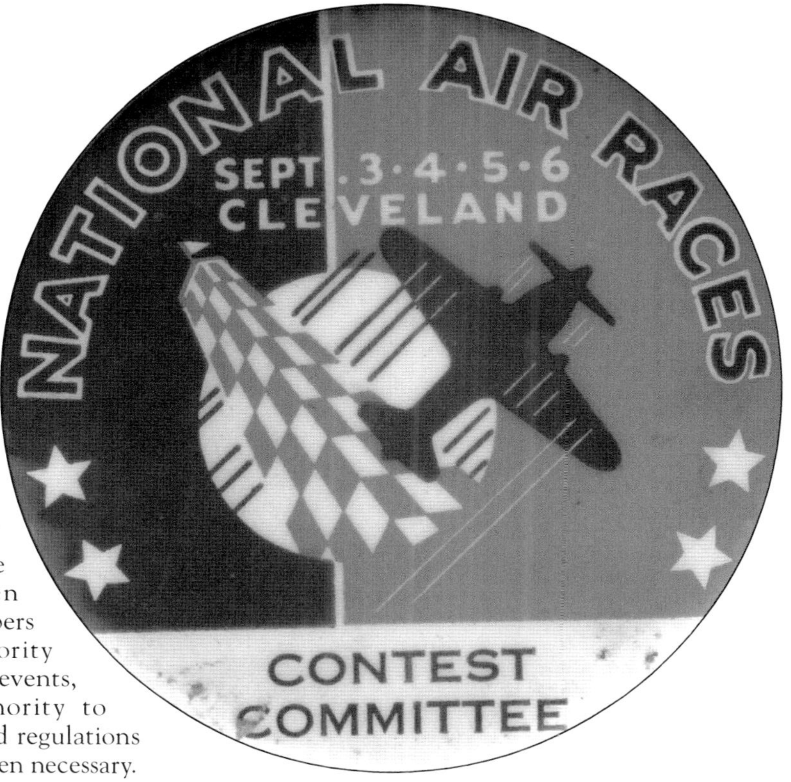

This is Shorty Fulton's National Air Races Contest Committee badge. Fulton served on the committee of the 1937 National Air Races as chief judge. The committee consisted of seven members. The members had complete authority over all competitive events, including the authority to interpret all rules and regulations and make changes when necessary.

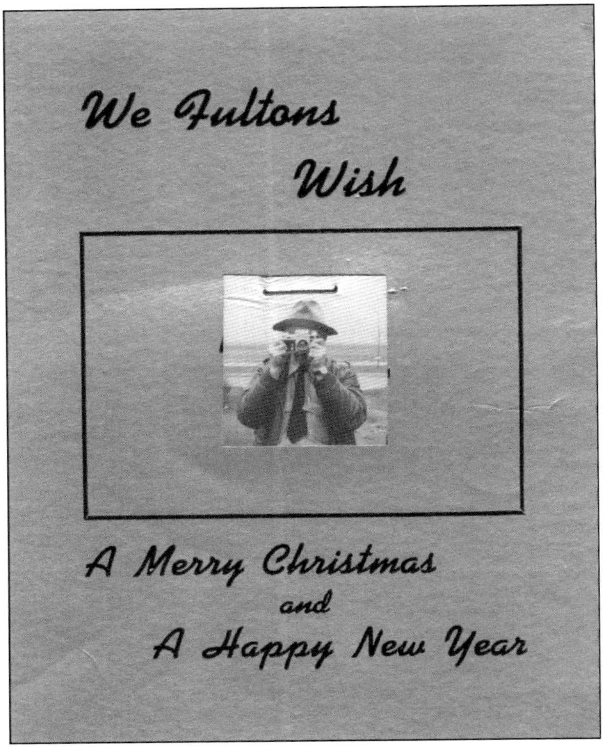

Shorty Fulton regularly sent Christmas cards to a variety of people and institutions, including family, friends, associates, government officials, Akron businesses and societies, and national airlines. Throughout the year, Fulton carried around his camera and took photographs of people he met and events he participated in. He often enclosed small copies of photographs of the recipient, or of events the recipient either attended or would be interested in.

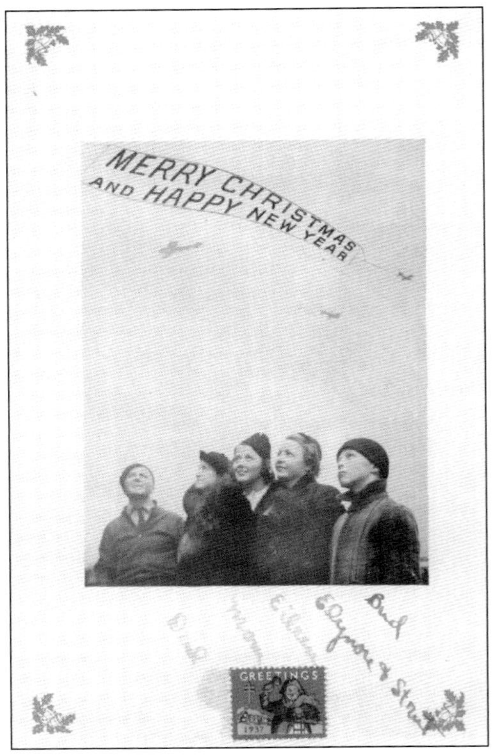

This 1937 Shorty Fulton Christmas card features the Fulton family. They are, from left to right, Shorty, Leah, Eileen, Elynore, Strut (dog), and Bud. Shorty Fulton regularly sent Christmas cards to family, friends, associates, businesses and societies, and national airlines. Throughout the year, he recorded people he met and events he participated in with his camera.

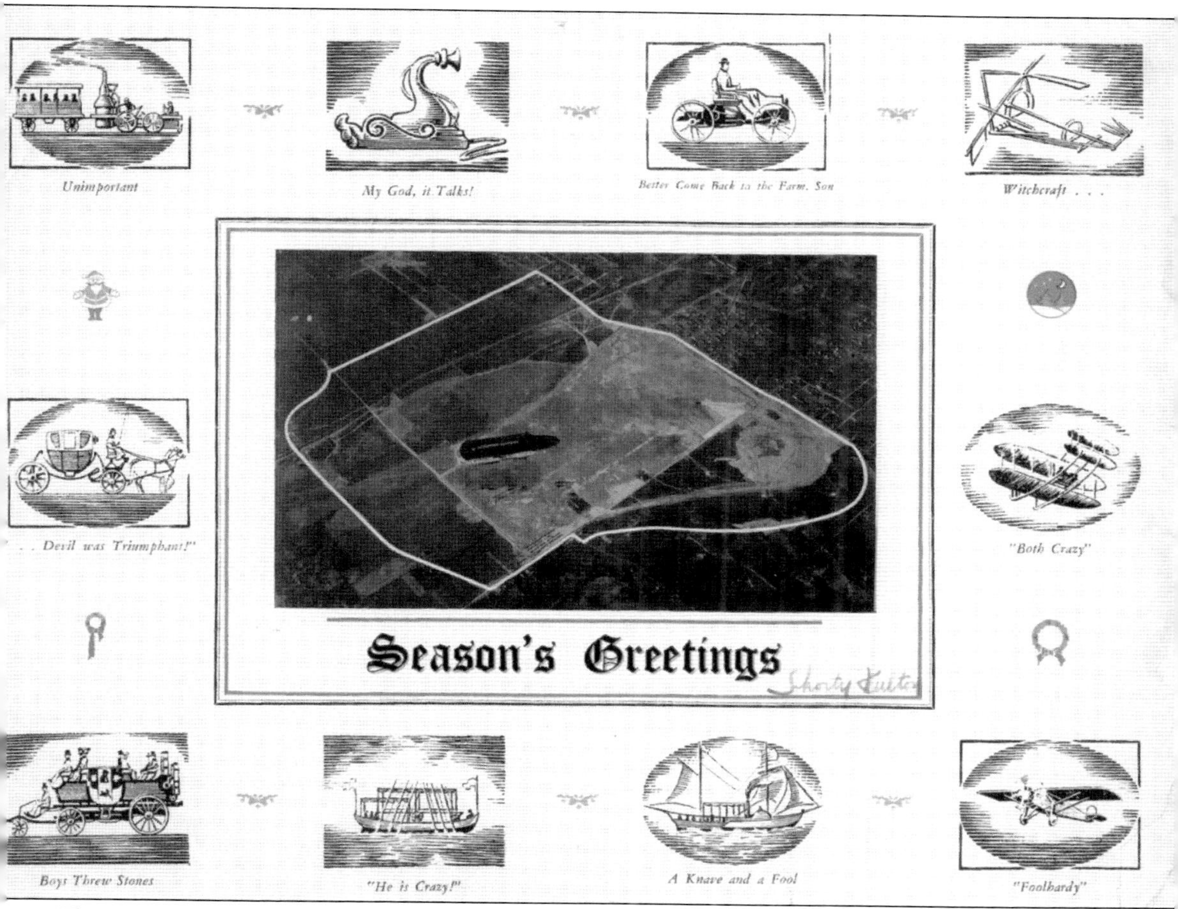

This c. 1930 Fulton Christmas card features the completion of the Goodyear Zeppelin Airship Factory. Note the border illustrations, which served to let folks know that the impossible simply takes a little more time.

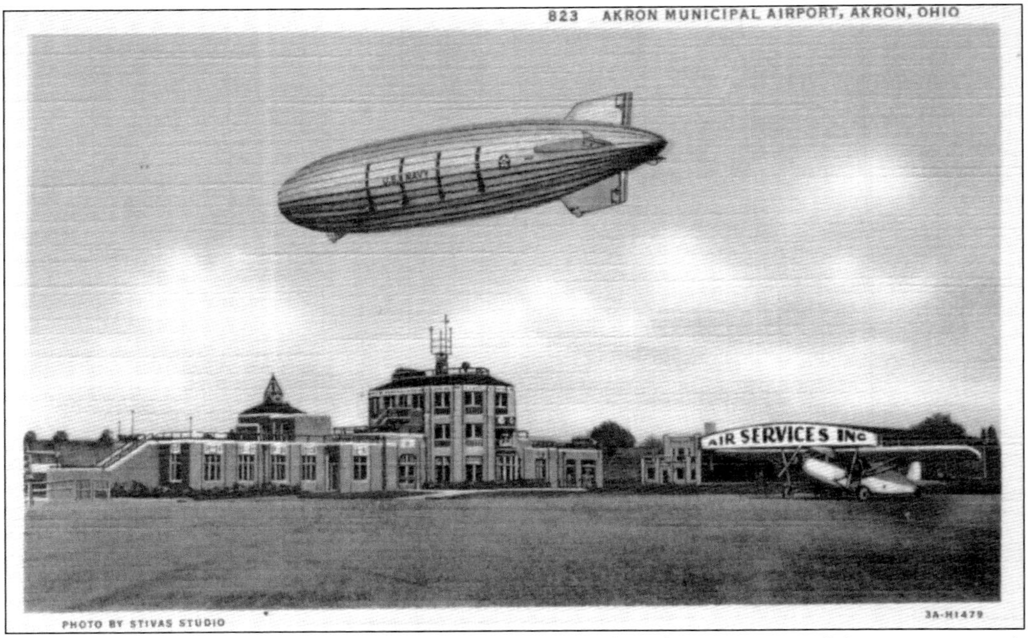

This example of an early postcard shows an airship over the Akron Municipal Airport terminal. Such postcards, a popular means of promoting the City of Akron, signified the importance of the airport to the community.

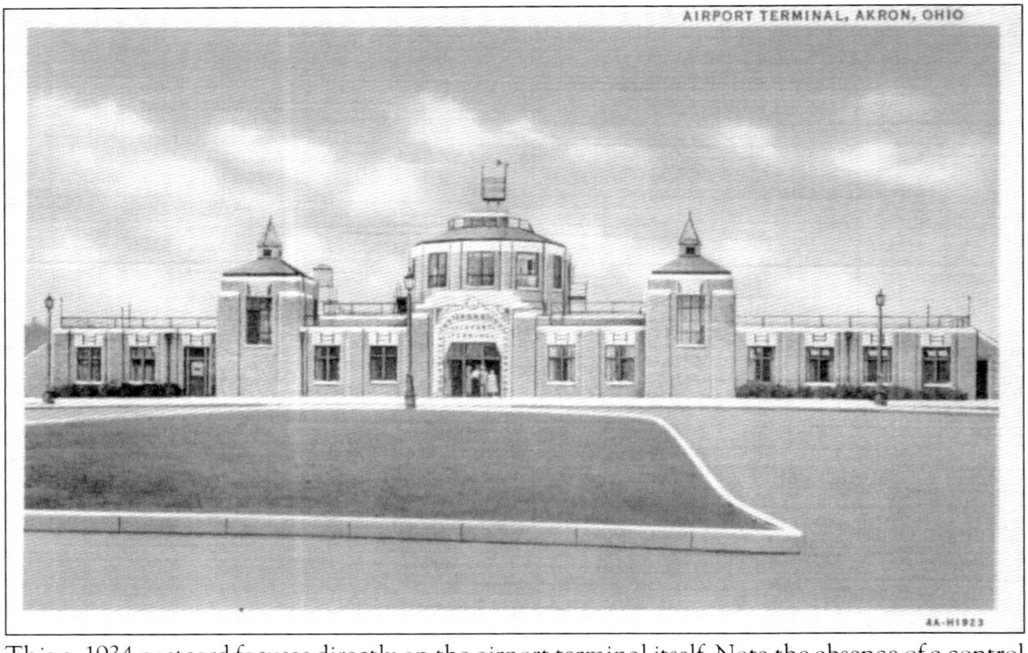

This c. 1934 postcard focuses directly on the airport terminal itself. Note the absence of a control tower. The top of the terminal only provided weather and radio information at the time.

Six

The College of Lighter Than Air

One of the most overlooked areas in exploring the history of aviation in Akron is the small, inconspicuous brick building located at the top of Triplett Boulevard. Known currently as an adjunct building for the Akron Public School System, the facility once housed the most advanced aeronautical research facility on lighter-than-air flight in the United States.

The Daniel Guggenheim Airship Institute was founded in 1929, when the construction of US Navy airships *Akron* and *Macon* was beginning. It was established as a cooperative project between the Daniel Guggenheim Fund for the Promotion of Aeronautics, the University of Akron, and the California Institute of Technology.

The airship institute was the first and only scientific facility dedicated to solving problems regarding lighter-than-air flight. The institute had to provide means for aerodynamic, meteorological, structural, and general physical research. This required the construction of a number of unique test stands.

The first was a vertical wind tunnel 6.5 feet in diameter with a wind velocity capability of 125 miles per hour. The wind tunnel was unique in that a vertical "jet" was used for testing. The choice of using a vertical system was made for better accessibility to the model. An airship model was suspended vertically into the tunnel for testing.

The Whirling Arm aerodynamic test stand was essentially a horizontal pipe measuring 32 feet to the center of the model, rotating at speeds of 175 miles per hour. The speed of the test depended upon the size of the model, since centrifugal force would increase its weight by 56 times. The gust tunnel, water tank, aerology laboratory, and aircraft metals research laboratory completed the composition of one of aviation's more interesting, yet unknown, stories.

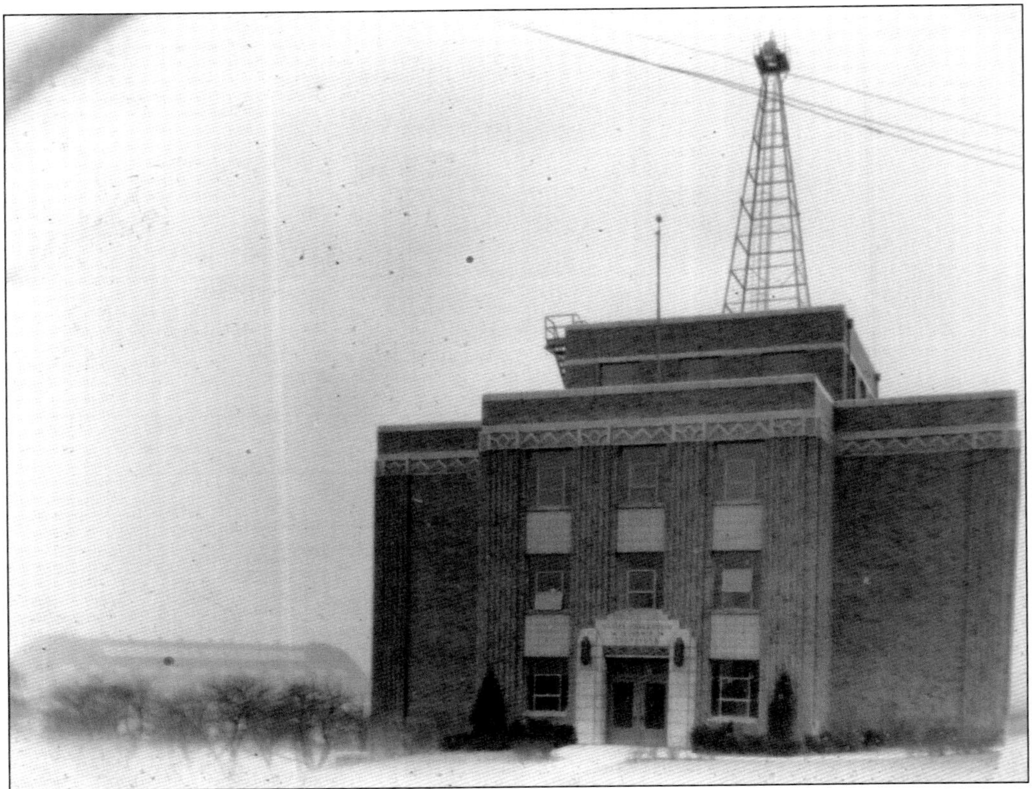

Daniel Guggenheim and his son Harry established the Daniel Guggenheim Medal for achievement in aeronautics and provided grants for aeronautics research at several universities, including the University of Akron. Designed by M.M. Konarski, the Akron Public Schools architect, the Guggenheim Airship Institute was established in 1929. The building, located across from the Goodyear Zeppelin Airship Factory, was dedicated in 1932.

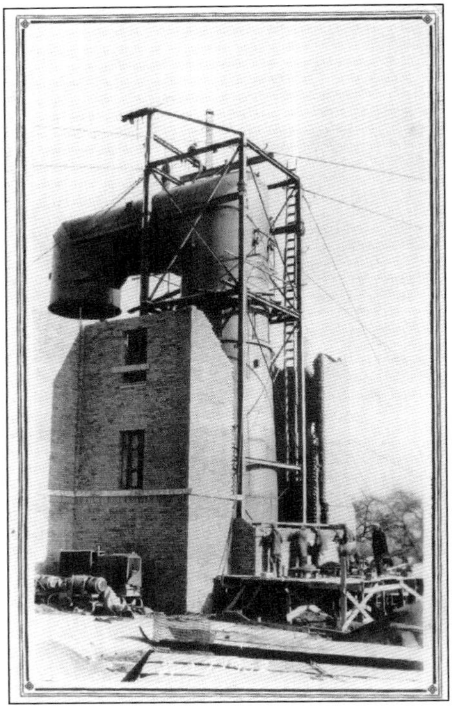

Shown here is construction of the vertical wind tunnel at the Guggenheim Airship Institute in Akron, Ohio. Daniel Guggenheim and his son Harry established the Daniel Guggenheim Medal for achievement in aeronautics and provided grants for aeronautics research at several universities, including the University of Akron. The institute was established in 1929, and the building, located on Triplett Avenue in Akron, was dedicated in 1932.

This 1929 photograph shows the exterior of the Guggenheim Airship Institute, designed by M.M. Konarski. The facade, created in the 1930s Art Deco style, can be seen today. The building, now property of the Akron Public Schools, still stands at the top of Triplett Boulevard, overlooking the Akron Municipal Airport and the airdock.

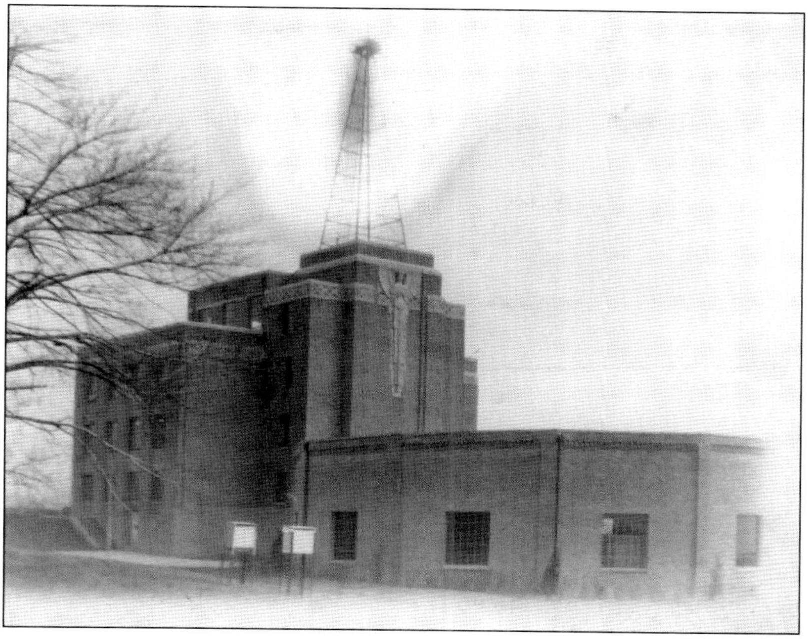

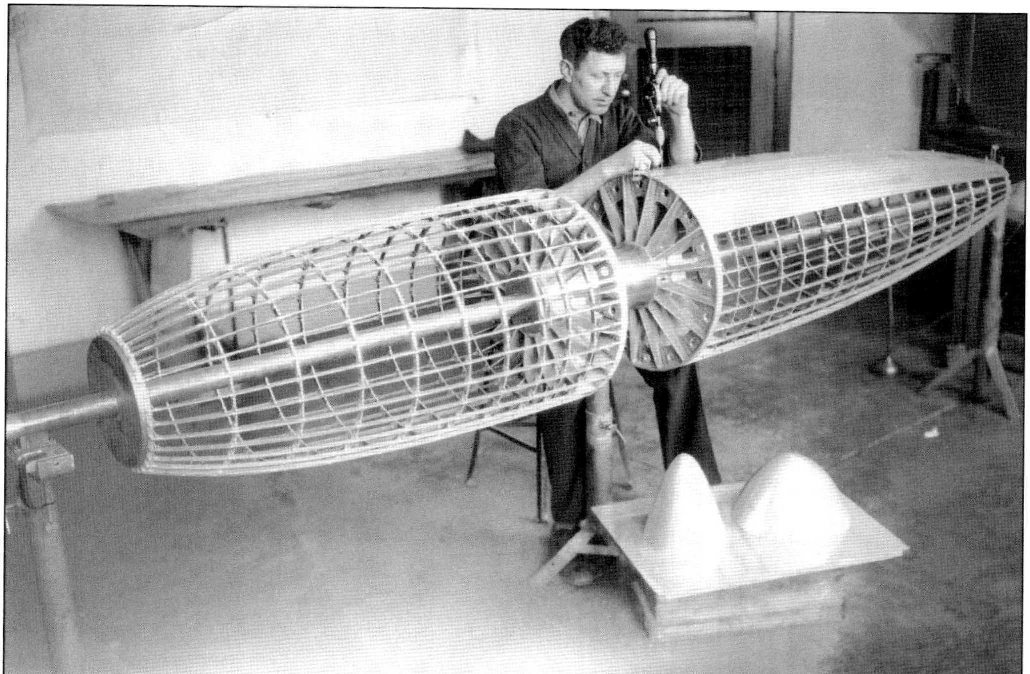

A man builds a model of the USS *Akron*. The model was later used for experiments in the wind tunnel of the Guggenheim Airship Institute operated by the University of Akron. It was the technical advancements in lighter-than-air flight in Akron that led to the development and construction of the institute, which existed from 1932 to 1949.

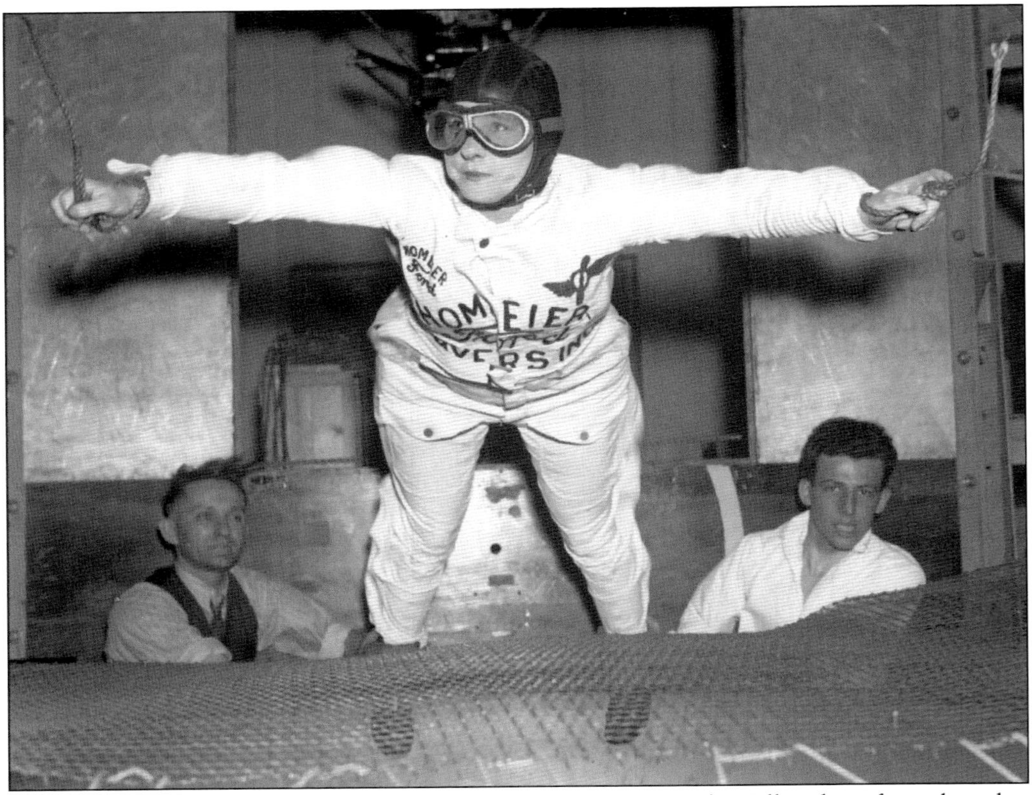

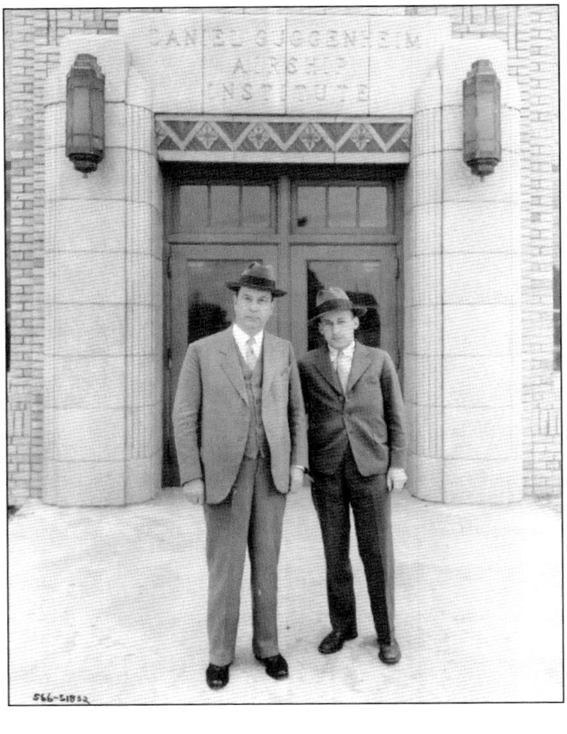

Babe Smith Walker dives from the side of a vent in the wind tunnel of the Guggenheim Institute at the University of Akron. Note the direction of the man's hair behind Walker holding her foot. The other unidentified man holds her other foot, while Walker herself holds on to rope lanyards. The side vent of the vertical wind tunnel could project winds of up to 125 miles per hour. It appears from this photograph that those speeds were reached, as Walker is nearly vertical.

Dr. George E. Zook (left), president of the University of Akron, and Dr. Theodore Troller, resident director of the new Guggenheim Airship Institute, pose together at the entrance to the institute during its dedication in 1932.

Seven

Naval Air Station Akron

The Naval Air Station Akron was commissioned on January 14, 1948, as one of 28 such activities strategically placed throughout the country for the purpose of providing facilities and instructor personnel for Navy and Marine Air Reserve personnel. Military direction was exercised by the chief of Naval Air Reserve Training activities from its headquarters near Chicago, Illinois.

Classrooms, projector rooms, library facilities, aircraft, and other training aids valued at approximately $7 million had been provided to the Naval Air Station Akron to allow training activities of the regular forces that approximated reality.

Naval Air Station Akron, at its peak, was composed of one Marine Reserve and 15 Naval Reserve Aviation units. Personnel consisted of 400 officers and 1,500 enlisted men. During the Korean War, two squadrons from Naval Air Station Akron were called to active duty. On February 1, 1951, Naval Aviation Fighter Squadron 653 (VF 653) mobilized and performed with conspicuous gallantry. Sadly, eight aviators from this squadron were killed in action. On October 22, 1951, Marine Fighter Squadron (VMF 231) was mobilized and served in Korea until the end of hostilities, with a loss of four aviators killed in action. The price these citizen soldiers paid was high, and their actions have never been forgotten. VMF 231 "Ace of Spades" is the longest-serving squadron in the Marine Corps, having been organized in 1923. It is still serving on active duty at NAS Cherry Point, North Carolina.

Decommissioned in 1958, Naval Air Station Akron's record of service and sacrifice makes a grand statement as to the nature and character of the men and women who wrote a stellar chapter in Akron aviation history.

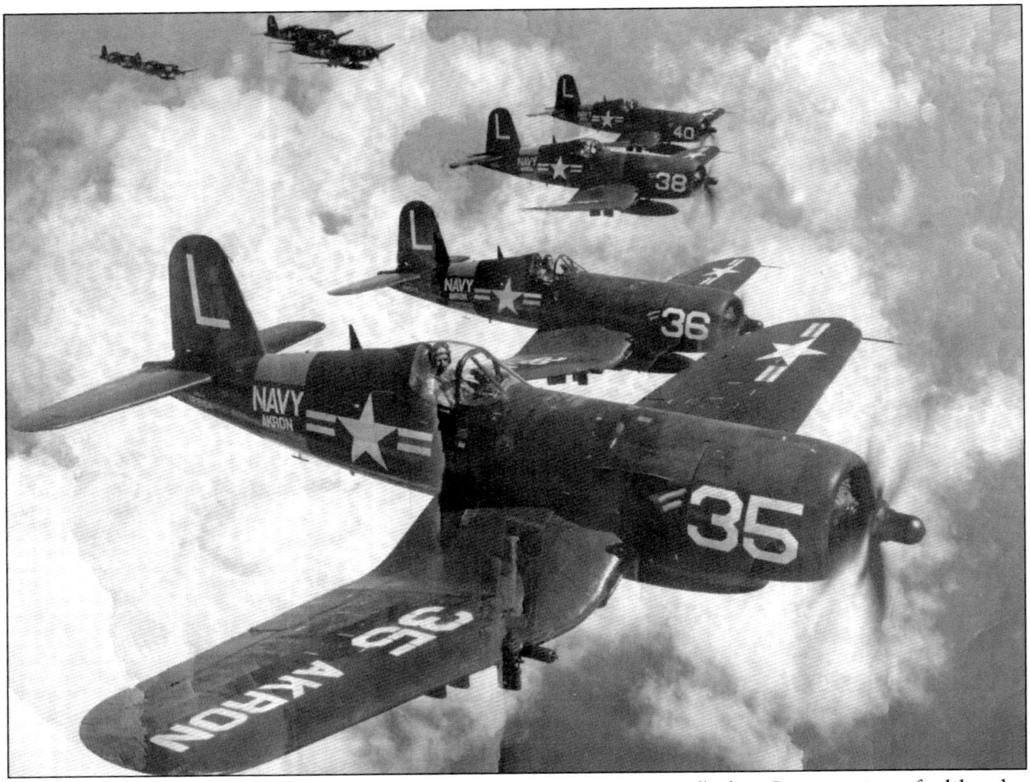

Seen here are eight Naval Air Station Akron FG-1 Corsairs in flight. Corsair aircraft, like the ones pictured here, were a familiar sight over the skies of Akron, Ohio, from 1943 to 1958, much the same as their airship counterparts.

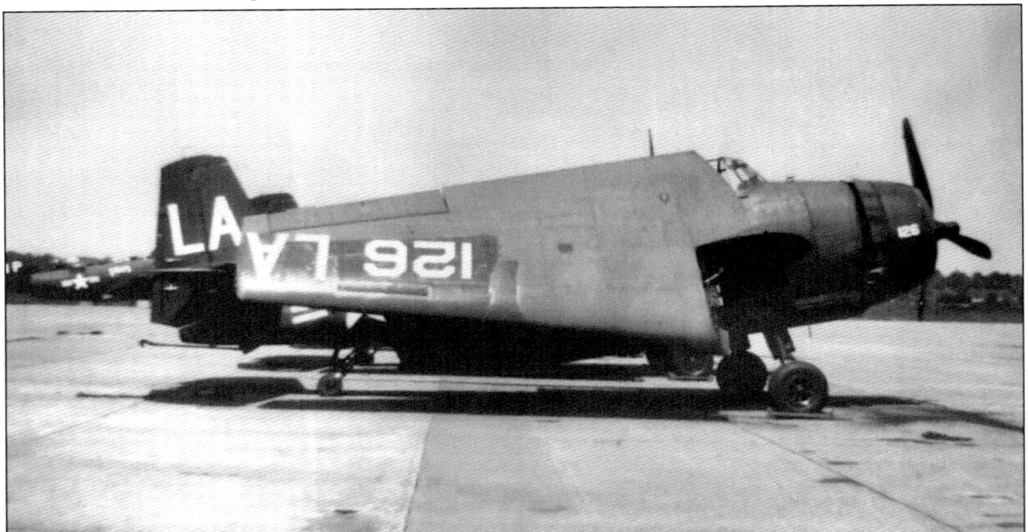

This is a TBM Torpedo Bomber. The US Naval Air Station existed in Akron, Ohio, from 1948 to 1958. Naval Air Station Akron operated a wide variety of aircraft, many of World War II vintage.

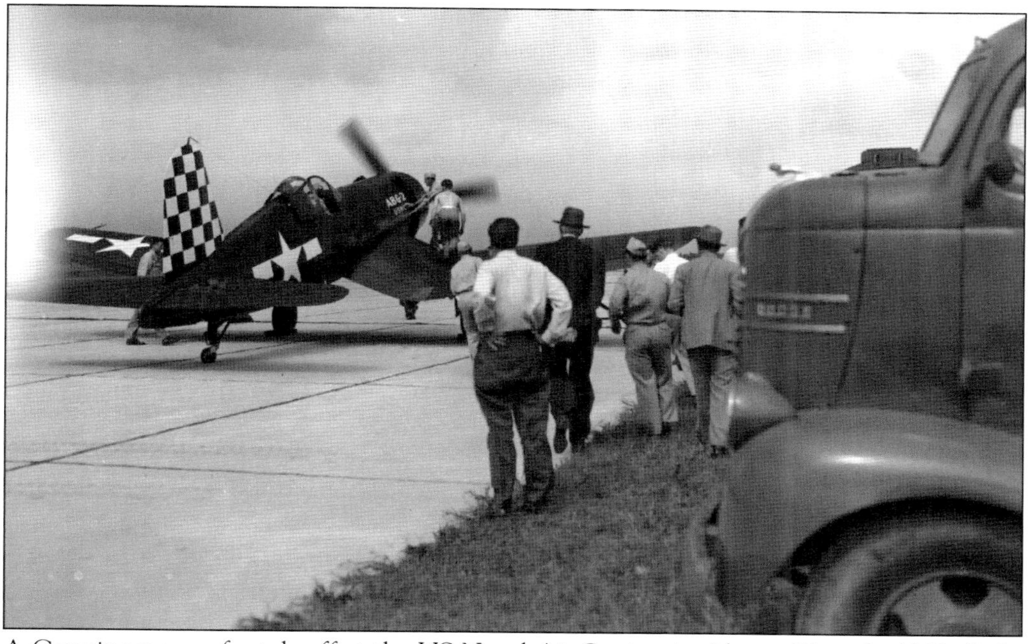

A Corsair prepares for takeoff at the US Naval Air Station in Akron, Ohio. In 1948, flight operations were not as formal and rigid as they are today. Note the position of ground personnel in relation to the aircraft taxiing for takeoff.

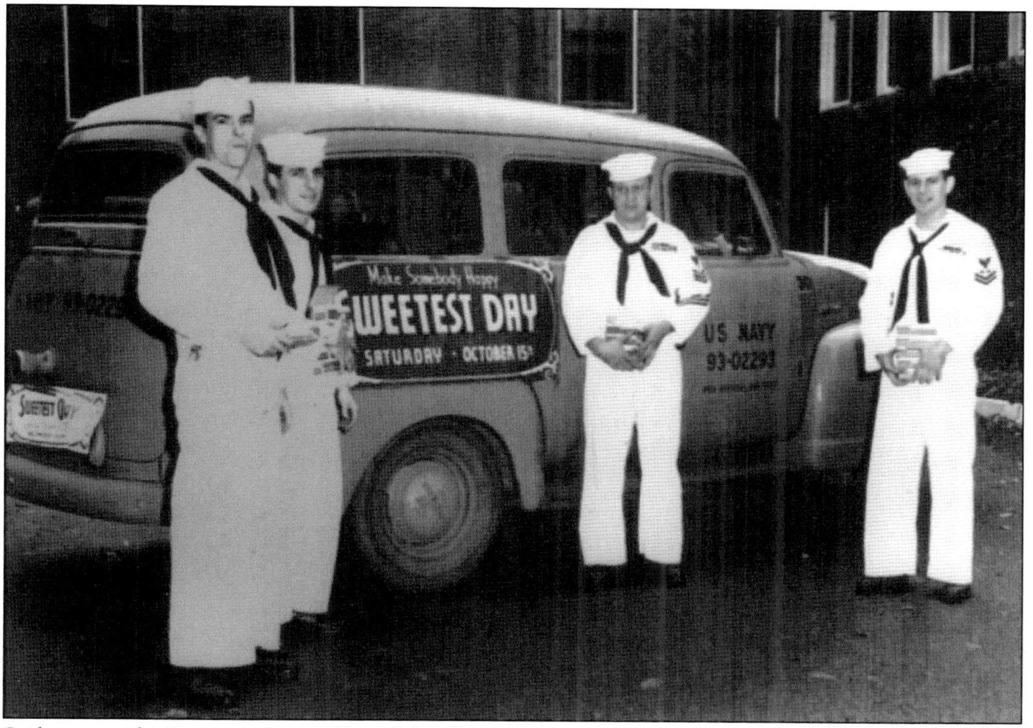

Sailors pose for Sweetest Day at Naval Air Station Akron. The air station was actively involved in community affairs. Many local high school graduates spent their service time at the air station.

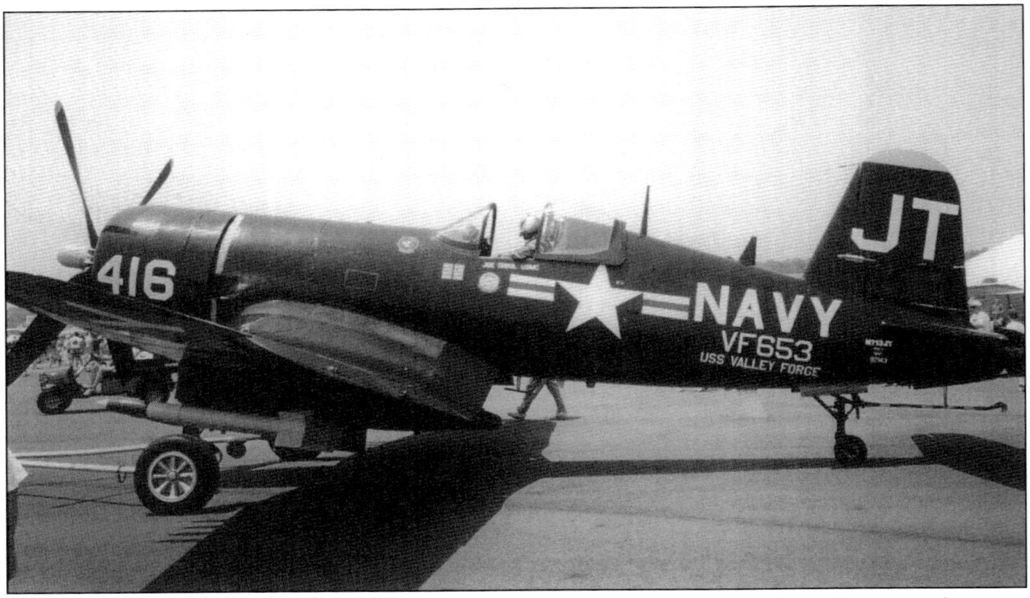

This is a USS *Valley Forge* VF 653 airplane. The markings of "fighting 653" were distinct, including the pilots' flight helmets, which were painted with red and white clown faces. The pilots' clown faces smiled, while the executive officer's helmet frowned, since the "XO" was in charge of discipline.

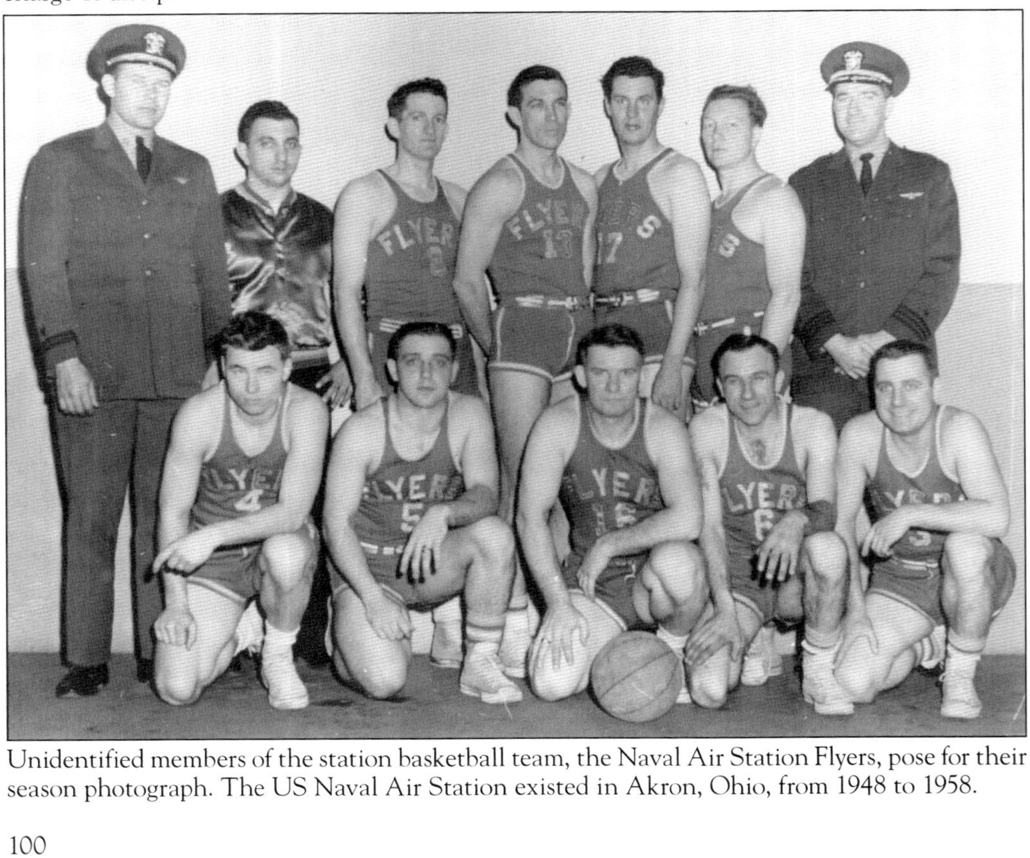

Unidentified members of the station basketball team, the Naval Air Station Flyers, pose for their season photograph. The US Naval Air Station existed in Akron, Ohio, from 1948 to 1958.

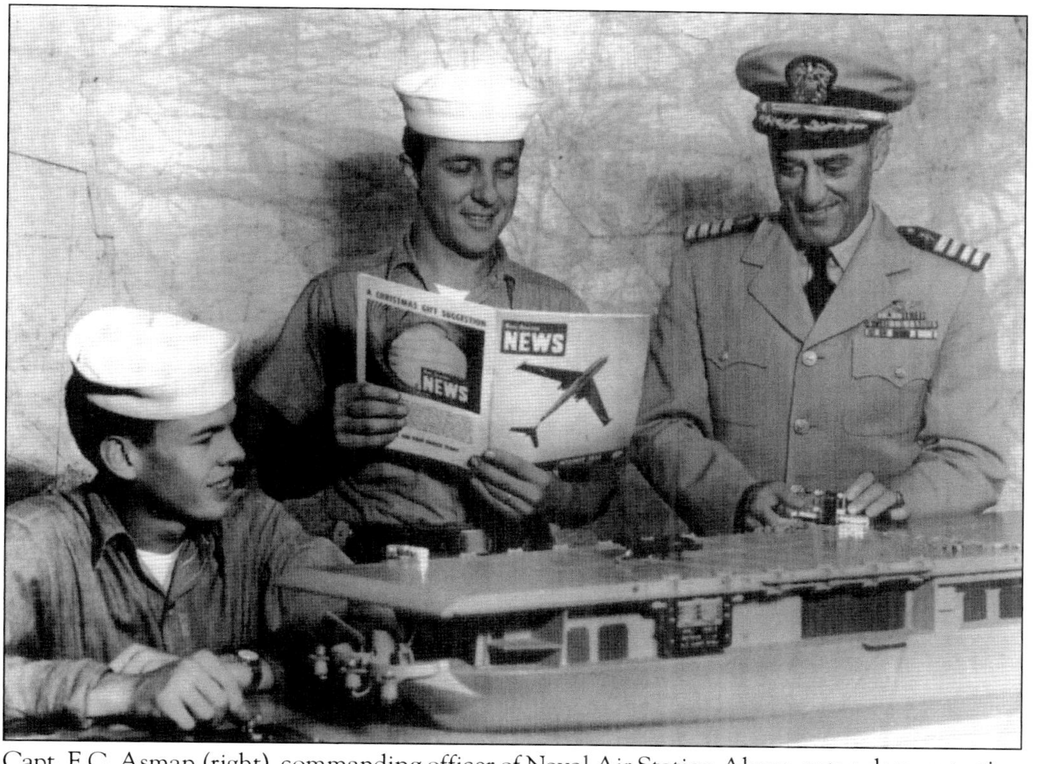

Capt. E.C. Asman (right), commanding officer of Naval Air Station Akron, gets a demonstration of the "deck landing mirror sight" aboard the USS *Akron*, the station's training model carrier. Biagio Lauretta, Training Device Man 3rd Class, is checking the working model against the November 1955 issue of *Naval Aviation News*, in which the mirror landing system was highlighted. J.W. Johnston, TD3, is operating the wave-off lights. The system is correct and authentic, even to centering the "meatball" for a perfect landing. The task was overseen by Chief G.W. Liebold, Aviation Electronics Technician Chief Petty Officer (not pictured).

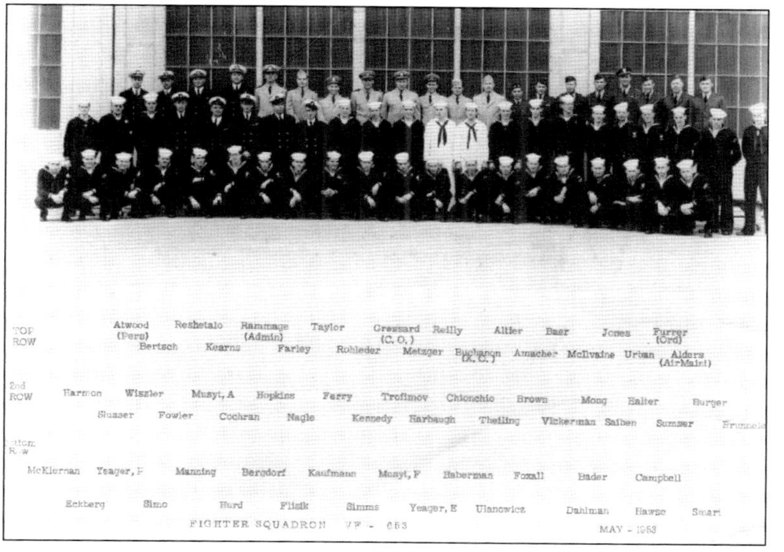

Shown here are sailors and officers from the fighter squadron VF-653 in May 1953. VF-653 was reorganized upon the return of the original squadron from service in Korea.

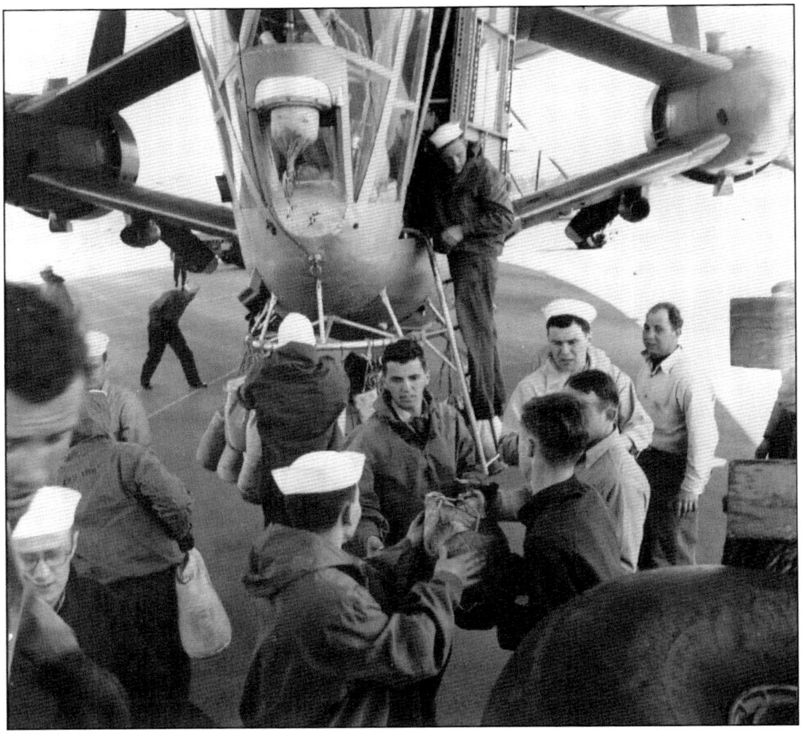

Sailors add a ballast to a ZP-651 blimp. A ballast is a weight carried aboard a lighter-than-air vehicle to offset the buoyancy of its lifting gas.

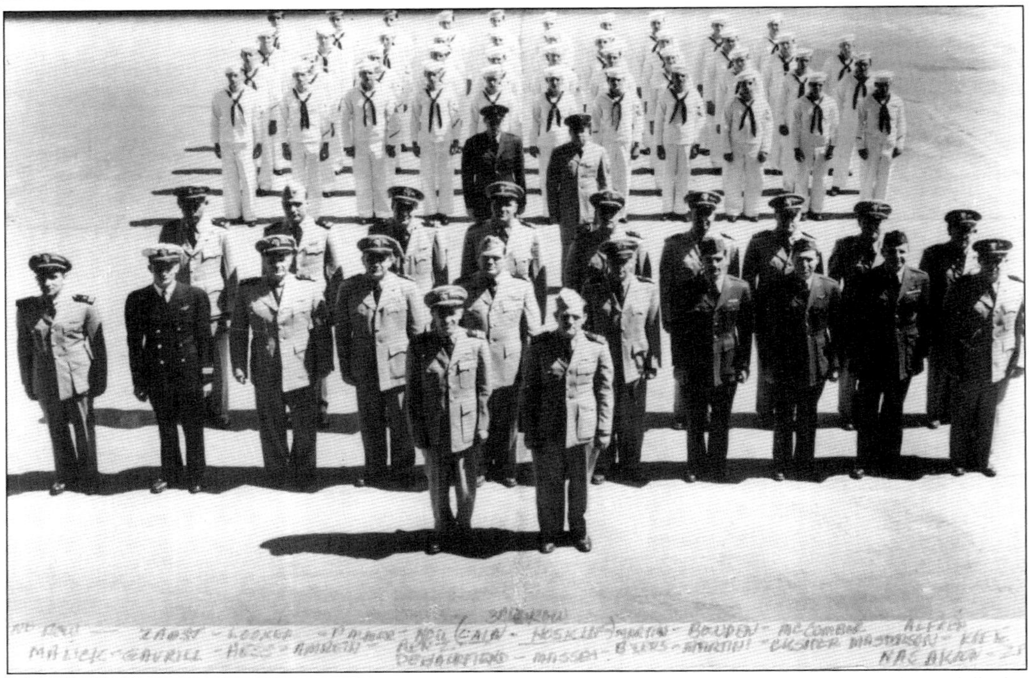

Naval officers and sailors of ZP-651 pose for a photograph. This airship squadron conducted flight training primarily at Naval Air Station Lakehurst, New Jersey. At the end of World War II, there were no facilities in Akron to hangar airships for operational duty.

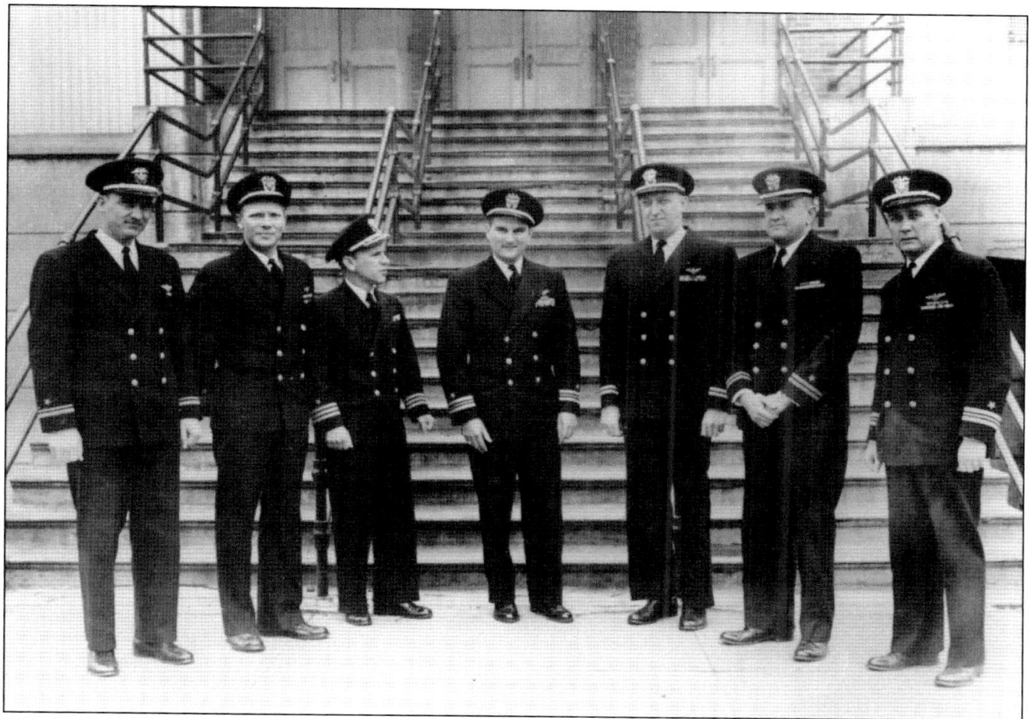

Unidentified officers pose in front of barracks. Most officers and enlisted personnel were married and had families. The average age of the station personnel was 34.

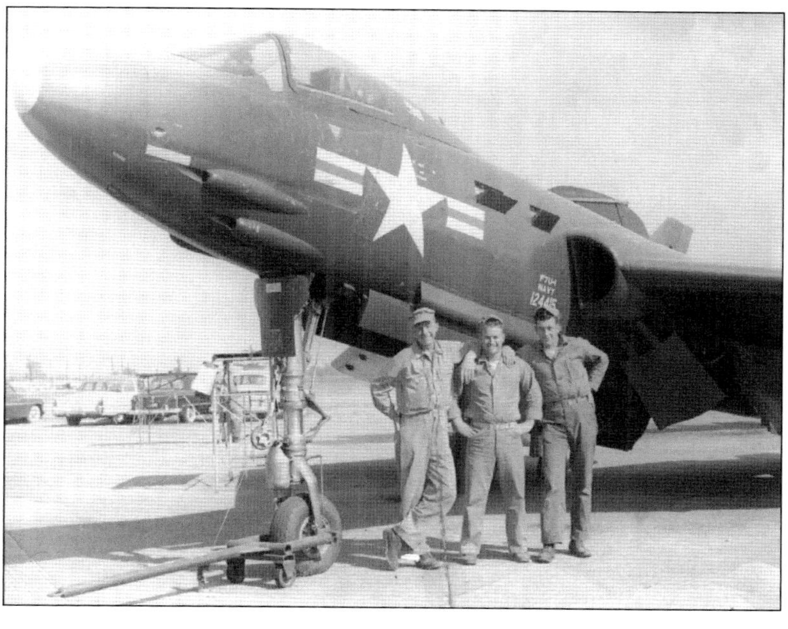

Esprit de corps was high, as evidenced by these three unidentified Marines standing in front of an F7U Cutlass fighter aircraft. The US Naval Air Station existed in Akron from 1948 to 1958.

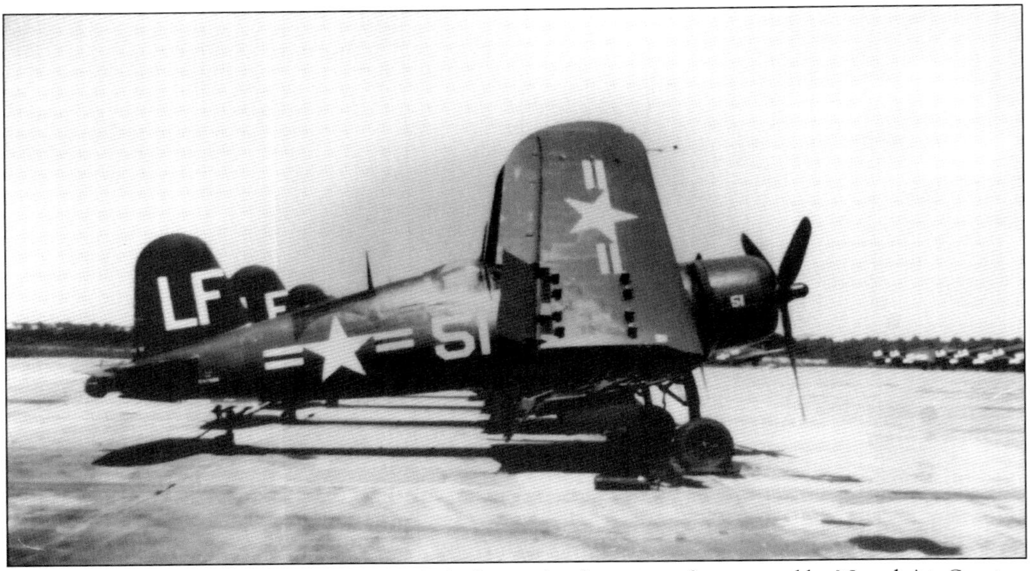

This photograph, taken on August 8, 1948, shows the first aircraft operated by Naval Air Station Akron. These Corsairs would be assigned to various fighter squadrons situated at Naval Air Station Akron.

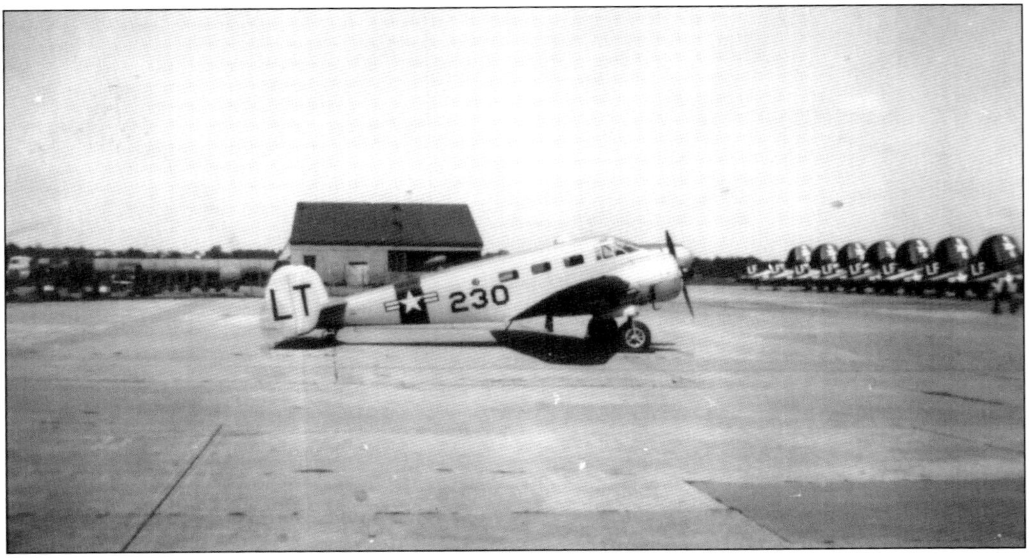

A SNB trainer transport rests on the apron. The SNB was a workhorse at the station.

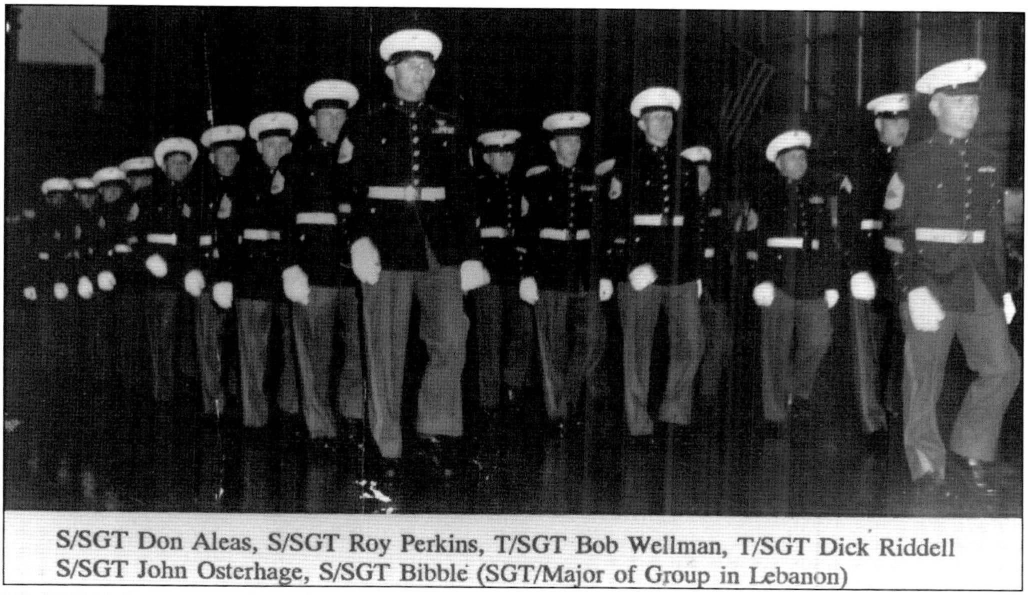

VMF 231 Marines march in downtown Akron. They are, from left to right in first two rows, S.Sgt. Don Aleas, S.Sgt. Roy Perkins, T.Sgt. Bob Wellman, T.Sgt. Dick Riddell, S.Sgt. John Osterhage, and S.Sgt. Bibble, sergeant major of the group in Lebanon.

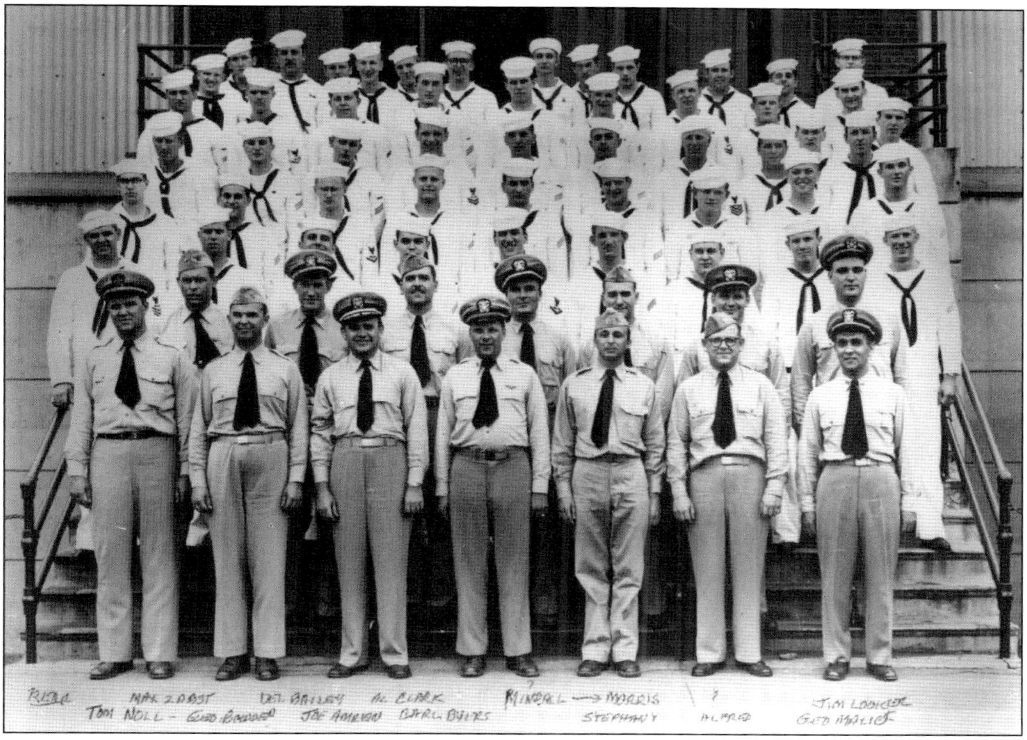

Officers and men of ZP-651 pose for a squadron photograph. The officers are, from left to right, (first row) T. Noll, G. Bowden, J. Amrein, C. Byers, ? Raindall, ? Stephany, and Alfred, G. Malick; (second row) M. Zabst, ? Bailey, A. Clark, ? Morris, unidentified, and J. Looker.

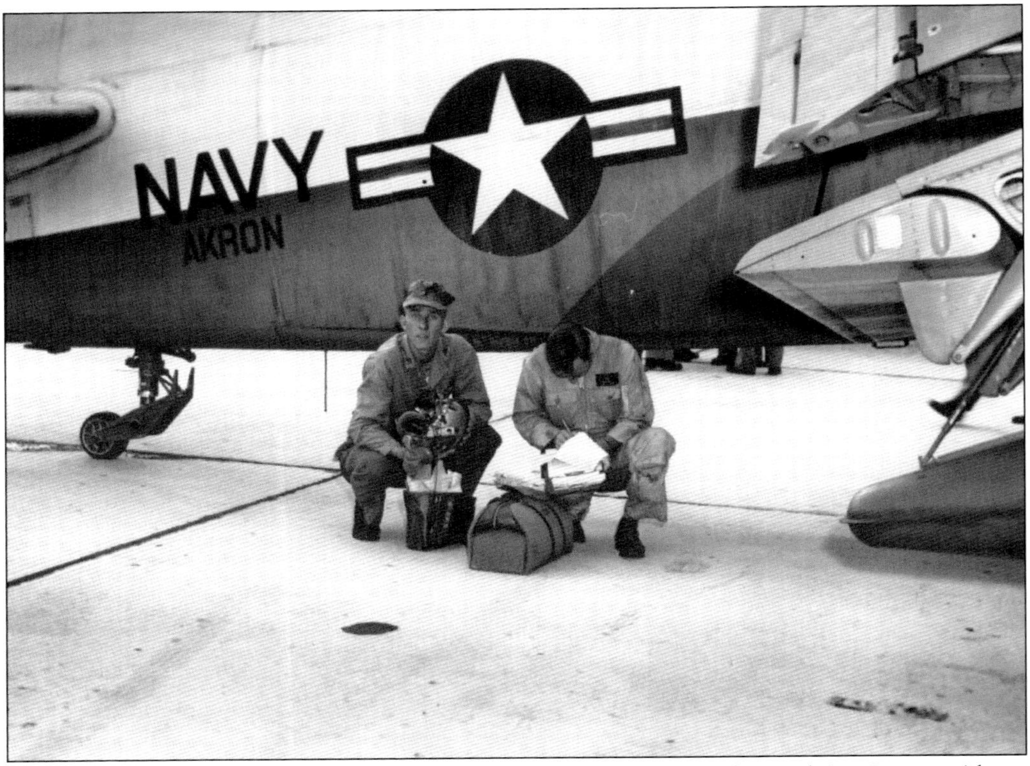

Here, two unidentified officers prepare flight plans prior to takeoff. Naval Air Station Akron aviators flew a variety of naval aircraft. These officers are kneeling next to a Grumman S2F "Tracker." This aircraft was used during the 1950s for everything from tracking submarines to delivering mail.

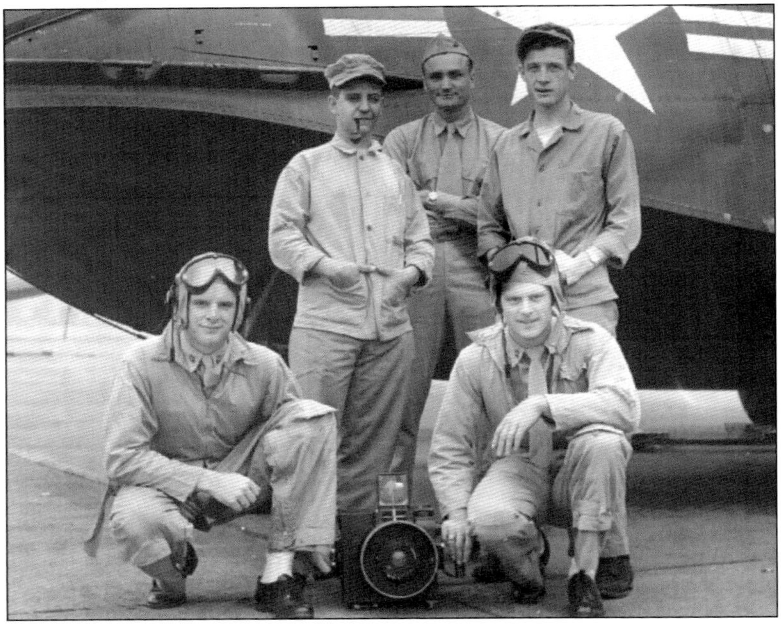

Pilots and aircrew pose in front of a patrol aircraft. Shown here are, from left to right, (kneeling) Bill Bickett and John Bicket; (standing) M.A. Kasyewski, unidentified, and Robert Allen. The men of Naval Air Station Akron came primarily from Ohio, Pennsylvania, and Indiana and would give new meaning to the term "weekend warrior."

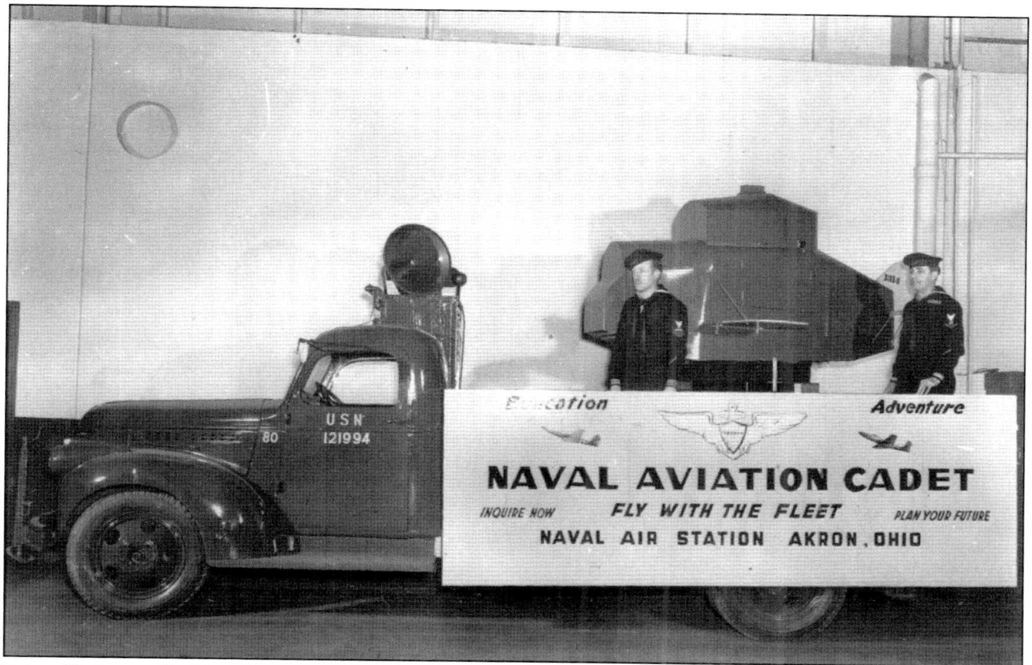

John Roberts (left) and Fred Ellis stand on the NAS Link Trainer. The trainer was used for training and as a recruiting device during parades.

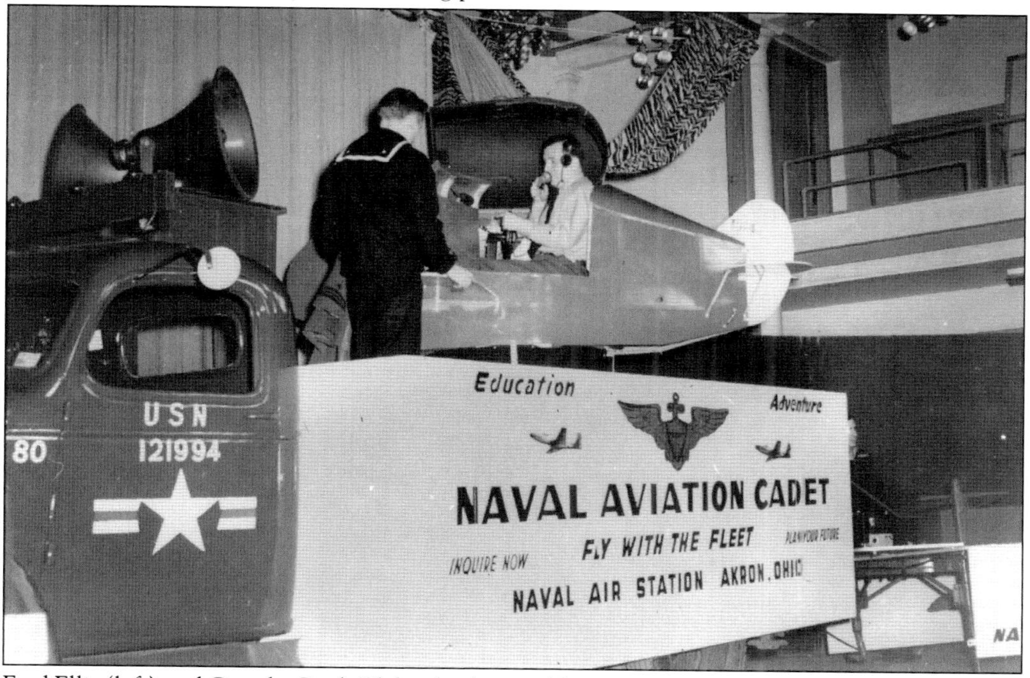

Fred Ellis (left) and Comdr. Cook Cleland, who would go on to command famed VF 653 (Fighting 653) in Korea, operates the speaker system on the NAS Link Trainer. The World War II–era Link Trainer was so effective in training pilots to fly on instruments that it saw service well into the mid-1950s.

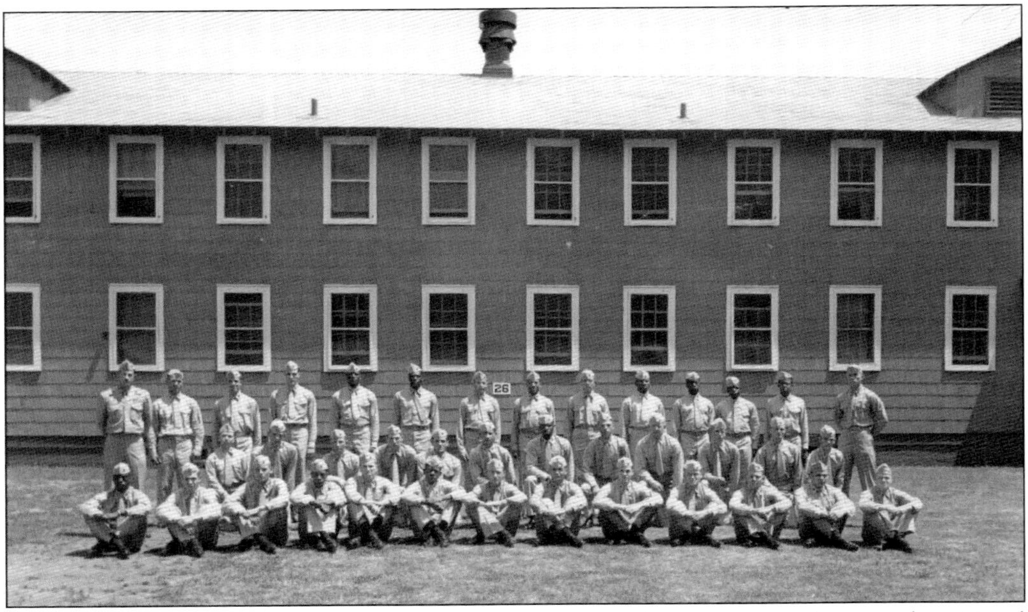

Unidentified Marine officers and enlisted personnel pose for a squadron photograph at Naval Air Station Akron.

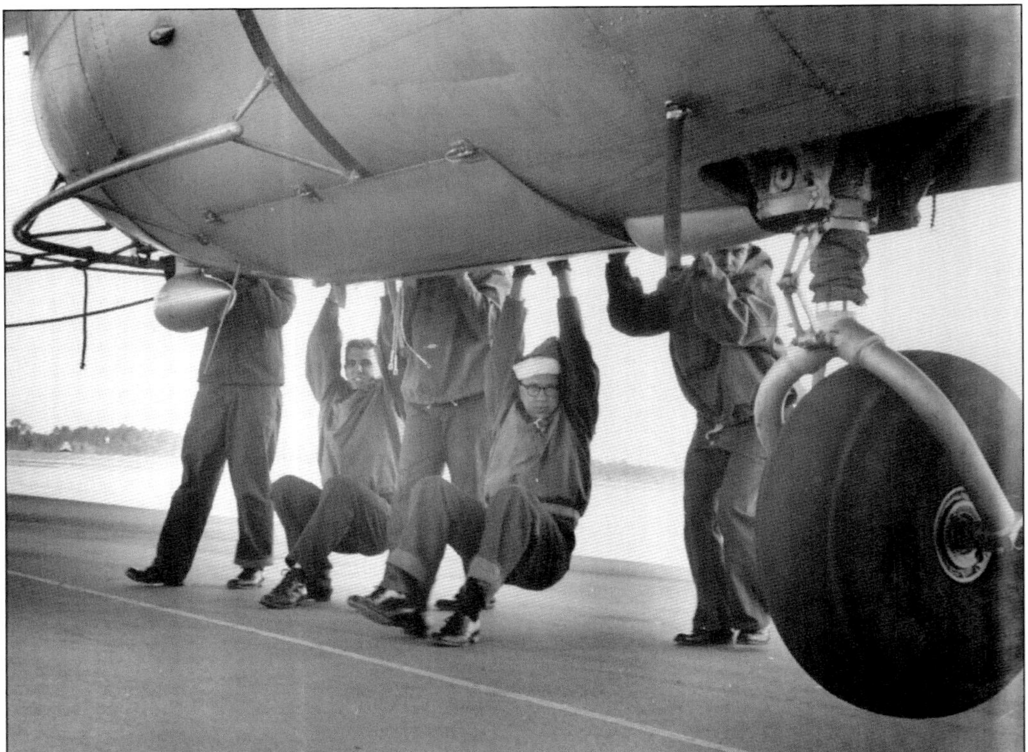

Life could be hard for ZP-651 sailors. Here, unidentified servicemen struggle to stabilize one of the squadron's airships.

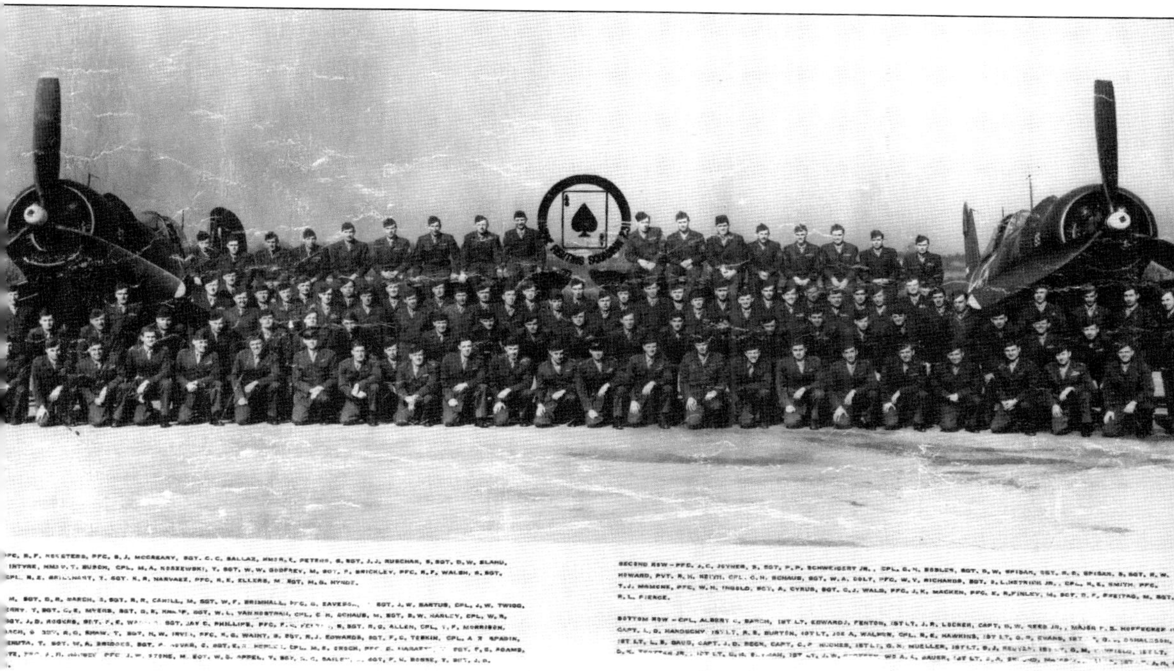

Marine Fighting Squadron 231 is seen here. In February 1951, the "Ace of Spades" Marines squadron was called to active duty in Korea. The squadron dates back to 1923 and still exists today. It is currently stationed at MCAS Cherry Point in North Carolina. Of the men pictured here, four would be lost in Korea: Maj. Frank E. Hoffecker Jr., killed in action; Capt. Donald K. Trotter, missing in action; Capt. Donald H. Clark, killed in action; and Capt. John W. Godfrey, killed in the line of duty.

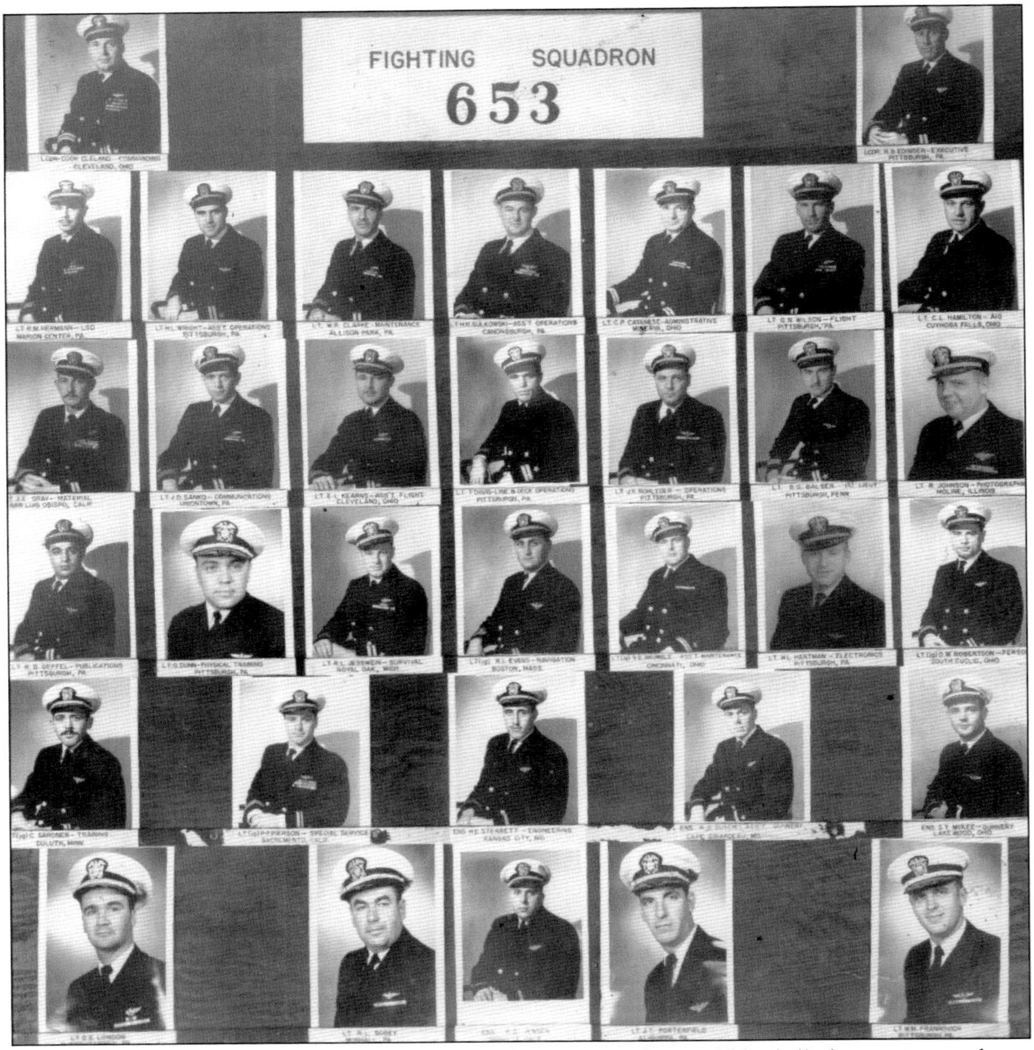

Of the officers pictured here, of Fighting Squadron 653, eight would be killed in action and two taken prisoner during the Korean War (June 1950 to January 1953). VF 653 was deployed aboard the US Navy aircraft carrier *Valley Forge*, stationed in the Sea of Japan. The squadron flew as bridge, road, and rail busters. Its missions were arduous and dangerous and required flying at low levels through mountainous terrain. Listed here are the names of those men killed in action or taken prisoner: Lt. James T. Porterfield, Lt. Donald E. London, Lt. Robert L. Sobey, Lt. William M. Frankovich, Lt. Hull L. Wright, Lt. Joseph D. Sanko, Lt. J.G. Channing Gardner, Ens. H. Edward Sterrett (POW), Ens. Roland G. Busch (POW), and Ens. Gordon R. Galloway. From Naval Air Station Akron, Squadron VF 655, Lt. Stanley Dunmore (not pictured) was killed in the line of duty. Author James Michener was embedded with the squadron aboard the *Valley Forge* during its deployment. VF 653's gallantry in action inspired the author to create a fictional account of their ordeal, *The Bridges at Toko-Ri.*

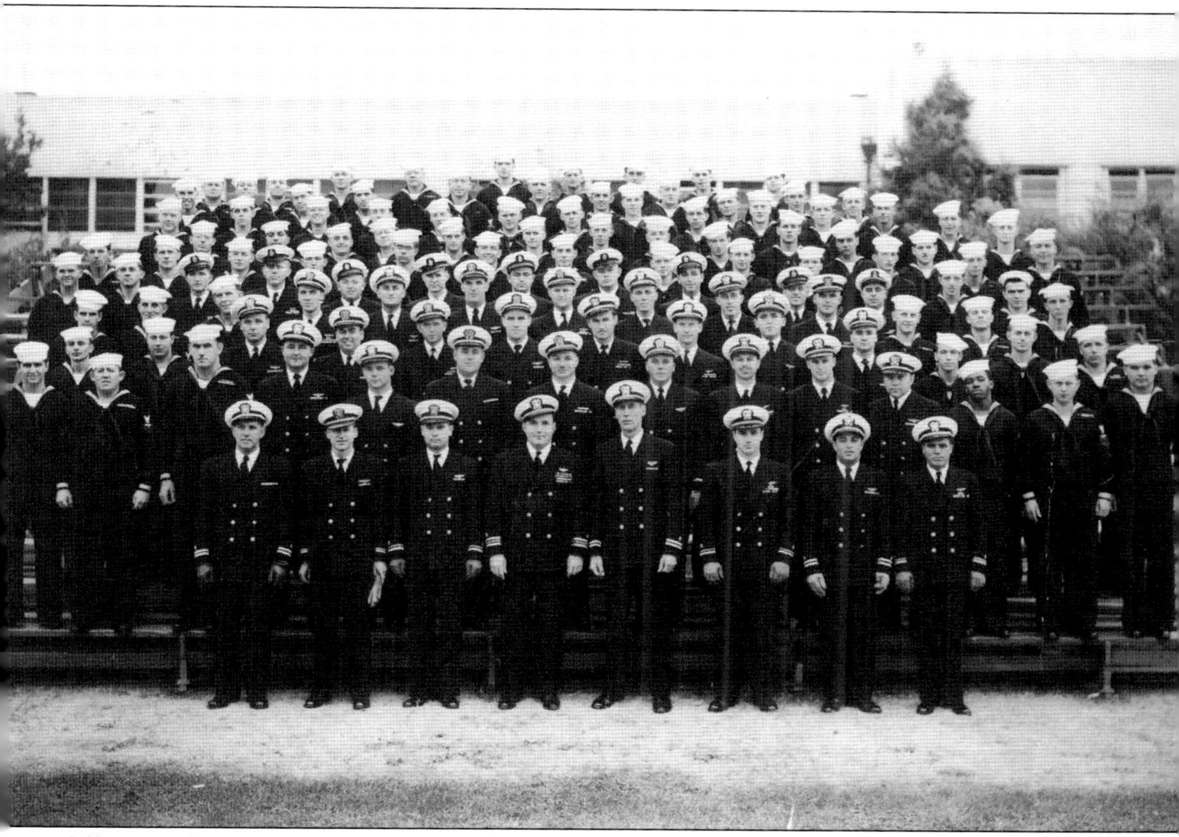

Officers and sailors of Squadron 653 of the USS *Valley Forge* pose for a photograph. Lt. Comdr. Cook Cleland (first row, center) was the commanding officer. The squadron was called to active duty in Korea in February 1951. Cleland's plane was hit by flak and was forced to land in Wonsan Harbor, Korea. He was rescued immediately by helicopter. During the squadron's duty in Korea, eight of its men were killed and two were captured and held prisoner until 1953.

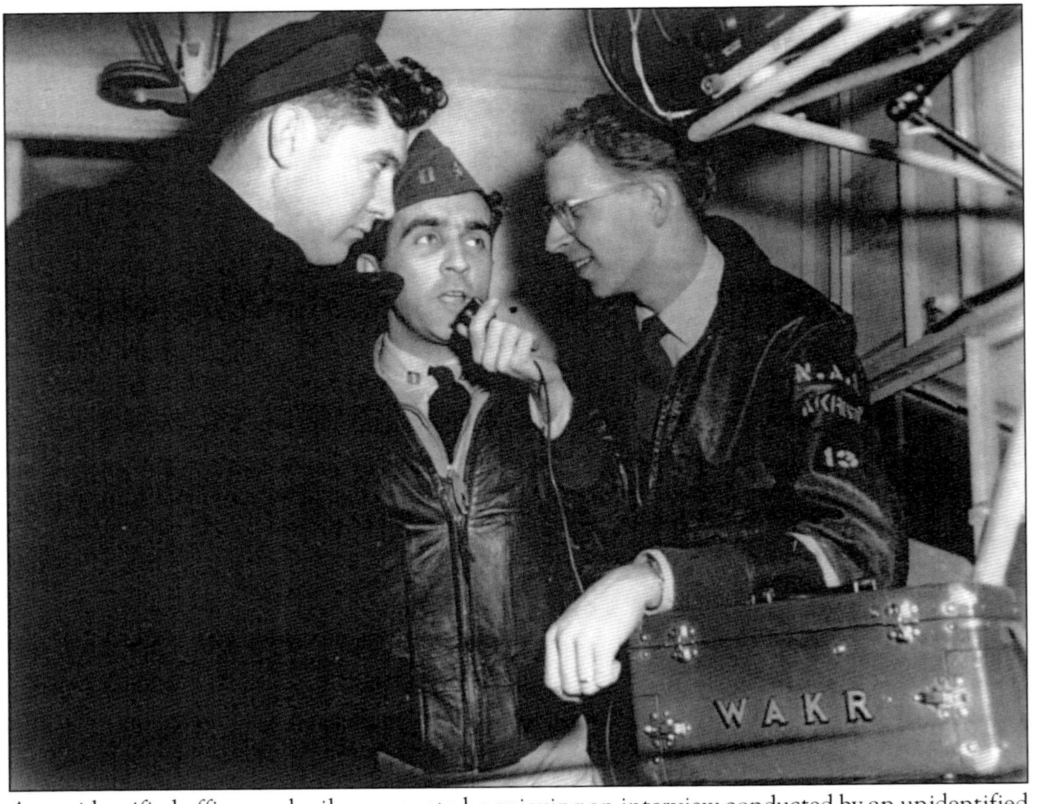

An unidentified officer and sailor appear to be enjoying an interview conducted by an unidentified man from local radio station WAKR. Note the stenciled "NAS" on the interviewer's flight jacket. The local media promoted Naval Air Station Akron on radio, television, and in the *Akron Beacon Journal's* ROTO section. ROTO was a Sunday magazine insert detailing life in and around Akron.

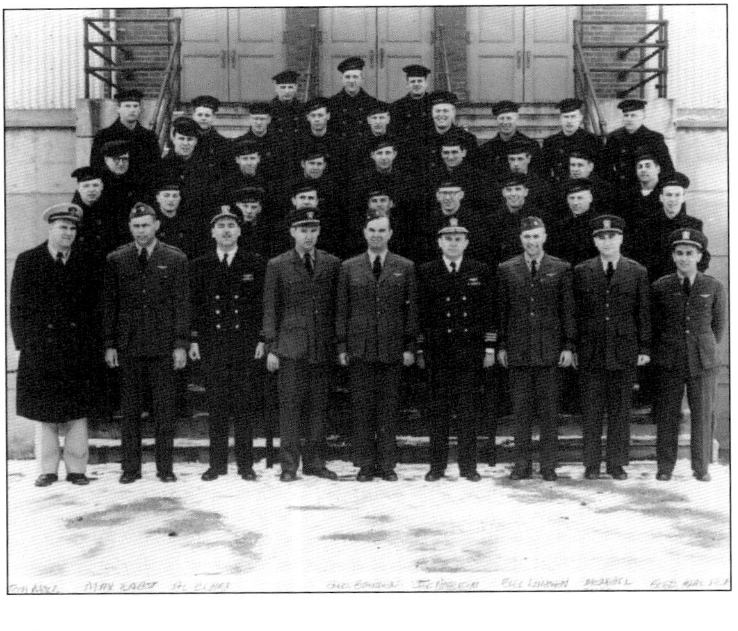

In this 1952 photograph, airship squadron ZP-651 poses in front of the entrance to Naval Air Station Akron. ZP-651 was unique in that flight training was conducted at Naval Air Station Lakehurst, New Jersey. Although Goodyear Aircraft Corporation was building the giant ZPG3W airship next to NAS Akron, there were no facilities for naval airship flight training.

Eight

The Aviators Visit Akron

During aviation's golden age, Akron Municipal Airport and the City of Akron became a home to those aviators and aviatrix who would eventually write their own pages in history. The aviation research and development activities in Akron in the 1930s and the National Air Races held annually in Cleveland made Akron and the airport a necessary stop. The list of visitors to the "port" reads like a who's who of early aviation. Charles and Anne Morrow Lindbergh, Douglas "Wrong Way" Corrigan, and Jimmy Doolittle were among the famous aviators to pay a visit.

A surprising number of women aviators called upon the "port" and Akron during those years. Among the women aviators were Helen Ball, a stunt flyer from Pittsburgh, and Gretchen Reighard, a glider pilot from Mansfield who financed her glider flying by parachute jumping. Lady Grace Drummond Hay, the first woman to circle the globe by air, visited the "port" via the *Graf Zeppelin* visit. Wiley Post became a frequent Akron visitor while working with the B.F. Goodrich Company on developing a high-altitude pressure suit. Hugh Herndon, Roscoe Turner, Capt. Al Williams, and the heroic Tilden Johnson called at the "port" often.

Akron had its own share of local aviation talent. Bain Fulton operated the first air service in Akron, and John Gammeter built the first airplane in Akron, flying regularly around the city. In later years, Ernie Stadvec, a returning World War II veteran, became the country's first aerial reporter for the local radio and television station, WAKR. Stadvec would also host a television show, *Captain Ernie's Flying Club*, in the late 1950s, educating students about aviation. Stadvec's children's television program may have also been the first of its kind.

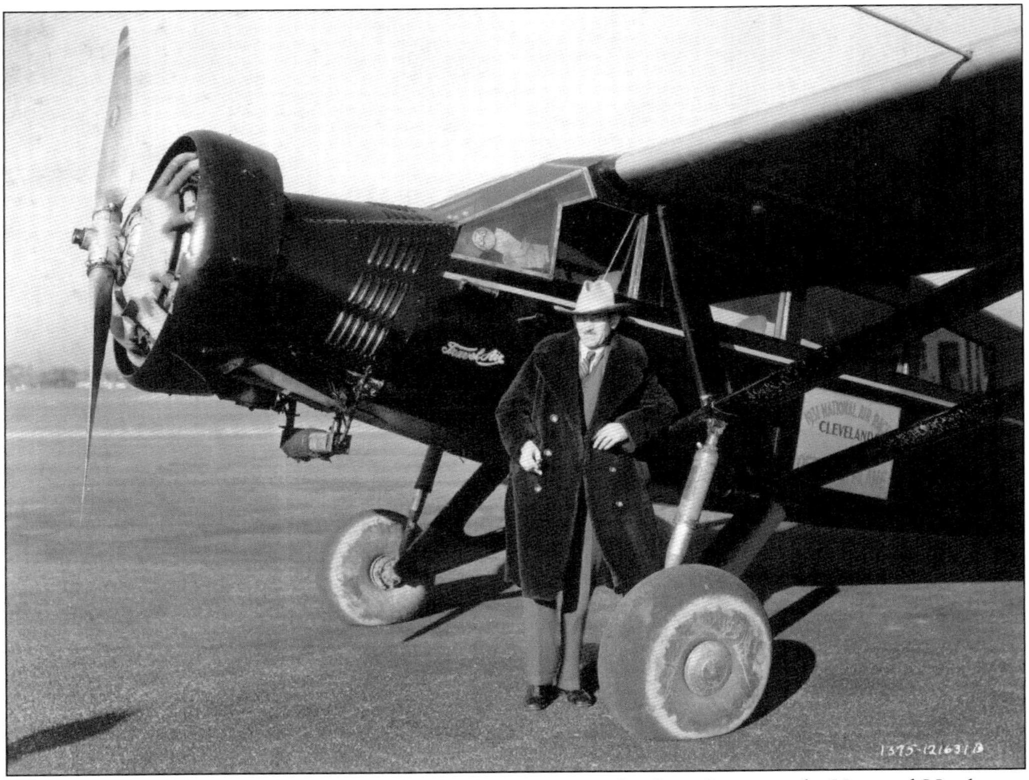

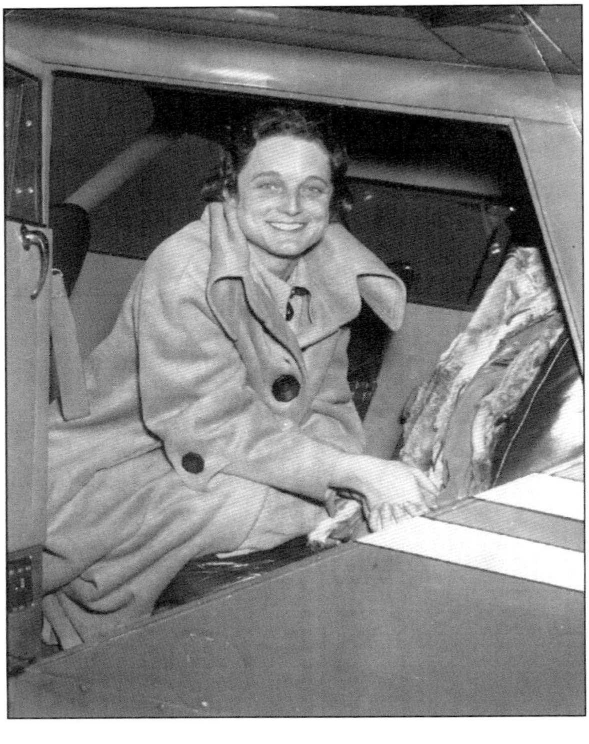

In this photograph, Howard Hughes is standing beside the Northrop "Gamma" monoplane in which he established the west-to-east transcontinental speed record of 9 hours, 26 minutes, and 10 seconds.

Louis Thaden (1905–1979) set aviation records and won many aviation races. In 1928, Thaden set the women's altitude record at 20,260 feet. In 1929, she set the women's endurance record of 22 hours, 3 minutes, and 12 seconds. She also won the 1929 Powder Puff Derby. Thaden was the first woman to win the Bendix Trophy, in 1936, and was the first woman pilot licensed by the State of Ohio.

Roscoe Turner was a racing pilot, stunt pilot (barnstormer), transcontinental speed record holder, and multiple National Air Race winner. For a few months, Turner flew with a lion named Gilmore in his cabin. Gilmore was with Turner when he set several transcontinental speed records in May 1930. Gilmore eventually grew too large to fly with Turner.

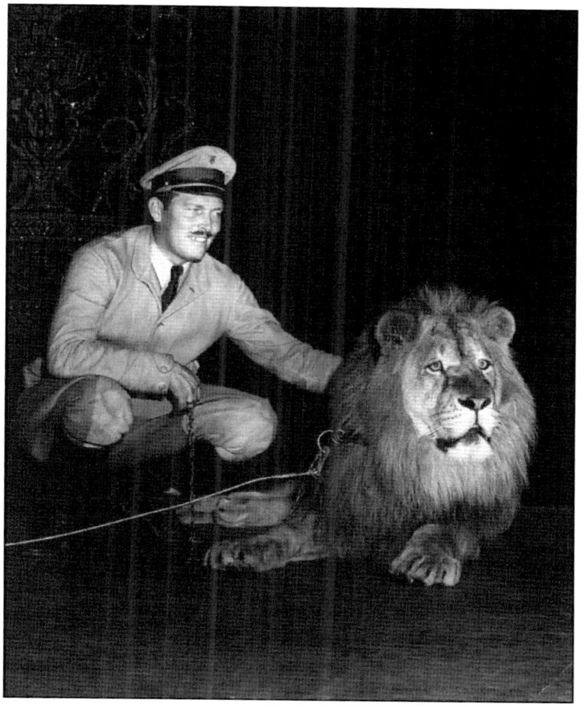

In 1931, Wiley Post flew around the world in the *Winnie Mae* with his navigator, Harold Gatty. He flew from New York to New York in eight days (June 23–July 1). Post died in 1935 in a plane crash in Alaska.

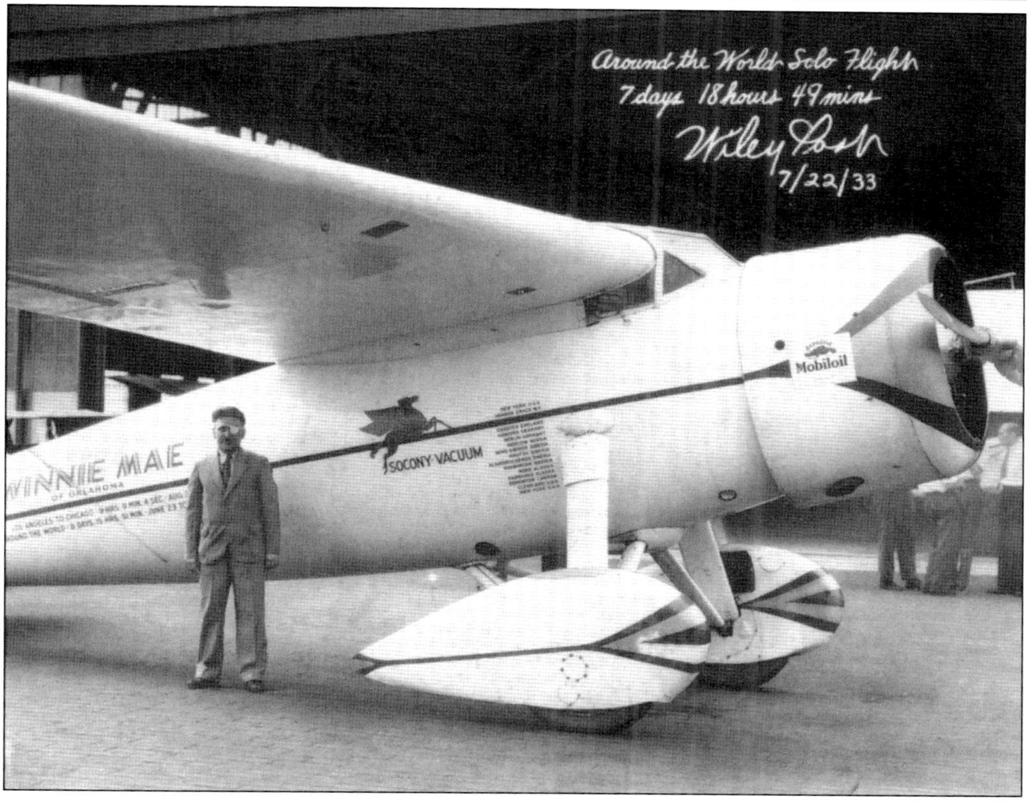

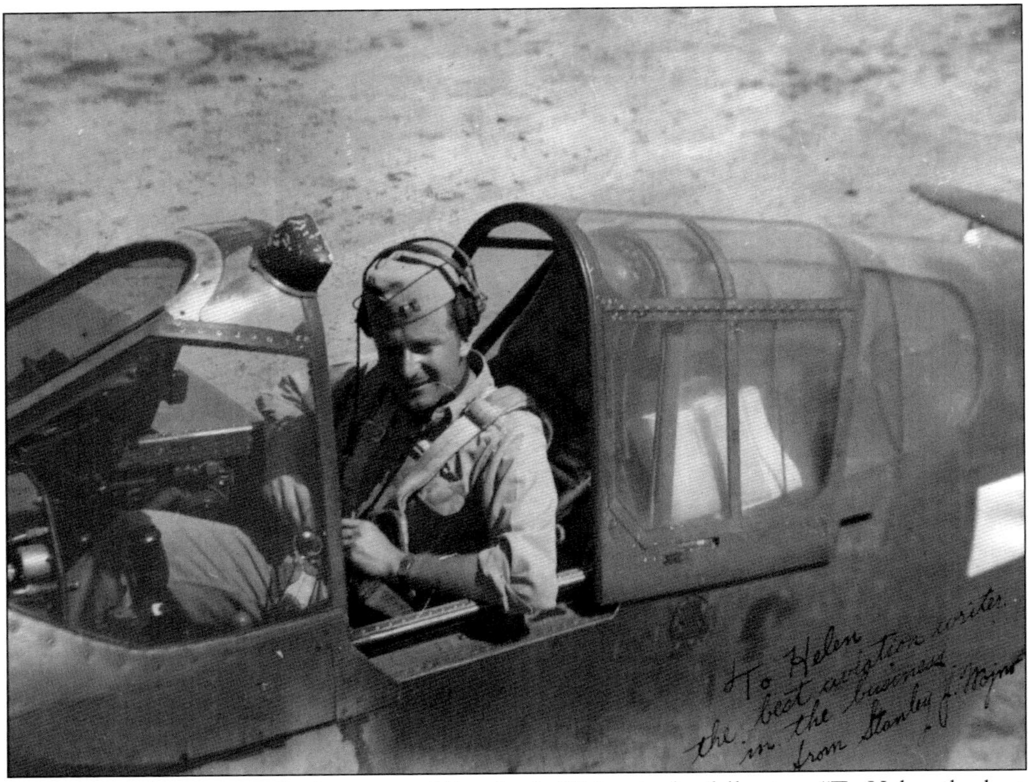

Written on this autographed portrait of Stanley J. Wojno is the following: "To Helen the best aviation writer in the business from Stanley J. Wojno." Stanley was born in Akron, Ohio, and was a graduate of North High School. He attended the University of Akron and was a lieutenant colonel in the US Air Force Reserve. During World War II, he served as a transport pilot in the China, Burma, India Operation. In 1994, Wojno received commendation and Chinese Air Force Wings from the Republic of China. Lieutenant Colonel Wojno died on February 25, 2008, and is buried in Holy Cross Cemetery in Akron.

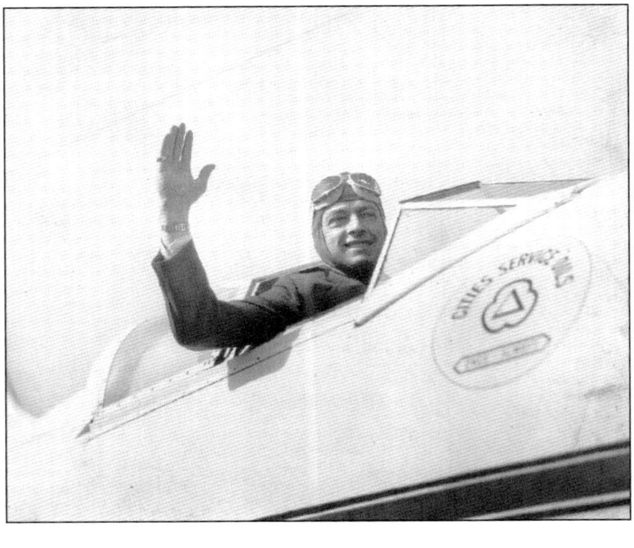

Hugh Herndon, the son of Standard Oil heiress Alice Boardman, sits in an airplane. On August 8, 1931, Herndon and Clyde "Upside-Down" Pangborn tried to beat the around-the-world speed record set by Wiley Post and Harold Gatty. Unfortunately, their plane was damaged when it slid off a runway in Siberia. Unable to beat the speed record, the pair decided to compete for the Japanese nonstop flight across the Pacific Ocean. On October 5, 1931, they landed in the state of Washington after flying over the Pacific Ocean in 41 hours and 13 minutes.

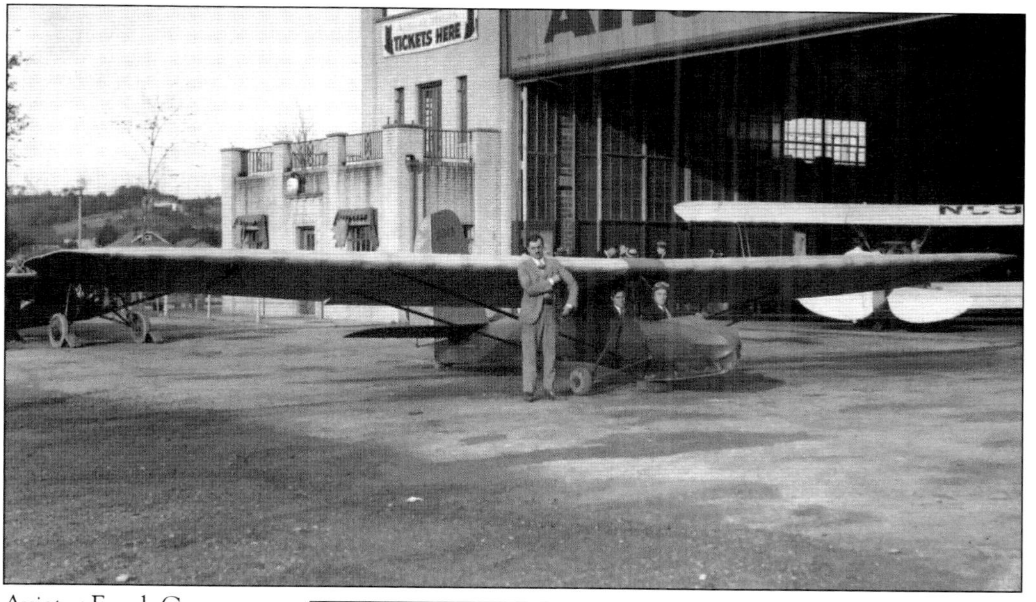

Aviator Frank Gross stands in front of his two-place glider. In 1935, Bill Bodenlos and Willis Sperry carried souvenir mail from Akron to Columbus, Ohio, in the four-place F-5 glider, designed by Gross.

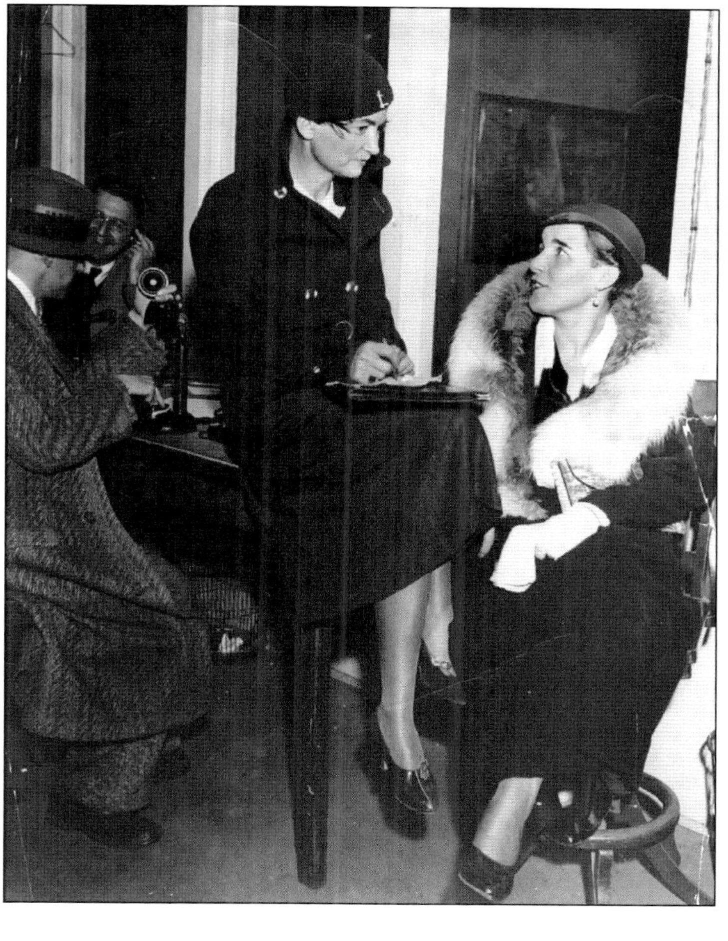

Helen Waterhouse (right), an *Akron Beacon Journal* reporter, interviews Antonie Strassman, a zeppelin aviatrix from Berlin, Germany, while waiting in a hanger at the Akron Municipal Airport. Strassman was one of Europe's most famous female pilots. In 1932, she moved to the United States. She was later revealed to be a Nazi spy.

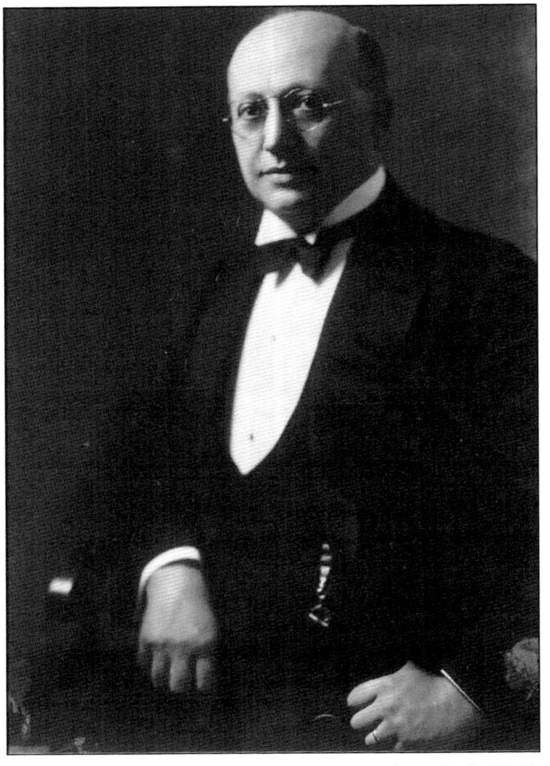

Dr. Karl Arnstein, Prague-born chief engineer of German zeppelin airships, was transferred to the Goodyear-Zeppelin Corporation in Akron, Ohio. Dr. Arnstein was the designer of the airships USS *Akron* and USS *Macon*.

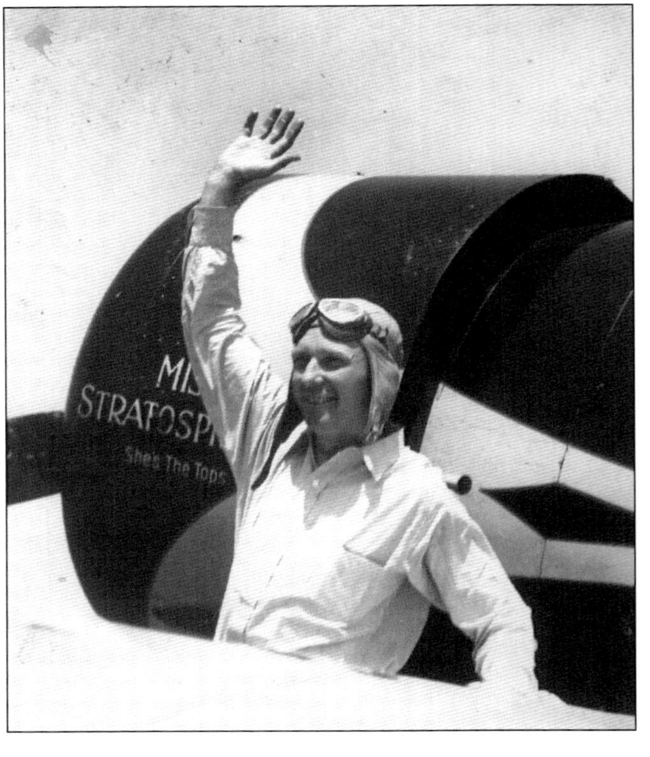

Clarence Duncan Chamberlin (1893–1976) was the second man to solo pilot across the Atlantic Ocean, and he was the first to carry a passenger, Charles Albert Levine. They left on a Bellanca monoplane from New York on June 4, 1927, and landed in Germany on June 6, 1927.

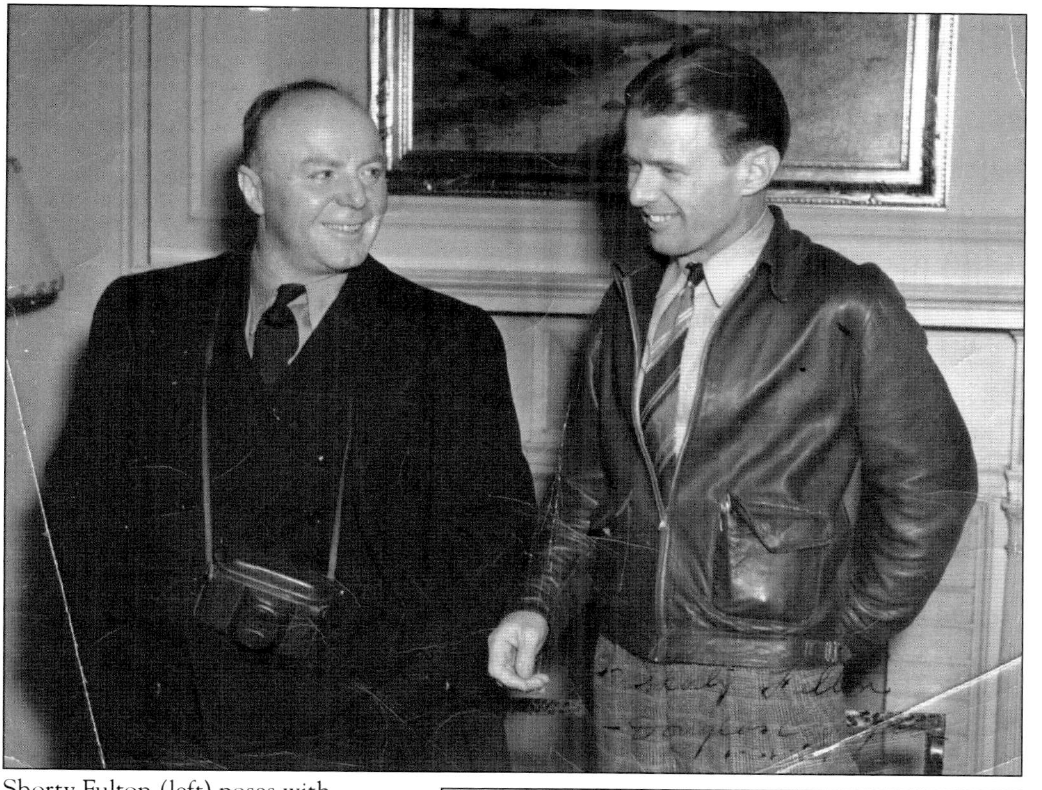

Shorty Fulton (left) poses with Douglas "Wrong Way" Corrigan. Corrigan was inspired by Lindbergh's transatlantic flight. Being of Irish descent, Corrigan wanted to fly from New York to Ireland.

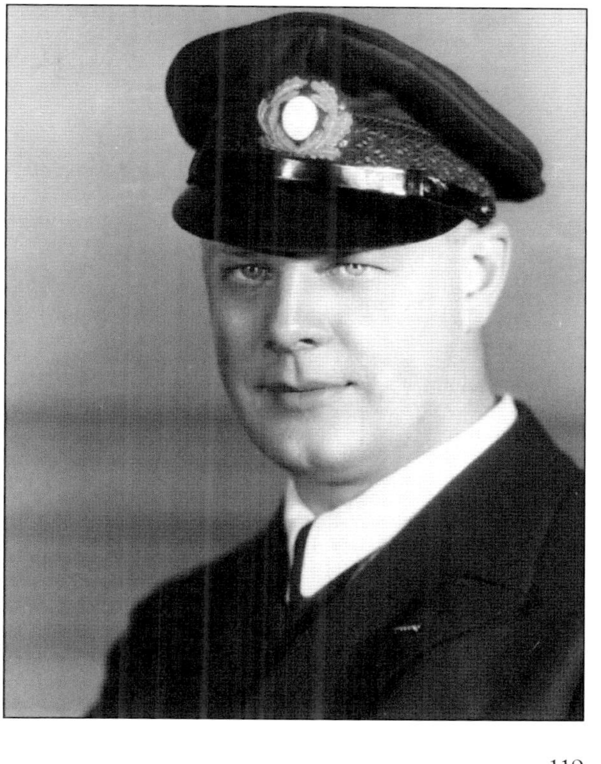

Knut Eckener was the son of Dr. Hugo Eckener, German designer and pilot of the commercial airships *Graf Zeppelin* and *Hindenburg*. Knut Eckener followed in his father's footsteps and also piloted both the *Graf Zeppelin* and the *Hindenburg*.

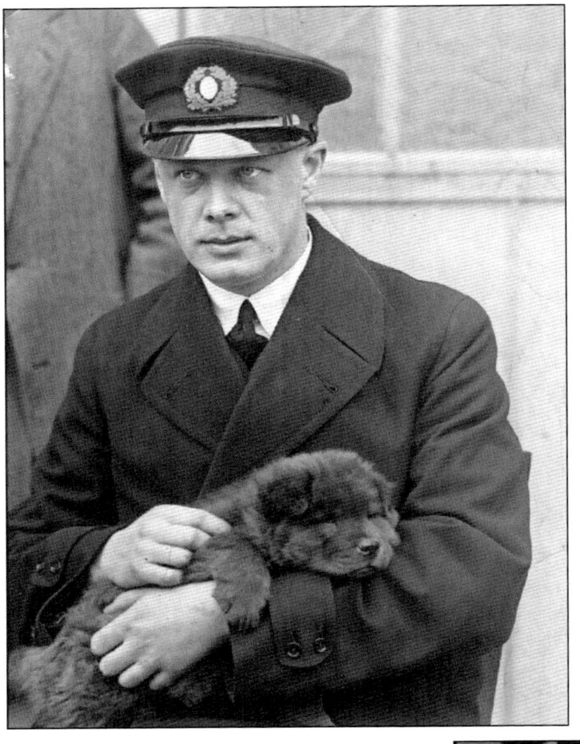

Knut Eckener is seen here with the zeppelin mascot, Vee-Dol, a chow puppy who was carried on the German zeppelins to ward off bad luck. Knut was the son of Dr. Hugo Eckener, German airship designer and pilot.

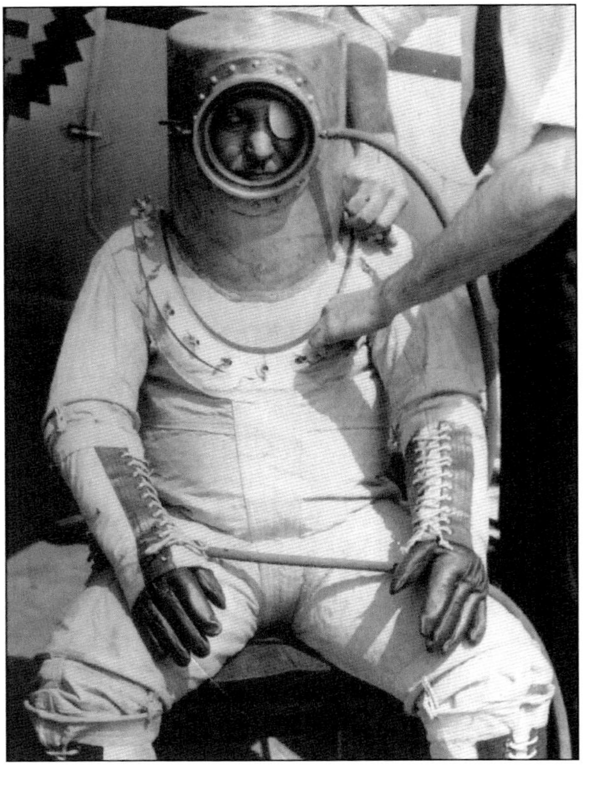

Wiley Post explored high-altitude flight. His airplane, the *Winnie Mae*, could not be pressurized, so he worked with Russell S. Colley of the B.F. Goodrich Company to develop what became the world's first practical pressure suit. In the suit, Post could fly to an altitude of 50,000 feet. During his high-altitude flights, Post discovered the jet stream. He died in 1935 in a plane crash in Alaska.

Wiley Post, seen here before donning his helmet, was a frequent visitor to Akron because of the scientific advances in aviation being made in the area. Post was concerned that the airship would replace the heavier-than-air aircraft in commercial air travel. That is one of the reasons he pursued such innovations as the pressurized suit, which is now common place in aviation. Note that Post's loss of an eye in a mining accident did not deter him from his dreams of flight.

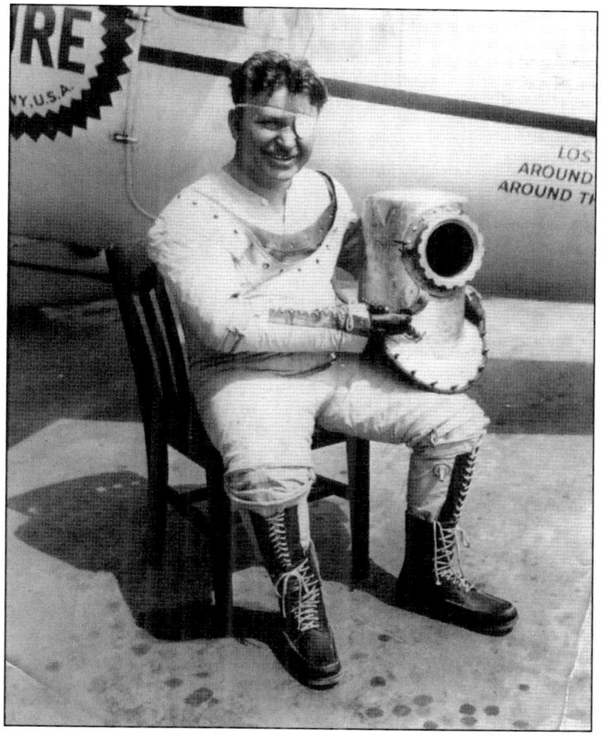

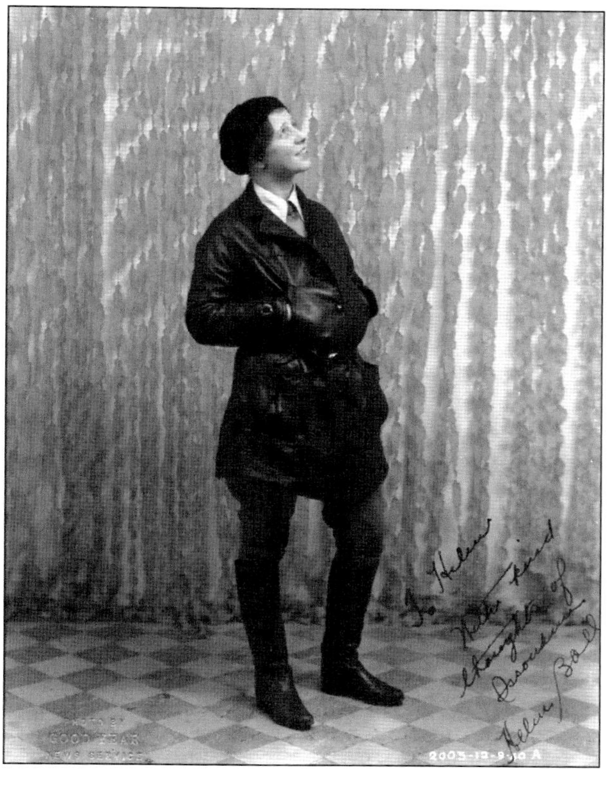

Helen Ball was a stunt pilot from Pittsburgh, Pennsylvania. This autographed photograph was given to Helen Waterhouse. It reads: "To Helen, With Kind Thoughts of Issoudun, Helen Ball." Note the flight clothes. Aviators, in particular women aviators, were not held in high esteem in the late 1920s. Whenever they were photographed, the aviators made certain their clothing was almost businesslike. Hence Helen's polished leather coat.

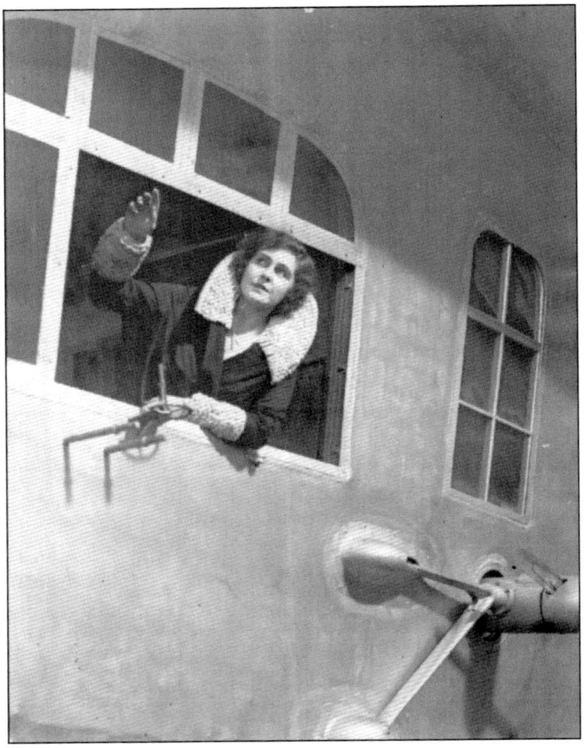

Lady Grace Drummond Hay waves goodbye from the *Graf Zeppelin* as it takes off from Lakehurst, New Jersey. Hay (1895–1946) was the first woman to travel around the world by air, in the *Graf Zeppelin*. She wrote articles about her aerial adventures in mainstream American newspapers in the late 1920s and early 1930s.

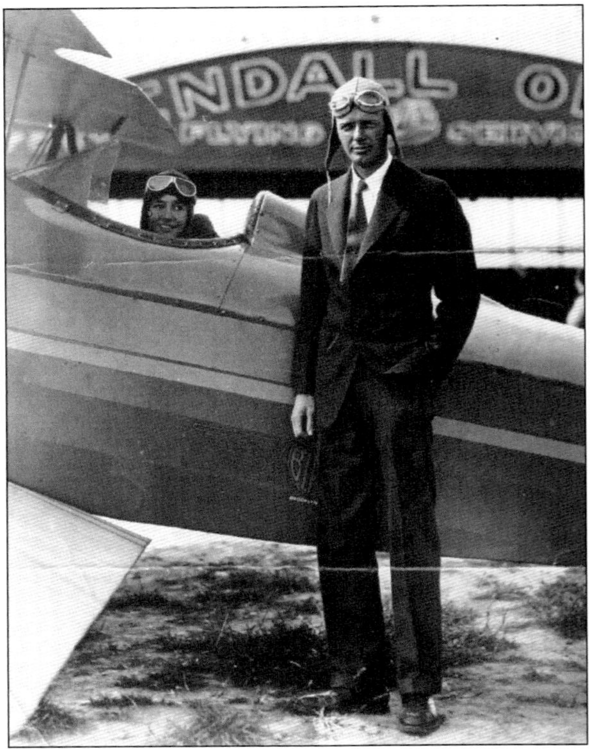

Charles Lindbergh is seen here with his wife, Anne Morrow Lindbergh. Charles Lindbergh (1902–1974) was famous for his solo, nonstop flight across the Atlantic, from Long Island, New York, to Paris, France, in 1927. He was presented the Medal of Honor for his daring flight.

In May 1921, Adm. William Moffett was appointed chief of the Navy's Bureau of Aeronautics. Moffett was an active supporter of lighter-than-air flight for both naval operations and for general use. Admiral Moffett was instrumental in the procurement of airships USS *Akron* and USS *Macon*. Admiral Moffett, along with 73 fellow airshipmen, died in the crash of airship USS *Akron* on April 10, 1933.

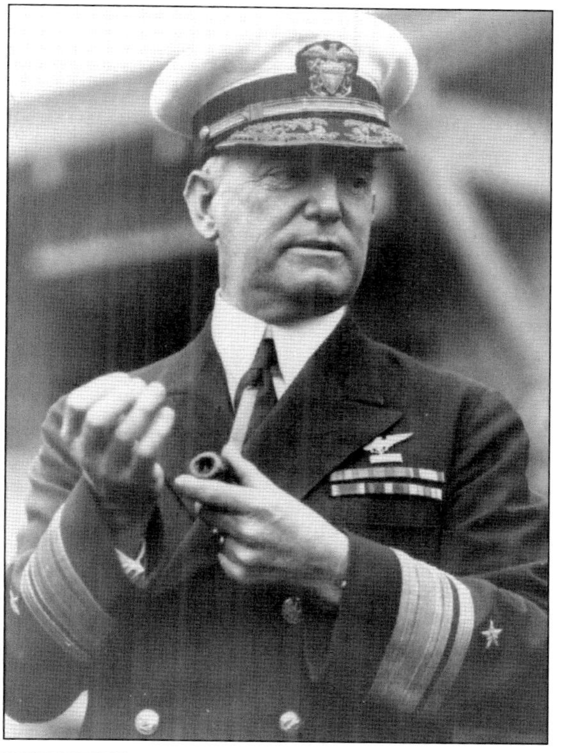

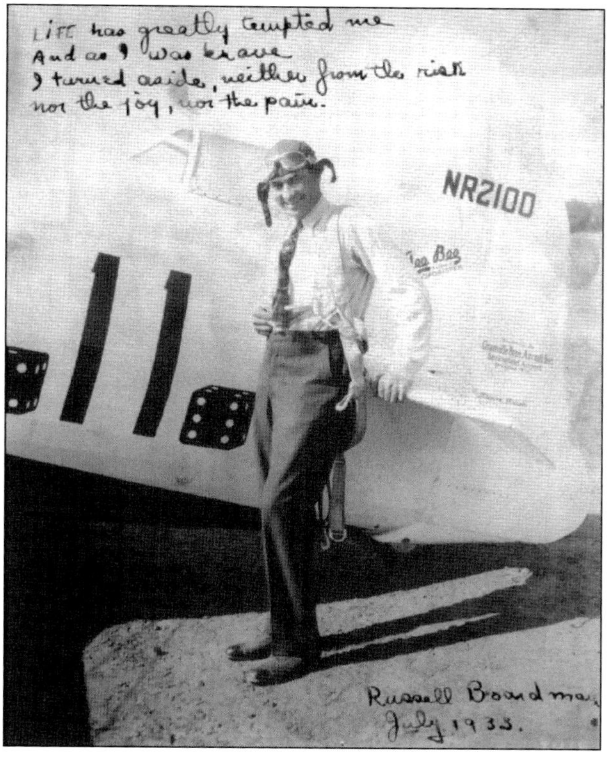

In 1931, Russell Boardman set a nonstop world record flight from New York to Istanbul, Turkey. He set the long-distance record in a Bellanca airplane with his copilot, Johnnie Polando. This photograph was autographed by Boardman. It reads: "Life has greatly tempted me and as I was brave I turned aside neither from the risk, nor the joy, nor the pain. Russell Boardman, July 1933." Boardman was killed in a plane crash two years later.

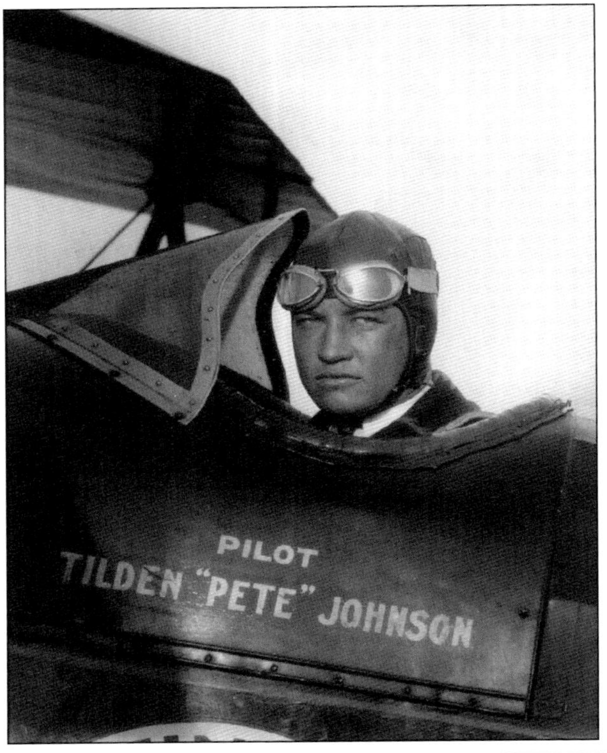

Tilden "Pete" Johnson was one of the youngest pilots in the airmail service. Airmail flights originated out of Cleveland, with frequent stops in Akron. On November 25, 1928, Tilden was killed while attempting to fly through a snowstorm near Massillon, Ohio. Tilden Johnson was 21 at the time of his death.

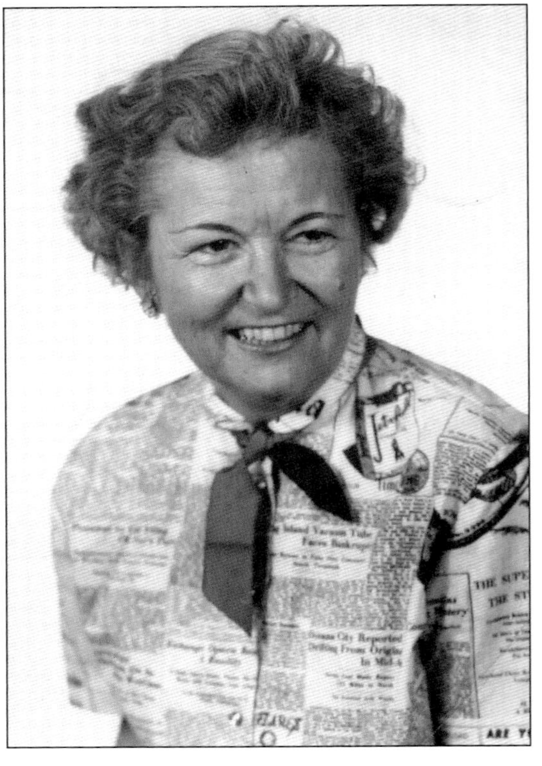

Helen Waterhouse (1892–1965) began working as a freelance writer for the *Beacon Journal* in the mid-1920s. By 1928, Waterhouse was selling so many stories to the *Beacon*, she was making more money than most staff reporters. John S. Knight, publisher of the newspaper, hired Waterhouse full-time as a way to save money. Waterhouse was the first woman aviation writer in the nation.

Maj. Alford Williams was an aviation pioneer. In his military career, he served in the US Navy, US Marine Corps, and US Army Air Corps. One of the pioneers of military aviation, he broke world air-speed records during the 1920s while a test pilot for the Navy.

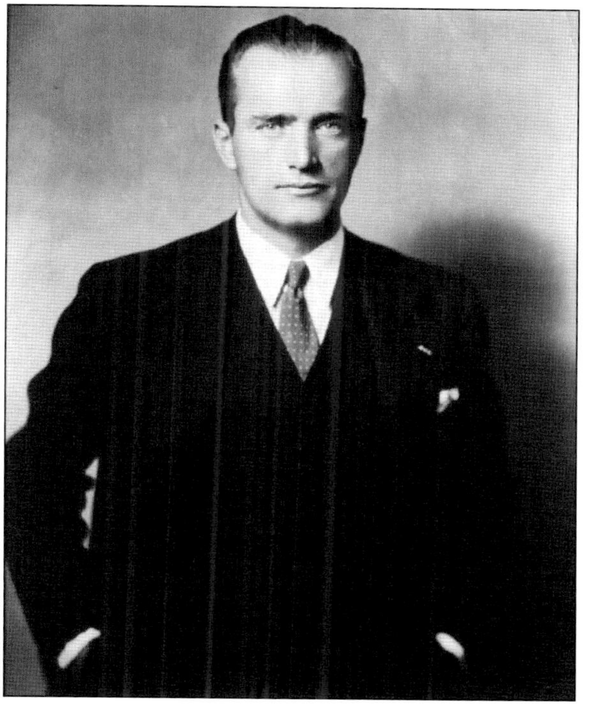

Jimmy Doolittle (1896–1993) was an aeronautical engineer and pilot. Shorty Fulton befriended Doolittle during the Cleveland Air Races. Fulton contributed gasoline and other assorted airport credits to Doolittle, which helped continue Doolittle's air-race career. During World War II, Fulton served under Doolittle in several air missions. One of those missions resulted in Fulton's imprisonment in a POW camp in Germany.

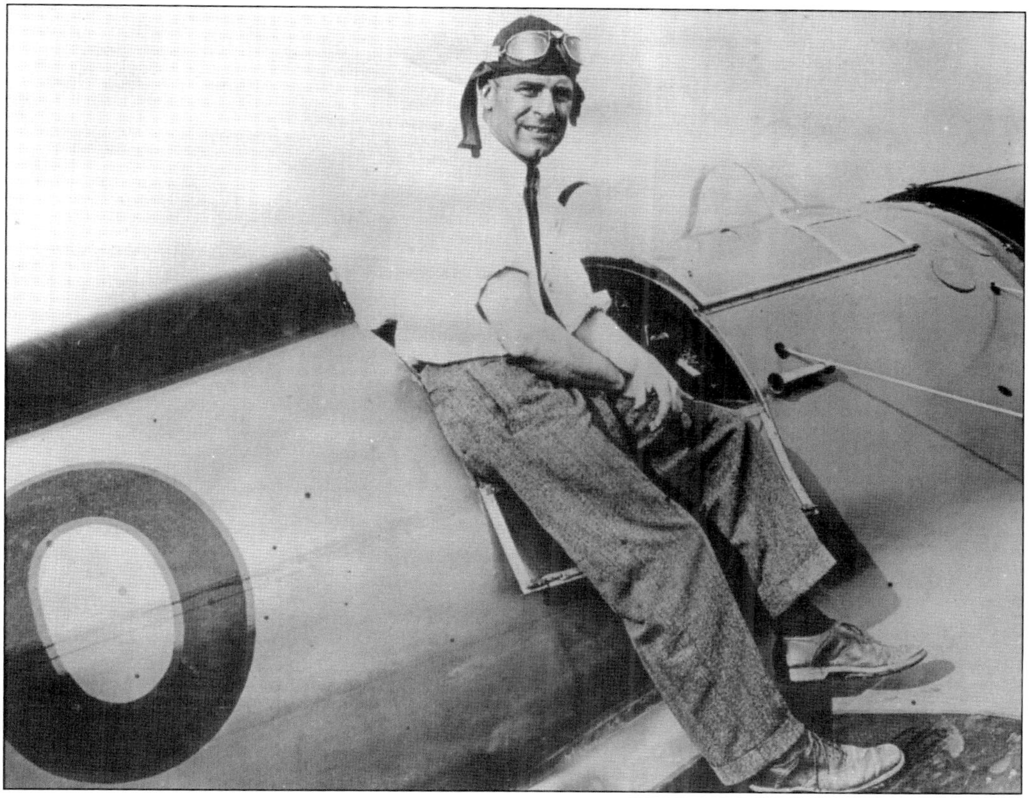

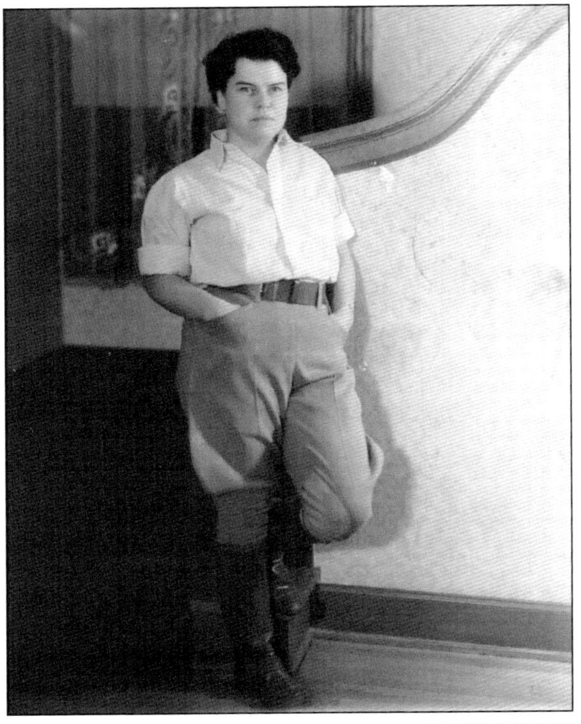

Gretchen Reighard was a glider pilot from Mansfield, Ohio. Parachute jumping helped finance her glider career. She was the first to jump from a four-passenger glider and was one of two to jump from a glider. She was one of six women in the nation who held a class-C pilot license. Reighard performed at the National Air Races in Cleveland in the years 1928–1938.

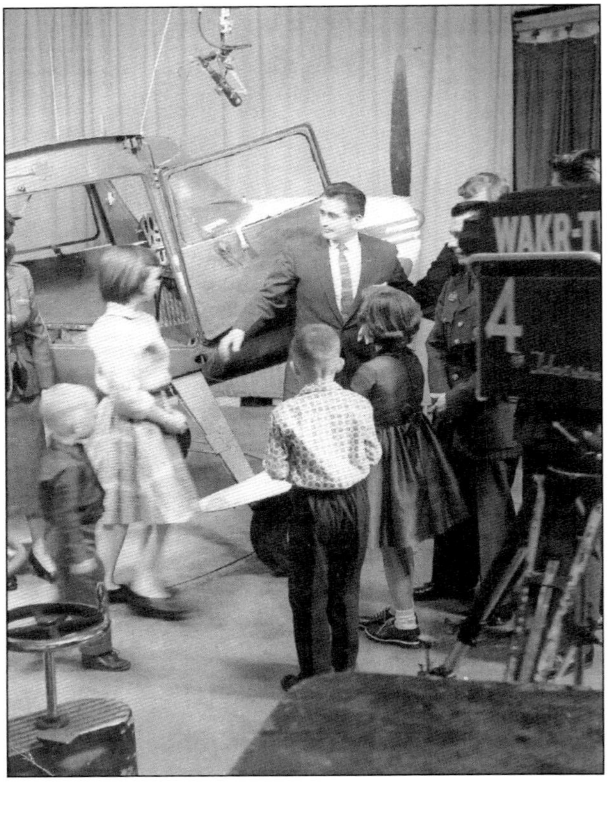

Ernest Stadvec would become the dominant aviation figure in the Akron area after World War II. Stadvec was an airport owner and operator in Copley, Ohio. He went on to become the first aerial reporter in the country, for Akron-based WAKR radio and television, and he hosted a local children's television program in late 1950s and early 1960s, *Captain Ernie's Flying Club*. On the show, a lucky child would get to sit in Captain Ernie's airplane while he taught the children the basics of flight.

THE NOT-SO-FINAL STORY

The history of aviation in Akron, Ohio, is best told by the airport itself. Now named Akron Fulton International Airport, in honor of Bain E. Fulton, the field still makes a powerful and lasting contribution to the Akron community.

Still active, the airport houses 106 aircraft, including two corporate jet aircraft and one helicopter. The airport plays host to numerous civic events, including air shows that continue to attract large crowds. The airport terminal, once the pride of Akron, still stands. However, it is now the home of a local business. The Art Deco designs of the 1920s and 1930s are still visible on the building's facade. The building that housed the Guggenheim Air Ship Institute is standing watch over the airport, almost in anticipation of a return to those glory days.

The Goodyear Zeppelin Airship Factory still stands at the southern end of the airport, rising majestically above the field. The building is now home to Lockheed Aerospace. Within the airdock's cavernous walls, Lockheed is busily creating lighter-than-air vehicles for the 21st century. All that remains of Naval Air Station Akron is a blue, faded sign emblazoned across the abandoned Goodyear plant D (the facility that built 4,006 Corsairs during World War II), announcing to all that Naval Air Station Akron was located there.

It all started with a runaway balloon flight in 1875. The blazing of the trail into aviation history continues not only in Akron, but in the next generation, heralded by Akron-Canton Regional Airport, as it continues to set new records in the field of aviation transportation.